Staying Legal

A guide to issues and practice
for users and publishers
of electronic resources

STAYING LEGAL

A guide to issues and practice
for users and publishers
of electronic resources

Edited by

C. J. Armstrong

LIBRARY ASSOCIATION PUBLISHING
LONDON

Published by
Library Association Publishing
7 Ridgmount Street
London WC1E 7AE

Library Association Publishing is wholly owned by The Library Association.

Published 1999

British Library Cataloguing in Publication Data
A catalogue record for this book is available from the British Library

ISBN 1-85604-276-6

Typeset in 11/13pt Elegant Garamond and CastleT from authors' disk by Library Association Publishing.
Printed and made in Great Britain by Bookcraft (Bath) Ltd, Midsomer Norton, Somerset.

Contents

Contributors

Chris Armstrong is Managing Director of Information Automation Limited (IAL), a consultancy and research company in the library and information management sector, which was established in 1987. Prior to this he worked as a Research Officer at the Department of Information and Library Studies, University of Wales Aberystwyth. In 1993, following several projects which pointed to a need for action in the area of database quality, IAL set up the Centre for Information Quality Management (CIQM) on behalf of The Library Association and the UK Online User Group; the Centre continues to monitor database quality and work towards methodologies for assuring data quality to users of databases and Internet resources.

Chris Armstrong publishes in professional journals and speaks at conferences regularly. He is a fellow of the Institute of Analysts and Programmers and a member of the Institute of Information Scientists, the UK Online User Group and The Library Association. He maintains close contact with the Department of Information and Library Studies and is currently Director of its International Graduate Summer School. The company's website can be found at http://www.i-a-l.co.uk.

Andrew Charlesworth is Senior Lecturer in Information Technology Law and Director of the Information Law and Technology Unit at the University of Hull. He chairs the University's Software Policy and User Regulation Group, and has carried out a range of consultancy work in the HE sector, including work for JISC, UCISA, the CATRIONA II project, and the Arts and Humanities Data Service. He is currently an associate editor of the *International review of law computers & technology*, and a member of the Correspondents Panel of the *Computer law and security report*. He is a former member of the British & Irish Legal Education Technology Association (ILETA) Executive Committee and the General Council of the Society for Computers and Law (SCL). His research covers the fields of information technology law, European Community law and intellectual property law. He has presented papers on computer misuse, computer software copyright, data protection, electronic publishing, social exclusion and the information superhighway, and legal issues of the Internet and World

Wide Web at conferences and seminars in the UK, Germany, Canada and Australia.

Michelle Green has worked in the commercial electronic industry since 1987. She was appointed Context's Marketing Director in 1990. Her duties include overall responsibility for Marketing, Sales, Customer Support and Subscriptions Administration departments. In addition she works with the other directors on strategic alliances and business development. Michelle Green is a dircctor of the Electronic Information Publishers Action Group (EIP). The Forum brings together individuals from EIP member companies who have direct responsibility for product support and development and wish to share experiences and help develop standards and general codes of practice for the benefit of the electronic publishing industry. In her capacity as former Chair of the Forum she has presented papers at key industry conferences.

Tony Hadland is Information Manager for the Group Property Services department of Barclays Bank PLC. His responsibilities include Information Security Management, Operational Risk Management, the Year 2000 problem, Data Protection compliance, Graphical Information Management (CAD and digital photography) and hypertext publishing His professional background is in architecture and building surveying. Former chair of the Building Surveyors' Research Group of the RICS, he has also been a member of that Institution's main research committee. Tony is a former freelance broadcaster and since 1981 has run his own small publishing house. He has contributed to books on surveying practice management, information management, retail bank design and cycle history. Currently he has five titles of his own in print, most of which deal with aspects of cycle technology.

Angus Hamilton is a solicitor in private practice in North London. Since 1986 he has conducted prosecutions under the Data Protection Act for the Office of the Data Protection Registrar and has advised corporations on data protection compliance. He is, together with Rosemary Jay – the senior lawyer at the Office of the Data Protection Registrar – the author of Sweet & Maxwell's *Guide to the 1998 Data Protection Act* (1999). He is also a contributor to *Liberating cyberspace* (Pluto, 1998). He writes a monthly legal advice colunm for the leading monthly computer magazine *PCPro* and is a regular contributor to *Computers & law*. His website is at **http://www.btinternet.com/~hamiltons/**; e-mail: **Angus. Hamilton@btinternet.com**.

Duncan Langford is a mainstream computer scientist, teaching at the University of Kent at Canterbury. He has specialized in the relationship between computing and professional issues, and is now regarded as an international expert in the field of computer ethics and Internet ethics. Dr Langford is a Founder Member of the International Advisory Board, Centre for Computing and Social Responsibility (UK). He was also a member of IEE/ACM Software Engineering Ethics and Professional Practices working groups (USA) and is on the editorial boards of the *On-line journal of ethics* (USA), *Journal of systems and information technology* (Australia) and *Information, communication and society* (UK). He has lectured frequently in Europe and North America, and has many publications in print on computer and Internet ethics.

John Lindsay is Reader in Information Systems Design at Kingston University. He was one of the agitators of Librarians for Social Change in the 1970s, ran the Need to Know Project at South Hackney School, was one of the originators of Gay Switchboard and has always been interested in the relationship between the politics of information and social organization. He is on the Executive of the Technical Board of the British Computer Society and runs the Transport Information Task Group.

Richard McCracken is Rights Manager at the Open University where the Rights Department manages the licensing of rights across all media as an integral part of the production and exploitation of the University's print, broadcast and multi-media materials. He lectures and tutors widely on the subject of copyright and related rights and is co-author of McCracken and Gilbart, *Buying and clearing rights: print, broadcast and multimedia* (Blueprint, 1995). He has been a member of both JISC and eLib working groups on copyright and has worked with TLTP and FDLT projects.

Charles Oppenheim is Professor of Information Science at Loughborough University. He has held a variety of posts in academia and industry. His professional interests focus on areas where the law and information overlap, such as copyright, data protection and freedom of information. He is an Honorary Fellow of the Institute of Information Scientists and a Fellow of The Library Association. He is a frequent contributor to the professional literature and gives regular conference presentations. The third edition of his *The legal and regulatory environment for electronic information* was published by Infonortics at the end of 1998.

Frederick W. Ratcliffe After ten years working in the university libraries of Manchester, Glasgow and Newcastle upon Tyne, Dr Ratcliffe was appointed University Librarian of Manchester in 1965. There he organized the merger of the libraries of the John Rylands and the University, becoming, in 1972, the first

Director of the John Rylands University Library of Manchester. In 1980 he moved to Cambridge as University Librarian and Fellow of Corpus Christi College, retiring from the former position in 1994 as Emeritus University Librarian. As librarian of one of the six copyright deposit libraries, Dr Ratcliffe was much involved in copyright issues, not least in relation to the new media. In retirement he is Fellow Librarian of Corpus Christi College in charge of the Parker and Butler libraries.

Dr Ratcliffe's work has also included a part time lectureship in medieval German; an Honorary Lectureship in Textual Criticism at Manchester; an External Professorship at Loughborough University; being the Sandars Reader in Bibliography, Cambridge; and the Chair of the National Preservation Office, 1984–94. He has contributed to many learned journals and monographs in the literature of the Arts and librarianship and was the author of *Preservation policies and conservation in British Libraries*. He served as a Justice of the Peace for 25 years and was appointed CBE for services to Cambridge and academic librarianship in 1994.

Heather Rowe   Since joining Lovell White Durrant as a banking lawyer 14 years ago, Heather has specialized in advising in relation to companies in the fields of telecommunications and computers and is now a partner in the Computers, Communications and Media Group. In addition to working on technology joint ventures, she has drafted, on a regular basis, turnkey projects in the computer/telecommunications field, outsourcing agreements, agreements relating to hardware and software supply and development, standard terms and conditions of supply/purchase in the information technology field, and EDI and network agreements.

A large part of her current practice revolves around the issues arising from the Year 2000 and the advent of EMU. Another major part of that practice relates to data protection, since the law in all EU member states is supposed to be changing to give effect to an EC Directive and there are a number of implementation issues that arise.

She is Chairman of the International Chamber of Commerce's International Working Party on Data Protection and Privacy, as well as having been appointed Chairman of ICC UK's Committee on Computing, Telecommunications and Information Policy. She is also Chairman of the Centre for the Study of Financial Innovation's Working Party on Regulation and the Internet and has recently been appointed Co-Chairman of Committee R, the International Computer & Technology Law Committee, of the International Bar Association.

Mark Taylor   At the time of writing, Mark Taylor was a trainee solicitor in Lovell White Durrant's Computer Communications and Media Unit, which he joined permanently in April 1999 on qualification as a solicitor. Prior to joining

Lovell White Durrant, Mark worked for IBM in software development. Previous publications include articles in *Computer law & security report* and *IT law today.*

John Williams is Professor of Law and Head of the Department of Law at the University of Wales Aberystwyth. He is the author of a number of books on the law and social welfare including *Social services law* (Tolley, 1996) and *Mental health law* (Fourmat, 1990). In addition, he has written articles on a wide range of legal matters including elder abuse, law and technology, and child law. He is a member of the Human Fertilization and Embryology Authority and chairs its Information Committee. He is an active member of the Citizens Advice Bureaux and is a past chair of the North Wales CAB Area Committee.

Introduction

C. J. Armstrong

Several years ago I heard a presentation on the legal ramifications of publishing on the Internet and I, along with the many other information professionals who heard it, was immediately struck by a great hole in my knowledge. Not just any gap that might be an irritation and leave me embarrassed at a pub quiz but one that was quite liable to have profound effects on my future professional life.

In the recent past, the nearest that most information workers came to legal risk lay in the agreeing of contracts with online vendors or information suppliers and the observance of copyright around the library photocopier. Now – as was made abundantly clear during that memorable presentation – the Internet has changed things.

I have no doubt that anyone who has been moved to pick up this volume must be at least partly Internet-literate and will not need to be told about web browsers or e-mail, about search engines or homepages, but at the same time I suspect that he or she may not have stopped to consider the extent to which the Internet has empowered anyone with access to a personal computer and a modem. (As nearly all PCs are now sold *with* modems, this is beginning to be a significant proportion of the population over the age of five!) Electronic mail means that written communications are easy and near instantaneous (and not always delivered to known recipients); browsers mean that users have access to a variety and volume of graphics, images, sounds, video clips and texts that once could only have been dreamed of in even the largest libraries; and the web space normally made available to users by their Internet service provider gives anyone – even that precocious five year old – the means to publish to the world. And for those who do not have their own PC, all this can be done from the library.

Electronic publishing is one of the most interesting areas. Once upon a time, all forms of publishing required the services of an intermediary – a publishing house whose publishers accepted the work, whose editors proof-read the work, whose designers were responsible for the style and whose marketing department targeted it appropriately. By these activities the publishing house guaranteed the work to its readership. Further, publishers have long experience of the laws of print-on-paper publishing and can usually be relied upon to ensure that their authors do not contravene them. In the brave new electronic world there may be no such buffer between the author and the reader, and it behoves those who provide access to the Internet to remain alert to the consequences of actions taken by both staff and clients.

The Internet also offers users an immediate ability to correspond with colleagues and friends around the world and a capability – unique in the experience of humankind – to conduct in-depth research, acquiring the relevant documents or resources from the home, the classroom or the library in real time and apparently without the need of expert help. This handbook includes material that will affect your attitude to both of these activities.

Electronic mail messages may not remain confidential or private despite the originator's intentions or endeavours, so what is typed – especially what is typed in the name of a company – should not be treated casually. The provision of web access to staff, clients or the general public effectively makes available almost any resource anywhere on any computer attached to the Internet. This could include pornography or other legally suspect materials, and – as intermediaries in that particular electronic publishing chain – libraries need to take cognizance of their role and legal position.

Finally, with regard to the Internet, it has to be remembered that it *is* worldwide: material viewed on the screen may originate in any other country and thus in any other jurisdiction. This may affect the legality of the material; it may also mean that the law of the country in which the information unit or library is situated may not be the relevant law to guide its actions.

But it is not just the Internet that should concern information specialists – *that* is just currently the most public face of electronic library activities. CD-ROM and online databases continue to be used and each presents unique legal concerns to their licencees. At a different level, users and providers must be alert to the issues surrounding legal deposit or security.

In assembling this collection of papers it is my intention to provide a first port of call for those information scientists and librarians whose work brings them into regular contact with the various electronic media. *Staying legal* is a handbook to alert readers to the relevant legal issues and the laws that surround them – it is not, most emphatically not, all you will ever need in the way of legal advice, but it is a guide that should be consulted before you begin publishing on the Internet, sending e-mails, creating webpages, accessing webpages, or letting others make free with your work stations. However, the bottom line is if something you read here gives you cause for concern, then get specific legal advice from a specialist in copyright, data protection or whichever of the other areas has suddenly become important to you.

The first three chapters do not deal specifically with legal issues such as copyright or liability: instead, they set the scene for readers. They offer a context for what follows. Duncan Langford examines earlier methods of communication on the basis that many assumptions made about communicating electronically are founded upon such individual and collective human experience. He talks of passive information, where a user simply accesses data of interest to them, and active information, where its direct publication becomes paramount; looks at likely areas of controversy and conflict; and examines possible developments. Where the first chapter touches on the larger, political, aspects of communication, the second – by John Lindsay – centres on the role of government and its agencies in the provision of information electronically. In Chapter 3, John Williams examines the rights and needs of various user communities for legal information and the extent to which these needs are met. There is some doubt that information technology alone can provide appropriate access but no doubt that groups such as children or vulnerable adults have a right of access that libraries – among others – may help to provide.

Following these are chapters that deal with specific areas of the law relevant to electronic publishing or publications. Charles Oppenheim covers the issues surrounding intellectual property rights and copyright, with definitions and explanations of the legal basis for copyright – both in print and electronic – before looking at some Internet copyright cases. In apparent contrast, in looking at legal deposit, Fred Ratcliffe in Chapter 5 takes as his starting point a quotation from *The Times* to the effect that copyright is finished. His erudite summary of the history of deposit brings readers right up to date, ending with the written answer by the secretary of state for culture, media and sport in December 1998 to a question on the *Report of the Working Party on Legal Deposit* chaired by Sir Anthony Kenney.

In Chapter 6 Angus Hamilton tackles the tricky ground of the Data Protection Acts of 1984 and 1998. As with so much in this volume, and as these dates indicate, the law is constantly subject to change, posing difficult problems for writers and editors. The new Act does not remove the old legislation but retains concepts and builds on the existing and established system. As there is also a transitional period during which both the 1984 and 1998 regimes will have relevance, the chapter covers the old legislation and looks forward to the new. This chapter is followed by one from Andrew Charlesworth dealing with the many issues of criminal liability and another from Heather Rowe and Mark Taylor on self-regulation of multimedia and the Internet, particularly in the area of advertising. Chapter 8 also touches on liability for content, discrimination and computer misuse, and considers some of the jurisdictional issues that can arise when advertising on the Internet.

It is unfortunate that a chapter on Civil Liability which was to complement Andrew Charlesworth's Criminal Liability offering has had to be omitted as, for various reasons, it just could not be completed for the absolutely final publishing deadline.

Chapter 9, by Richard McCracken, covers agreements, user licences and codes of practice. Rather than presenting a model licence, the chapter details the issues and points to be considered in preparing, drawing up and agreeing a licence. The message is to prepare well – and this chapter is a good start!

The final two chapters differ slightly from those that have gone before. Tony Hadland deals with security within a library or information unit. While not strictly a legal issue, the link is unarguable and the advice on the precautions to take timely. Finally, Michelle Green provides a commercial viewpoint with her chapter from the information provider's angle.

It is undeniable that the Internet offers the information profession a wealth of opportunities and an enormous fund of resources. While it has often been suggested in the past that the Internet offers some sort of freedom of speech or freedom from censorship, or is in some way immune from the legal process, it has become clear that this is very far from the case. The Internet is *not* a tool to be used casually despite the fact that it is inexpensive to use and offers much material that is completely free. Most information units now offer an environment in which information and library staff, employees of the parent organizations and/or the public are given access to work stations linked to a network in turn linked to CD-ROMs, online databases and the wider world of the Internet. Management has a responsibility for ensuring that all such activities remain legal and thus, from the point of view of the company, safe.

This handbook should alert readers to areas where there may be risks and should highlight the type of risk as well as its significance. It may even, in some cases, offer a partial answer, but *Staying legal* does not set out to be more than a guide warning readers of areas to which they should attend. Any reader who feels that he or she may have a problem – or even the potential for a problem to develop – should seek appropriate legal help.

Used wisely and appropriately, electronic resources are no more risky in legal terms than print publications. Wisdom comes from understanding what is appropriate to each individual activity. I hope this volume helps in this undertaking.

Chris Armstrong

1

Universal access to information

Duncan Langford

Introduction

This chapter is intended to establish a context for debate on the electronic exchange of information. After providing some general background, it considers issues relating to this field, and looks ahead to likely developments.

We begin by briefly looking at ways in which humans have, in the past, obtained and distributed information, with the intention of establishing the strengths and weaknesses of these earlier methods. Although an examination of earlier methods of communication may at first appear irrelevant to the consideration of computer-related issues, analysis of the earlier 'non-electronic' aspect of information access is actually of particular importance. This is not least because many basic assumptions made about communicating electronically are, understandably, founded upon previous individual and collective human experience. As much of this experience must, inevitably, relate to earlier forms of communication, lack of awareness of the applicability of earlier behaviour to an electronic setting may result in the transfer of inappropriate assumptions.

Information itself can, of course, be defined in a huge variety of ways. For the purposes of this analysis, however, I suggest an approach to communication in which information may be appropriately divided into two distinct categories. These two essentially different methods in which exchange of electronic information between humans takes place can be described as the *passive* and the *active* presentation of data. These terms are defined below, and their relevance to the transfer of electronic information compared and contrasted.

The discussion then moves to a general overview of the considerable differences in human society that have resulted from the availability and growing predominance of electronic communication. Using a series of examples, it is argued that differences between 'traditional' means of information interchange and electronic communication at every level inevitably result in far more than a simple change in scale.

Some important issues that relate to the reliance upon electronic media in a twenty-first century society are then highlighted. The use of 'real world' examples of both successes and failures of differing forms of electronic communication allows examination of some very different problems caused by electronic storage and transmission of information.

The chapter concludes by summarizing the current position, giving particular attention to areas of debate and potential conflict. It ends by examining likely future developments, giving particular emphasis to the inevitable changes in public and private behaviour.

History

However impressive the Internet may appear, it may be argued that it is really just the latest of many aids that have evolved over millennia to aid human interaction.

This perception is important, because in most spheres of human activity experience is cumulative – when learning, we tend automatically to apply previous knowledge. When an individual employs a new communication tool it is usually appropriate for that person to apply previous experience from other areas of communication. So, for example, just as the first printed books imitated existing manuscript documents, so early computer displays imitated printed material.

However, when considering appropriate conduct in the handling of electronic information today, such a 'natural' progression of behaviour may be less relevant. Indeed, if applied unthinkingly to communication in this area, previous knowledge of human interaction may not be helpful. Communicating through computers, using networks and the Internet, is quantitatively and qualitatively different from all earlier human experience.

Let us for a moment consider exactly what the communication of information has meant at various points in history.

Information has probably always been communicated verbally; it has also been inscribed on clay or papyrus, and, later, written and then printed on paper. Once in written form, information has been transported between individuals and organizations, by foot and by horse, and, of course, by sea and later air. Such early means of transmission had several things in common. Before the arrival of broadbased communications, such as newspapers and books, transmitted information was *specific*, by which I mean it tended always to be between a known source and a known target. It was also specific in the sense that the information *itself* tended to relate to a particular topic, rather than to matters of general interest.

When in the fifteenth century development of printing technology allowed the spread of 'non-official' information, those in authority moved decisively to control it. For example, for centuries the Vatican insisted upon papal approval for all published texts, while as late as the eighteenth century the introduction of newspapers in the United Kingdom led to government attempts at control through a newspaper tax. A growing potential audience and the increasing spread of printing technology gradually reduced the ability of governments and others to control printed information, but in most countries statute law remains precise about what may and may not be officially published even today. Although copyright is clearly relevant here, this is not solely a copyright issue. Restriction of information on anything that the State considers might be used against authority (whether opposition manifestos or recipes for bombs) is also common.

When considering individual access to information and its transfer between individuals, a major concern has always been one of *relevance*. The perception of the possessor of information concerning its relevance to a potential recipient has frequently played an essential part in whether information has been communicated at all. As an old saying goes, 'knowledge is power', and while of course there are exceptions, from the prehistoric priesthood onward, those possessing information have sometimes appeared to see their primary role as preventing, rather than encouraging, the distribution of knowledge. Again, using a religious example, the promotion of a particular pattern of information has frequently been accompanied by the rigorous suppression of dissenting or competing information.

This position is still largely true. Those in positions of power – commercial power, governmental power, industrial power – guard their secrets jealously. While millions may be spent on general product promotion, commercial confidentiality can prevent members of the public from finding out more specific data. During elections, politicians may speak encouragingly of 'open government', but restrictions on the publication and distribution of government information still often remain in place. While there are signs in the UK that this may well be changing – the Government Information Service 'Open Government' site is certainly an excellent start[1] – too often those organizations possessing information prefer to decide for themselves what should and should not be made available to others.

What, though, of the role of the individual? Here there has been a dramatic change, beginning with the growth of secular education in the sixteenth and seventeenth centuries. Until then the language of European education was Latin, and, because books and teaching used Latin, those people without a knowledge of the language were automatically excluded from the collective body of knowledge. The first *Bible* printed in English appeared after the establishment of the Church of England by Henry VIII; until then, reading the *Bible* involved learning Latin or Greek, the languages of scholars. Use of these languages meant, of course, that information could normally be readily made available and distributed to the cognoscenti, while preventing direct viewing by the wider public.

This exclusion of those without specialist knowledge is analogous to the present manner in which physical access to computers is restricted to those individuals who can afford them, or who work for those who can afford them. Of course, insufficient knowledge of specialist computer skills effectively prevents access, too.

The spread of wider education and increasing enfranchisement in the twentieth century overcame many of the earlier constraints on the free exchange of information. In the developed world, universal general education has for most of this century been accepted: most individuals are now literate. In Britain the State stranglehold on the distribution of information has been eased – no longer is approved information published by being nailed to a church door; no longer is official approval needed before books or newspapers are produced.

However, this does not mean there are no longer any constraints: control (often invisible) remains. It certainly appears that the most highly controlled and restricted aspects of information exchange are inevitably those that are the most popular, and have the highest profile. For instance, publication of a specialist book is far less restricted in its approach and contents than similar material published in a newspaper, which itself is in turn less restricted than a television programme. A popular terrestrial television programme is likely to be more severely controlled than one appealing to minority interests or broadcast by cable – and so on.

The inverse relationship between popularity and freedom from control is one significant reason why the rise of communication through the Internet has been greeted with widespread official concern – the Internet is a truly global medium that cannot be effectively censored or controlled.

In summary

People have always had the ability to communicate with each other, but history has shown that the possession of information does not automatically lead to its distribution. Those in authority, whether commercial or governmental, do not necessarily accept any need to pass on or distribute information, or to facilitate such actions by others. Although the ability of the general population to appreciate and participate in media distribution of information has greatly increased, the control of conventional methods of communication is still firmly in the hands of authority. This authority, in most countries, is fully prepared to encourage, or enforce, the imposition of what it considers appropriate standards. As the size of a potential audience increases, the degree of such control is likely to increase in proportion. The Internet is a radically different method of global communication, and, unlike traditional print and mass media, it cannot be controlled.

The Internet

To properly appreciate the issues involved, it is necessary to describe very briefly what the Internet actually is, and how it may be used.

Essentially consisting of a globally linked set of computer networks, the Internet was originally developed and has for many years evolved without any central control or direction. Since its inception it was largely used for the transfer of textual information, through electronic mail and other means. The introduction of the World Wide Web (WWW) added a very 'user-friendly' graphical interface. No longer is Internet communication limited to standard typed text; it may now include colour pictures, digital sound and even full-motion video. Suitably connected individuals are able to use both new and established aspects of the Internet, 'posting' e-mail and news items to specialist text-based newsgroups, and also 'visiting' web 'sites' and viewing their contents. More sophisticated users may themselves become publishers by creating their own websites.

In order to access the Internet, a computer is normally connected by an ordinary telephone link to an Internet service provider, or ISP. The ISP then makes an onward connection to a national 'backbone site', and thus to the wider Internet – which is essentially a collection of connected backbone sites. Apart from a computer and the appropriate software, the only other equipment needed for a user to make these connections is a modem, a cheap and simple device to connect a computer to a telephone line.

It is important to appreciate that the censorship of textual information circulated through the Internet is virtually impossible, while the control of websites is only practicable by the ISP concerned. However, this apparent measure of control is illusory: a censored site may readily move to another ISP, potentially even in a different country, where more favourable rules may apply.

Connection to the Internet means a computer is linked through an ISP to the global community of networked computers. Once this connection has been made, data may be freely exchanged with any other similarly connected computer. In addition, the advent of World Wide Web sites allows the easy viewing of graphically based information, while providing both companies and individuals with the opportunity for global publishing.

Categories of information

So far, when we have discussed 'information' it has been considered as a monolithic whole, as a shapeless mass that has only one aspect, that of communicability. While this may be generally true, the task of considering how electronic information can best be examined will be helped by distinguishing between two distinct categories of information. I define these categories as the *passive* and *active* aspects of information interchange.

Passive information

This first category is concerned with the availability of information, and the freedom an individual may have to obtain *specialist* data; that is, data that would normally be the preserve of a specialist group. Essentially, some cultures (and, within cultures, professional groups) can be considered as 'information rich' – exclusively possessing information that may nevertheless be of interest or relevance to a much wider group. Often, secure in their possession of such specialist material, these professional groups place bars on the sharing of information outside their membership. Membership of the group itself can then normally be achieved only by a series of tests, designed perhaps as much to exclude the unsuitable as to enlist the appropriate. Most professions seem to operate a similar approach, which has given rise to a description of the development of professions as a 'conspiracy against the laity'.

A typical result of this state of affairs is a situation where specific information, whilst theoretically available within a society to everyone able to read it, is in practice limited to those who are concerned professionally with it. Medical information tends to be the exclusive preserve of doctors, legal information that of lawyers, and so on. This is unfortunate, as a desire and need for such information are not restricted to those dealing with a subject professionally. Those concerned as clients or patients usually also have an interest. However, an educated member of the public wishing to build an informed opinion on such a 'specialist' subject would have to devote considerable research time to reading books and specialist journals to a high level. Clearly, in these circumstances, answering a specialist question by simple access to specific data is not normally possible.

In strong contrast, the electronic publication of specialist information potentially allows any connected individual located anywhere in the world systematic access to data previously restricted to specialist groups. This information may already have been theoretically available to those who were able to spend the time and resources necessary to track it down, but the sheer scale of the Internet and the volume of specialist information contained make it probable that even a knowledgeable expert can be materially assisted by reference to electronically held data.

It is now the case that even the most complex specialist material can be found through a simple Internet search. An example of a typical area where this has made a considerable difference to individuals is the field of medical information.

It is possible to use World Wide Web search engines (software applications that are used to seek out data) to obtain specific information. Given a suitable word or phrase, a Web search engine can readily produce a list of webpages containing references to that data. For example, I used a search engine to look for any mention of 'bronchitis', which produced 2601 instances of global information and discussion on the topic. For obvious reasons I did not access them all, but those webpages I investigated ranged from helpful and friendly advice from sufferers of the condition to detailed medical information.

As well as containing information, some specialist webpages provide specific onward pointers or links. For example, besides allowing general searching of the World Wide Web, the search engine Excite! has many pages of information which have already been collected and collated under various headings – for those interested in medical information: for example, Figure 1.1 shows part of the Excite! list of medical conditions,[2] with onward links to considerable further information.

The increasing spread of global presentation of specific information in this way has had several important consequences. One of the most interesting is not just the informing but the enfranchising of individuals. People can now not only access previously hard to obtain data, but may themselves group together to provide shared information and support through the Internet.

An excellent example of how the Internet provides a previously impossible resource in this way is the case of UK academic Ken Spencer. Shortly after a hol-

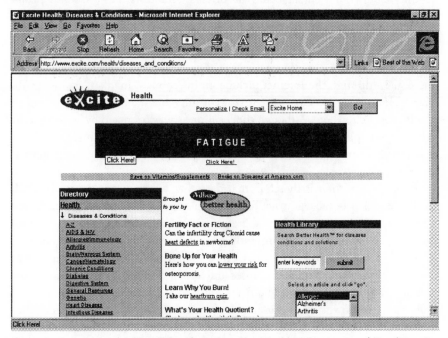

Fig. 1.1 Excite! search engine classification under 'Health – Diseases and Conditions'

iday in England, he developed a mysterious illness, thought at first to be an allergy. After a period of increasing pain and disablement, a friend noticed similarities between his condition and Lyme disease, thought to be restricted to more tropical climates. His doctor suggested the diagnosis to the rheumatology consultant, only to be categorically assured that there was no Lyme disease in the UK. Believing his illness to be misdiagnosed, Spencer found specialist information on the web that convinced his doctors that he was indeed suffering from Lyme disease, despite previous assurance to the contrary.

The first class of passive information is therefore that which allows material to be made available electronically. While it may previously have been available in other forms, the easy electronic availability of material permits individuals who could not before have obtained access to gain desired information. Of course, it also allows those who could previously have viewed information only with difficulty to do so readily.

A second class of passive information is that which would have been (and often still is) subject to official restrictions or outright banning. In this case, before the advent of the Internet it would have been both possible and practicable for an authority to place an absolute prohibition on the publication and distribution of specific information. A recent example from the UK relates to the Joint Enquiry Team (JET) report concerning child abuse, prepared for Nottinghamshire County Council but embargoed by it for legal and other reasons. Many people felt that this information should have been published, and, despite serious efforts to prevent it by Nottinghamshire legal officers, it is now available widely through the Internet.[3]

Previous examples of information that, despite legal attempts to contain it, was distributed through the Internet include an infamous Canadian legal issue, the Karla Homolka trial. This case created considerable interest and discussion on the Net and elsewhere. Although the local press was restricted by court order in what it could print, Canadians with Internet access were for the first time able to learn easily from other reports – principally in the US – what was happening on their own doorsteps.

Passive information is therefore that data that would normally not be easily available, either because it is not ordinarily physically accessible, or because it is physically widely distributed and therefore hard to collect. Once published on the Internet, such data becomes instantly globally accessible and later attempts to control or limit its distribution are doomed to inevitable failure. The widespread availability of passive data enfranchises individuals, by freeing them from the limitations of official channels and official publications. However, it is important to reflect on the downside of this new enfranchisement. Wider issues, including freedom of speech and the freedom to contain personal data, are also involved.

Active information

Active publication of information extends the role of an Internet-connected individual even further. From being merely a passive seeker and consumer of information, albeit on a global scale, such a person is now able to become both publisher and distributor. In direct contrast to the situation throughout recorded history, connection to the Internet essentially means that access to simple global broadcasting and communication is available to virtually anyone, anywhere.

The usefulness of the Internet to those individuals who share a common interest in a specific medical condition was mentioned earlier; in this case, a low percentage incidence of an illness in a specific population may nevertheless result in a large number of concerned individuals globally. The Internet also allows such people to communicate directly, for example in providing support, personal experiences of particular drugs and treatment and so on. It allows them to work together and gives them the ability to act together, perhaps as a pressure group.

Other benefits of communication through the Internet may be less tangible. Those individuals prevented by bodily or other disadvantages from moving freely around the physical world often suffer social isolation. Such isolation may potentially be overcome by encouraging linking to the Internet, with subsequent free movement around the electronic global village, a community of which they can be full members.

It is also possible to use active publication of information through the Internet to overcome political barriers to freedom of expression. The UK's *Guardian* newspaper of 12 December 1996 reported on the way in which attempts at news censorship by the Serbian government in Belgrade were overcome:

> When Serbia's Slobodan Milosevic, faced with large anti-government demonstrations, tried to shut down the last vestiges of an independent news media last week, he unwittingly spawned a technological revolt.
>
> Tens of thousands of students, professors, professionals and journalists connected their computers to Internet websites abroad when the government closed independent radio station B-92 for two days. The station made digital broadcasts in Serbo-Croatian and English using audio Internet links, and using its website, continued reporting on the protests, which were set off by the government's annulment of municipal elections won by the opposition.
>
> B-92, which has been the main source of news here, was allowed to broadcast again as the government eased its response to the protests and hinted that it might reconsider the annulment of the elections.
>
> But the experience has made protestors aware of the tremendous potential at their fingertips. Independent journalists have rushed forward with plans to bypass govern-

ment transmitters, news agencies and television studios, using the Internet to carry their message across Serbia and to the outside world.

Clearly the Internet can provide a voice not just to those who were previously without one, but to those who have been more actively disenfranchised.

As the number of individuals connected to the Internet has grown, so the number of different uses made of 'personal' webpages have increased enormously. The opportunity offered to individuals of telling the world about issues of importance to them has been seized with enthusiasm.

There are many tens of thousands of individual webpages, covering the whole range of human experience and interests. For example, some people use the opportunity of a personal webpage to promote themselves as a prospective employee, with a suitably impressive CV and biographical information. Others take a more personal approach, with lists of their interests, often defining themselves by including ongoing links to their favourite webpages – some personal pages consist of little more than lists of links to other sites. Fans provide information on every sport, their pages often packed with colour photographs and statistics, while television enthusiasts of all flavours produce often incredibly esoteric information about their chosen programmes. Many specialist interests are supported. Genealogical issues are a good example of the advantage of the Internet in assisting specialist interests – however unusual your name may be, the chances are that somewhere in the world there is someone who shares it.

Apart from personal information and leisure interests, the easy publication of personal webpages gives a voice to political and pressure groups, however unrepresentative they may be. Many are benign, but others promote extreme fascist and revolutionary views and other controversial material, such as pornography.

Commercial examples of active publication of information range from small local firms to major international companies. Of course, only the quality of the displayed material, rather than the size of the company, is obvious when viewing a webpage; the electronic playing field is a level one.

The growth of the World Wide Web over the past few years has been extremely rapid. From a largely academic network, the Internet has undergone an explosion of private and commercial growth. It is now, for example, considered routine for most companies to promote themselves by including their web address in paper or television advertising. Such company websites normally consist of a page or series of Internet pages, which typically allow a company to both present help and advice to users and potential users of their product, while additionally displaying a variety of advertisements.

Of course, as was mentioned above, private individuals and pressure groups enjoy the same opportunities. The introduction of the Internet, and especially the World Wide Web, has allowed individuals virtually unfettered access to a global medium. Possession of a suitably networked computer allows a user to both scan and collect passive data, and, for the more technically aware, also provides the ability to easily promote their own information nationally and internationally.

Essentially, networked computers allow spreading of information by companies and individuals in a way that is directly analogous to traditional broadcasting or publishing on paper. However, once distributed electronically, such 'published' information is potentially seen by very large numbers of individuals indeed – far more than could ever be possible using the traditional media – while, in addition, Internet publication cannot be effectively controlled or censored.

Disadvantages

Apart from the changes made by easy global broadcasting, the most important difference between electronic and 'traditional' information lies in the ease with which electronic information may be manipulated. Apart from simple transmission of an original, it is possible to produce indistinguishable electronic copies. There is no limit to the number of identical copies that may be easily circulated through local, national and international computers.

There are several interrelated issues that must be addressed here, the first of which is the *validity* of electronic data. How much reliance may be placed on the fact that it is actually what it purports to be? The issue of validity is of equal importance whatever aspect of electronic information we are considering: an electronic message or an electronic contract is equally vulnerable. The presentation of information electronically, for example on a webpage, cannot be taken as proof of its authenticity – even when claiming to be genuine, such material can be and sometimes is totally spurious. Even when a document is demonstrably authentic, we need to know whether it is a current draft, or merely an obsolete early version, and, of course, whether it may have undergone any unauthorized changes since it left the author's computer. Essentially, if we are no longer sure of its authenticity, no reliance can be placed on electronic information.

A subsidiary but related authenticity issue concerns the *depth* of retrieved information. For example, as we have seen, searches of the Internet may produce specialist information not otherwise generally available. However, how much data is actually required to form an accurate view? While an expert in the field may be able to accurately interpret the full position from a limited volume of material, a less experienced reader could well form a false impression.

A second important issue concerns the potentially enormous *distribution* of electronic material. Even with modern photocopiers, mass duplication of printed documents is not a trivial exercise. In strong contrast, identical copies of electronic documents may be cloned with a keystroke, and dispatched around the world with another. When such copying of documents is both invisible and triv-

ially easy, the security of information must be considered important. It is also crucial to remember that the distribution of an electronic document may eventually
be far wider than the original author ever intended, and copies of it may be kept
indefinitely. Long-forgotten electronic memos may then, in the memorable
words of one businessman, 'return to haunt you'.

This issue is also related to the problems of free speech and free expression
provoked by Internet links, which encourage free speech by the simple fact of
their existence. It is no longer possible to close national borders, but some countries – China is probably the most notorious – are nevertheless attempting to keep
out information they consider inappropriate, and to prevent unauthorized connections between their citizens and the outside world. For technical reasons, this
is not a strategy that can survive a large volume of Internet traffic, or a citizenry
determined to circumvent the restrictions. However, such attempts do not always
involve straightforward issues of free speech against political repression. Other
countries, such as the UK, may for example have a far more restrictive attitude to
sexual matters than have their electronic neighbours. Such countries consequently face similar problems in attempting to prevent their citizens from obtaining access to material officially considered illegal. However, such attempts are
almost certainly doomed to failure – preventing electronic cross-border traffic is,
in practical terms, impossible.

Easy copying of information can encourage the infringement of privacy: without appropriate safeguards, information that is personal in nature may be readily
passed on to others. This issue concerns both commercial and private information – one case I found particularly distasteful involved a person who, for motives
of revenge, distributed intimate photographs of a former lover on the Internet.

The ease of copying electronic material also opens up the likelihood of copyright infringement, both of text and images. Through ignorance and indifference,
particularly on the World Wide Web, such copying is extremely widespread.
Indeed, Internet abuse has led many major companies such as Viacom (which
owns Star Trek) to employ specialist lawyers to pursue such illegal use of their
material.

While local defaulters may of course be pursued, a major problem for
enforcement of statutory rights in this area is the supra-national nature of the
Internet. When Nottinghamshire County Council lawyers, based in the UK,
threatened the owners of a website in the United States with legal action over
their publication of the council's JET report, the threat of legal action in the US
(to be taken under UK law) was clearly hollow, however understandable the
attempt.

Essentially, the fundamental technology of the Internet makes any form of
external control difficult. To prevent anyone with even modest technical knowledge from Internet access is quite impossible – it would be as difficult to enforce

as a ban on the use of fax machines. In addition, widespread public access to powerful computer codes means transmission of material cannot be effectively overseen and regulated. This is true even though US export regulations classify cryptographic software as munitions, and prohibit their export. However, these regulations cover software only in electronic form (for instance sent on disks or via the Internet). The US Government embargo has been legally circumvented by exporting software code in printed form, and, once it was safely abroad, scanning it back into a computer.[4]

It is therefore quite unrealistic to suggest the electronic transmission of material can be effectively monitored and policed, even if the technical means existed to do so easily – which they currently do not.

Open defiance of local laws can most clearly be seen, though, in the spread of international websites offering many varieties of commercial pornography. The case here is directly analogous to an earlier issue, that of telephone sex lines in the UK. These caused much public disquiet but, when eventually banned by local telephone companies, such lines did not vanish. Their owners simply added several digits to their numbers and moved their operations outside the legal jurisdiction of the UK.

Finally, there is one serious practical disadvantage which is frequently overlooked by enthusiasts of widespread electronic information. In order for an individual to participate, there is a basic need for appropriate equipment, infrastructure and technical knowledge. While many homes in the developed world may already have a computer and telephone link, such things are by no means universal. Without them or a suitably equipped and sympathetic employer, individuals must be automatically disenfranchised from the benefits of the electronic society.

Despite the many advantages offered by the widespread use of the Internet, there are clearly associated problems. The nature of electronic information itself needs to be considered – is it actually dependable, and does it represent what it appears to represent? Even when the information is correct, the possibility of widespread distribution, whether wanted or unwanted, may lead to problems. National statutes can be infringed by unwanted actions, ranging from the distribution of copyrighted material to unacceptable publications. However, global enforcement in an environment without global authority may not be simple.

Changes in global society

The advent of globally networked computers has radically changed the ways in which an individual is able to both receive and transmit information. Internet communication and experience are totally different, both in scale and type, from anything humans have previously encountered. What changes will these radically transformed facilities have on civilization – both our local communities, and, if such a thing exists, our global society?

There are several relevant points that can immediately be established. First, the history of technical development has shown computer power roughly double every 18 months. While prices have remained fairly constant, the power of machines has greatly increased. Barring an extraordinary shift, it is quite certain that this pattern will continue – computers will become far more powerful, with greater memory capacity and expanded capabilities, while their cost remains constant. However, the increase in the number of individuals connected to the Internet and the networking of computers will continue to accelerate. There are currently moves to connect domestic televisions to the Internet, and massive promotion of Internet connection continues. The commercial bandwagon of Internet provision is still gathering speed. Today most homes in Europe have a telephone; by 2004 it is likely that most will probably also have a networked computer.

The combination of these two developments – the rapidly growing power of computers and the increasing pace of networking – must play a considerable part in changing our society. The most immediate result will undoubtedly be a disenfranchising of those without networked computers – the effect will be similar to the spread of satellite television, where those who can afford to enjoy additional services can be seen as forming a distinct group. Missing out on a connection to the Internet, though, could have a more significant effect, from limiting children's education to depriving adults of increasingly essential specialist information: libraries could provide a very real solution.

Further developments in the use of the Internet are likely to exacerbate the differences between 'haves' and 'have nots'. In the case of passive information, for example, legal judgments (for example, the Louise Woodward case) are beginning to appear on the Internet; government publications are being made available there, and many other organizations are beginning to shift their focus from paper to electronic information.

Active information has even greater possibilities. Online shopping is becoming practical, with specialist shops appealing to a potentially huge audience (see for instance the Internet Bookshop[5]), while such varied ideas as electronic voting from home and video on demand are no longer limited to science fiction. Such moves may lead to increased social isolation, where face-to-face encounters are replaced by the exchange of electrons over a network; on the other hand, those already experiencing social isolation, through physical disability or rural location, say, may be able to participate more fully in society than would otherwise be the case. Those members of society who lack the skills to use computers effectively may face marginalization, their views more difficult to obtain, their contributions less relevant to current concerns, and their involvement in society more limited in content and condition.

There are many potential advantages of universal access to information, but, in order for everyone to benefit from them, the definition of 'universal' needs to be continually kept in mind.

Conclusions

We have considered the way in which previous expectations of information interchange have been affected by the introduction of a globally linked network of computers known as the Internet. We have seen how connection to the Internet is both simple in concept and easily achieved in practice, and how, once connected, a user may readily obtain access to a vast hoard of information. It has been suggested that electronic information potentially falls into two groups – *passive*, where a user simply accesses data of interest, and *active*, where the direct publication of information becomes paramount. It was pointed out that censorship of Internet material is certainly non-trivial, and indeed may well be technically impossible. Some advantages and disadvantages of electronic communication, storage and transmission of information were considered. Transformations in social behaviour consequent upon these technical advances seem inescapable.

With the intention of forming a background for later discussion, in this chapter we have considered the broad picture involved in the electronic exchange of information. It has been stressed that the changes in both computer equipment and networking seen in the developed world over the past few years are likely to accelerate. The effects on both individuals and society must be profound.

References

1   Government Information Service:
     http://www.open.gov.uk [visited 02/07/1998].
2   Excite! health/diseases and conditions page:
     http://www.excite.com/health/diseases_and_conditions/ [visited 03/071998].
3   Nottinghamshire County Council *Joint Enquiry Team (JET) report*:
     http://www.jeremy.bc.ca/jetrep.htm (the gagging attempt)
     http://www.double-barrel.be/mirrors/dlheb/jetrepor.htm (the report itself)
     http://insight.dcss.mcmaster.ca/org/efc/pages/nottingham/ (discussion)
     [visited 03/07/1998].
4   PGPi Scanning Project:
     http://www.pgpi.com/project/ [visited 03/07/1998].
5   The Internet Bookshop:
     http://www.bookshop.co.uk [visited 03/07/1998].

2

Open.gov.uk?

John Lindsay

Introduction

This chapter is a little different from others in this book. Its concepts of electronic law, the information society and open government create an interesting circular argument. If government makes and implements laws and if government delivers laws to make government 'open', then is the process of law itself to be open? Are we all a part of government now?

Government makes laws about government. One law that the government has made is that government is to be open. Are we simply to describe something: 'This is the law and this is the government' or are we to engineer something: 'This is the government in the information age'?

Enthusiasts for the information society suggest that the new media will lead to a withering away of the state and a global democratic village in which all participate. Their opponents suggest the new technology will lead to an increasingly wide gap between the information rich and information poor, and increase the Big Brother control of government over the people.

This is, however, a book aimed at information professionals through The Library Association. This suggests that one question we should ask is, 'What is the proper role of a professional in this environment, and what is the role of an organization constituted by a royal charter with a special social responsibility for information and society?'

Even more precisely – just as the members of the Circle of State Librarians are employed by the State and are part of the civil service, so librarians in public libraries, schools and universities are only slightly less directly employed by public service organizations – does this mean that they are also a part of the process of government?

Professional librarians *are* part of the process of open government, executors of policy as well as observers and commentators on process.

My perspective in this chapter is that of an information systems engineer. We are engineering a society and we can describe its mechanisms; one of the mechanisms is government. As engineers, we can decide on the forces and trajectories, the vectors; we can decide what sort of object we are building and how to realign and re-engineer its components. For any one of us to undertake this alone would be an exercise in megalomania and delusion, though the information age might encourage us to think we could achieve the illusion. But as a part of a professional society duly constituted within this process, we *do* have to consider our collective role. As members of trades unions from time to time we become an active part of the process; many of us, too, may be members of political parties in which we will then also play a role – perhaps even as elected representatives of the people and therefore further agents of government?

In a book called *Staying legal*, this chapter offers the personal approach of someone for whom changing society is more important than staying legal. It describes some of the political forces that are now shaping the new landscape of public and private spaces, of competition and cooperation, of ownership and control. These are elaborated in looking at information, communication and interchange. The last term might be 'computation' rather than 'interchange', but it is not yet clear in the world of information professionals what the real impact of computation will be. This is followed by a worked example on information in transport, an area in which no progress seems to have been made since 1934. Next comes a consideration of some of the very basic shifts in word meanings and power with which professionals must be concerned. To justify never accepting defeat, the conclusion is that the profession, through the structure of information planning, might be able to play a hitherto untried role in reshaping the information landscape.

What is government for?

I must presume that we – reader and writer – have some sort of shared reality which includes a recognition of a tension between a civil society, in which we citizens participate in a collective responsibility for organizing a domestic economy, *and* a class war, in which exploitation and expropriation of surplus labour value from one class by another maintains an unequal distribution of power, wealth and access to resources. Individually we will emphasize one pole or the other differently at different times. I must also presume that we recognize that developments in technology are not a determinant but a consequence of a resolution of this tension in different ways at different times. Government is one of the forms by which this tension may be recognized and articulated. So, even to discuss open government is to take a stance.

As information professionals we play some intermediary role between the citizen and civilization. We are part of the social construction of reality.[1] Part of that reality is now mediated by a combination of computing, telecommunications and television. By means of a computer connected to a telephone everyone has the opportunity to become a publisher. One role of information professionals is to understand that a consequence of this reality is that what was concrete and material now has become virtual and abstract. Just as books and journals meant we had to produce new methodologies – such as shelf organization, cataloguing, classification, standards, citations, and so on – now we need to engineer new codes, structures and notations. The experiences of everyday life, the Internet and information retrieval are a model for what I mean: as the profession matures, new methods will evolve, become accepted, taught, and ultimately enter the rigours of syllabuses and examinations, while in the meantime our *ad hoc* solutions will begin to become concrete.

A little history

In case the discussion so far is too abstract, what follows is a digression into a moment of autobiography in order to show how I have understood this in the past.

My professional practice started in a public library in South Africa at the end of the 1960s when the stranglehold of apartheid tightened to exclude blacks from 'white' public libraries. Part of my job was to check the *Government gazette* for banned publications and remove them from the stacks or the incoming mail. That time must have been the exact opposite of open government. Thus, at least, we have a benchmark. But it was also the time when offset lithography from paper and aluminium plates was produced, of the first electric typewriters, of dry process photocopiers and of wax stencil electronic cutters. These machines made it possible to turn readers into writers and people who could not come into libraries could, with a little help, become publishers.

By the middle of the 1970s I was running the Need to Know Project at South Hackney School in London. It started from a very simple proposition, that in order to live in an urban society you had to be information literate. This meant that we had to study what people needed to know, devise methods of teaching it and produce materials. Telephone directories, bus timetables, road maps, government forms, and the local council were all mysteries to people who had never travelled half a mile outside the line between home and school. Again, the new technologies of photocopier, offset lithography, video camera and magnetic tape extended our vocabulary of production and consumption.

At about the same time, I was involved with a small group of people who shared a vision as a consequence of the Gay Liberation Front. We believed that the process of 'coming out as gay' in part starts when you realize that you are not the only one in the world. This means being able to connect! So we started a Gay Switchboard that had one simple idea: a telephone number so widely advertised that anyone who wanted to know it could not possibly remain ignorant of it. Someone answered this telephone 24 hours a day. I built the information system to support this telephone so that any query could be best answered. The telephone was another technology, but behind it were 5 x 3 catalogue cards organized by a classification and a filing sequence.

In the early 1980s it was clear that the computer and the telephone were going to be a significant technology through the digitization of data and that the potential for organizing the most important component of civilization, the management of cities, would open a new way to see political power. It would influence the shape of development, particularly in the big cities of the Third World. The problem of urban information and developing countries led to the Information for Development Coordinating Committee and the Development Information Plan.

The thread of this self-indulgence is simply the intertwinings of political power and its absence, organizational form and its articulation, and information with its social construction of reality mediated by new technologies – new technologies which change the relationships of production and consumption, distribution and exchange.

Force fields

Can we identify some of the force fields and tension points where the information society is going to find pressures building up?

The Library Association espouses noble sentiments in the principle of freedom of expression, in access to information and in the role of information in a democratic society. We can ignore the quibble that one can have access to data but not to information, as for the moment, information is what we do; being prohibited from having access is itself a kind of information. But the sentiments seem noble, even if it is not clear what the individual or the organization should do when impediments to these freedoms are encountered.

The law specifies data protection and privacy. This too seems a noble sentiment. I am opposed to people doing things with data about me which I don't know about or to which I have not consented. In the United States the principles of ownership of information have been elaborated by Branscomb, but nothing like that has been produced in Britain or Europe.[2] European integration seems likely to take us further into a minefield of conflicts between freedom of information and data protection. We have to ask, does this mean that the personal data subject must be left out of information freedom?

However, it is not just data subjects who provide us with problems. Sex, drugs and bombs seem to touch raw social nerves where the synapses respond by passing laws. An issue that I have had to examine in some detail is pornography.[3] It seems that children's access to the Internet combined with the depiction of children, laws about drugs other than alcohol, tobacco, tea and coffee and political responses to illegal terrorism produce complexities of thinking that are additional to those encountered when the same issues surface within the traditions of paper book publishing and arguments about censorship.

These areas will provide us with a complex discussion of open government in the digital age, given that the process and the product of government are concerned with the policing of the medium within which the discussion takes place as well as with the result. Are children participants in open government? Are children able to discuss their own participation in discussions about their own sexuality?

Another area where I see an interesting circularity is in intellectual property rights and the leveraging of intellectual property advantage. Freedom of information is expected to sit in harmony with the defence of the ownership of electronic information as private property. Indeed, a popular metaphor seems to be that information is the same as groceries, or any other commodity. I would argue however that it is not. Is a discussion about the nature of intellectual property, when it is concerned with the digital and takes place in the digital medium, part of open government? What needs to follow the discussion?

Another area is in the building of infrastructure. From the days of roads, canals and railways, communications networks were understood to behave differently from other markets and to need a special legal and regulatory framework. Newspaper, radio broadcasting, television, telephones, even theatres and book publishing similarly carry a baggage of peculiarity. It is no different with computer-based telecommunications. For nearly ten years, compliance with a European Commission regulation on open procurement and standardization required any public sector organization to write compliance with open systems interconnection (OSI) into all procurement tenders. This effectively prevented knowledge of TCP/IP networking and subsequently of its utilization until, in 1992, this impediment was simply swept away. The history of how the change happened has not been written and perhaps never will be, so there is much that is unexplained. How much it held back understanding of the Internet in Europe, and how much that cost, is unmeasured.

The privatized and tightly regulated national PTT (Parts, Telephones and Telecomunications) did not show itself at the forefront of progress. In the UK, it was from within higher education that the Joint Academic Network (JANET) was built. This was almost entirely through central government funding – either through top-slicing of the budgets of universities or by pressure within individual universities for expenditure – even though the network was procured to run over British Telecom plc (BT) lines. When the Internet came, there was an installed base of high-bandwidth networking in place and an educated workforce with some understanding of the technology.

Within the universities there was a continual battle between the open society and its enemies. The battle was over whether the polytechnics could have the same access as the universities, then over whether improvements in bandwidth would be accessible only to six high-level research universities or comprehensive, and then over whether access would be given to further education, public libraries, working hospitals (rather than teaching hospitals, where there was a turf war over whether the Department of Education or Health would carry the cost) and museums. In time, with the development of cable television companies, the market opened up so that procurement increasingly threatens to break the level of interconnectability and ubiquity. That the Joint Academic Network has survived and functions as it does is a triumph.

Within individual universities the battle was fought at a lower level. Should undergraduates have access to electronic mail; should they be able to have web-pages; should access to databases and CD-ROMs take place only in the library; what is electronic plagiarism; how is compliance with data protection managed within X.500 open systems; how many levels of passwords and security are needed; how often have they to be changed; who is taking these decisions; which of them are necessary; and which are just a bureaucratic response of those whose jobs and power extend as a result?

And throughout all this, librarians must be proud that they took a lead in open access, interoperability and user education. In 1984, Elizabeth Rogers at Sussex University had already produced a leaflet listing the open public access catalogues (OPACs) that were accessible along with what was then an almost incomprehensible complexity of access paths.[4] Migration from there to Z39.50 and the Web via networks, campus-wide information services, Gopher and Veronica, has not been a straight line, but the resources of higher education libraries are more available than they ever have been. The same is not true of public libraries.

It is also the case that the organization of knowledge has not proceeded at the pace of the technology. While enthusiasts speak of Moore's law for the increasing performance of processors, the time taken to put a journal into circulation has hardly changed since journals in libraries began. The vast proliferation of data available has increased the complexity of knowing. The explosive impact of the Internet on social knowledge, on knowing about power and its distribution in society, has barely begun.

It is not, however, simply the development of the Internet that has opened discussion on open government. There are also the political responses to two more fundamental transformations. The first is the collapse of the social democratic agenda.

For at least 50 years there existed an optimism and an enthusiasm that the worst excesses of capitalism could be ameliorated by social policy and that, through planning, productive processes could be coordinated. But thirty years of sharply oscillating boom and crisis have eroded that confidence while the disintegration of state capitalist organization in the USSR has apparently left a free-market rhetoric triumphant despite the obvious limitations of its failures.

The second transformation is the end of history, or at least the end of theory. There is an enthusiasm for suggesting that there can be no explanation, but rather a post-modernity, a relativist reductionism which moves in favour of disconnected, hypertextual digital realities and television bites.

Through liberalization of markets, privatization, competitive tendering, contracting out, service level agreements, what has become of the civil contract? However, for the rhetoric, it is worth remembering that half the gross domestic product is still taken through taxation and disbursed in some way through public expenditure.

The result of such activities appears to have been a galaxy of quasi-autonomous non-governmental organizations (Quangos) with citizens' charters, performance targets and webpages.

Is open government going to consider levels of taxation and their raising and expenditure? Is it going to consider the process of law making and enforcement, and above all else the relationship between the governing and the governed?

Information

This is not an essay on politics but one on information systems engineering aimed at information professionals, so what is the role of information in this process? I want to break 'information' into three parts. The first is information as it has been historically understood within librarianship: documents – files or the output of communication and decision taking. There are a great many documents in libraries. The second is communication, the political process by which people share and construct information. The third can be called interchange, the actual transactions processing events either between machines or among people but always involving the execution of processes that might involve the taking of decisions. It is unfortunate that the word information has come to be a carrier of so many meanings but I would suggest that this is the result of digitization and virtualization.

If we start at the local level of the borough or district council, there were in the beginning blue books, mayors' minutes, budgets, agendas and minutes; then planning applications, rubbish collection, dog licences and trading standards;

education, social services, housing. This is the level that government most practically impinges on the daily lives and commercial activity of the citizen as civil and economic object. At this level the citizen is concerned with a vast web of interrelations which when they work normally are transparent yet when they break down become Kafkaesque. Yet at this level the electronic society has had almost no impact at all. Some local authorities have websites that provide a variety of mainly promotional materials. Computers used as word processors are almost ubiquitous in many departments but information engineering is almost totally absent. An explanation for this is difficult. Partly it lies in the inertia of the bureaucracy and partly in the absence of effective pressures for change, but the re-engineering of business processes, the reduction in cost and waste in local administration, is almost untouched.

The additional complexity of local government reorganization and unitary development plans has made the layer between local and central government difficult for the individual citizen to understand. Webpage organization and information retrieval capacity make it no easier. There has been a tendency, though, for the front doors of public buildings to become more open and for one-stop information points to parallel the work of the non-governmental organizations such as Citizens' Advice Bureaux. Studies of citizens' empowerment are thin on the ground.

Also thin on the ground are actual studies of information flows within government. My impression is that the relationship between the local department with responsibility for expenditure and the central government department releasing the funds is much stronger than horizontal local coordination. This has been a consequence of the strengthening of the central state during the last 20 years under the policy of liberalization of market forces.

This takes us to central government and the heart of the problem.

The Government Information System – as the Central Computing and Telecommunications Agency (CCTA) now subtitles itself – runs the Government Information Service 'Open Government' website.[5] This must the starting point. For official government information at every level it is probably the only URL we need. It is likely to remain the case that all others will be pointed to from it. Local authorities' URLs are organized within it in alphabetical order. Because the CCTA is the naming organization for the 'open.gov.uk ' domain we might safely presume that it will maintain its integrity. We might also presume that anything that has a 'gov.uk' name space is part of government and that anything that does not is not, but I suspect that this will prove a dangerous presumption.

Webpages are still a very thin layer of the totality of governments documentation: they are a long way from being systematic and must drive specialist librarians in this field to despair. Anyone needing to go into official publications in detail is referred to the Standing Conference On Official Publications (SCOOP) and its newsletter.[6]

British governments – through a variety of policy statements linked to the process of privatization and the removal of power and influence from local government under the rhetoric of the free market – have instituted a number of citizens' charters and official regulators. As to how these have functioned as two-way transmissions between the 'users', or 'customers' or 'consumers', and the service providers, I know of no study that contains reliable measures of relative influence and that compare them with local government in terms of information flows, decision- and action-taking mechanisms. In this area we are weak on theory and evidence of practice beyond the anecdotal experience. Just as the boundaries of public and private are shifting, so too are those of what is and is not government.

One incident though is worth a little detail. After the break in the regulatory framework prohibiting use of anything other than OSI-compliant technology, the shift to TCP/IP, the decision of the Internet Architecture Board to admit commercial activity and the consequent explosion of Internet use, a series of manoeuvres took place within various government departments that was to have influence in this area. There had been earlier government initiatives on the role of information technology in society (as far back as 1982, the 'IT Year' had prompted librarians to remark on the need for more on 'information' and less on 'technology'), and there had been a programme to build Government Open Systems Interconnection Protocol (GOSIP), coordinated across Europe and the United States – but none of these had the impact of the Internet.

In part, a government committed to the market was in some difficulty when it came to stating what that government was going to do, which did not stop a number of ministers making statements that showed varying levels of ignorance of what was happening. There were a series of meetings in London that were open to almost anyone who was interested, followed by the setting up of a series of Consultative Open Groups (COGs). At the risk of drawing an unjustifiable political conclusion, it seems possible that for the first time the state was proven to a large number of people to be completely wrong-footed, not knowing what was going on or what to do. The openness of the response was also exceptional and might be indicative of future directions.

The COGs proliferated, grouped, subdivided, grouped, blossomed and now seem to have died. They did throw up two interesting questions: how much discussion can you have in the global village and how are decisions going to be taken or actions implemented and managed? From time to time issues will emerge that one individual may consider important, but this is no way to open up government. The significance of this component of what amounted to free consultancy to the CCTA and its influence on government policy in the future remain open to question.

Another thread that might have influence on the future of electronic information is the privatization of HMSO. This presumably removes one further player from open government and is in interesting contrast to the role of the Government Printer in the United States.

Further consideration of different components of the responses of parts of central government would extend this chapter unmanageably but the pattern seems clear: a combination of contradictory policies and individuals playing their own power games in a situation that lacks clarity.

Government in the UK does not stop at the national boundary. The European Commission is involved, whatever the meaning of subsidiarity, and is also responsible for large expenditures in research that impact on the development of technology and its interconnectedness. It is also further removed from the citizen, apparently impenetrable, its website a small exception to that impenetrability.

Large research resources have gone into re-engineering government processes and methods through simple transition to electronic processing (STEP) or electronic data interchange (EDI), but almost without impact. The problem of the local council is writ large in the Council of Europe although, as I finished a draft of this paper, Lorcan Dempsey drew the attention of the LIS-Link list to Project CIRCE:[7] 'funded by the British Library Research and Innovation Centre, [Project CIRCE] is looking at frameworks for the delivery of community information through public libraries. An important part of this will be to advance consensus about open approaches for distributed access. CIRCE is a collaborative project of Gloucestershire Libraries, UKOLN, Project EARL and Croydon Libraries.'

Part of government and the one in which the citizen has least influence is that of relations among governments, foreign policy. But there is one whose policies have the potential to impinge on us all – the United States. This is partly because it is the militarily most extended, partly because the technological developments tend to happen in that marketplace first and partly because of an enthusiasm for extra-territoriality. There are two cases that are worth remarking on in detail as they point clearly to the issues.

The first is the 'clipper chip' – the idea that secure networks can be built by building security into the client. That kind of security in networks implies a loss of security to the state and therefore secure networks cannot be allowed, except for the State's. The requirement of the clipper chip was that no network security through encryption could be implemented or exported from the USA without the State's having access to the algorithm. Indeed at one stage no security algorithms could be exported.

Indeed security (in the computational sense) must be an issue of open government, for if citizens are to have information freedom, they must be able to protect themselves against intrusion. But if they can defend themselves against intrusion by the State then do they, at some point, become enemies of the State? And how can the State know?

The second is the Telecommunications Act. This was a law passed by the US Congress prohibiting the passing of offensive (read 'sexually offensive') material over networks. Its international significance was that it applied to companies that were internationally supplying telecommunications, so in order to procure a contract with an Internet service provider in Britain, users had to agree to comply with a requirement which was law in the US but not in Britain. Fortunately and heroically, the American Library Association took the law to the Supreme Court, where it was ruled illegal.

Our discussion of government should also consider international organizations, such as the agencies of the United Nations. A first example is UNESCO and its General Programme for Information. The British Government withdrew from UNESCO in 1985, the principal unstated reason being the commitment of UNESCO to the general availability of information and communication, which was considered unacceptable. There is a certain irony in this, given the ineffectiveness in general of UNESCO's operations, but the principle of availability is important. The argument about access to information and freedom of expression is also important to the vast majority of the planet's population, not only to the small and privileged minority who currently have access.

A second international example is the World Intellectual Property Organization (WIPO). The issue of copyright has been an international one at least since inception of the Berne Convention in 1886. Internationally formed policies on electronic intellectual property have an impact on the *laws* of the nation states and might have an impact on *activities* according to whether they match the mood and are policed. My jaundiced interpretation is that the WIPO process was taken over by some particularly interested parties of database content providers, who then attempted to extend the definition of intellectual property beyond its previous limits. All praise to The Library Association, which made available the resources to ensure enough argument that this 'extended definition' was defeated. These battles, like that with the European Commission on TCP/IP and reverse engineering, will return and place a special responsibility on professional associations.

A third example is the International Standards Organization (ISO). Standards and markets – measures and trades descriptions – have gone together since earliest times and the electronic age seems to have made no particular difference. Companies battle over achieving proprietary control of a market, gaining advantage, and then supporting standards when they lose it. In 1998 Java and

Microsoft's Internet Explorer were the source of two such legal battles in the USA that may yet have international repercussions. The alliances being formed to promote open systems seem to make the formal treaty processes of organizations such as ISO irrelevant. The OSI, TCP/IP issue has been referred to already. A new generation outside the relative formalization of the Internet Architecture Board (IAB) has grown up and so, at some stage, we will presumably see the pattern repeated.

Communication

From government information as formal, legal, printed documents, we now step to communication in the government process, the making of laws. What I have considered in the previous section is what might have been seen historically to be information in the mainstream sense of the tradition of librarianship. It is predominantly concerned with organizations and their output of documents, which can then be catalogued, classified and put on shelves – even if virtually.

There is a slide from the document to broadcast multimedia that will make the continuation of this tradition impossible. How is communication between the government and the governed to be conceptualized?

There has been some experimentation with virtual town meetings – democracy and decision taking, but my earlier remarks on **open.gov.uk** being government controlled seem to me true at every level – it is just not possible to facilitate communication, that is, information – decision – action, without a structure. Once there is a structure then we are back into information systems design. A virtual street-meeting to discuss rubbish collection might be feasible, but how are larger political processes to develop? Three examples will illuminate this development.

The process of formulating a freedom of information act might be a straw in the wind, but a White Paper has been published on the Internet (*see* **http://www.open.gov.uk**). The United Kingdom Committee on Online Democracy (UKCOD) has promoted a discussion on the White Paper.[8] UKCOD is funded by the Rowntree Trust and supported by America Online (AOL), Sun and GX Networks. The discussion has in turn been supported by the Cabinet Office and the minister concerned. My view is, however, that all this is a gloss on reality. There will be no new information; all that will happen is a change in the management of information.

Secondly, the Department for Education and Employment (DfEE) funds the Higher Education Funding Council for England (HEFCE), which conducts an arcane exercise called the Research Assessment Exercise (RAE) in order to evaluate HEFCE expenditure. There is an important sub-layer to this in that the social construction of reality has not yet been publicly discussed. Now, however, the consultative document on the future of the process has a discussion list attached.[9]

Lewisham local authority – the third example – has implemented a tellytalk system, whereby video-conferencing is linked from sites around the borough to borough offices with a scanning capacity, so that the concerned citizen can bring in a query and any necessary documents. The Friday afternoon I went to have a look, however, the doors were locked, despite a notice to the contrary, and there was no list of opening times.

These are intended only as examples of what might be.

As professionals we are involved in a strange migration from the local to the global which might prove to have some interesting impacts on concepts of self in the age of the virtual identity. As plans to make access to Internet-based communication ubiquitous through wiring up public libraries, schools and colleges as well as universities are announced, the role of the public librarian as someone who might have some understanding of what is going on will change in interesting ways. The enormous enthusiasm of *New library: the people's network*[10] coupled with marketing ploys by BT and Microsoft promises to open up a range of new professional issues. These will go far beyond the limits of the citizen's communication with government and are capable of changing the relation between citizen and government. This cannot happen without organization.

Interchange

The area of open government in the electronic age goes furthest from what was traditionally librarianship and deepest into what I consider to be information systems engineering. This is the facilitation of interaction between the citizen and the actual processes of government through EDI. The present (Labour) government in Britain is making much of this. It seems eminently sensible that much of our execution of processes is amenable to electronic communication and information systems design. However, experience is likely to show that the power struggles among the various participants unfortunately will make the exercise futile. The government.direct Green Paper seems a very small innovation for the scale of the issues to be addressed, although most of the discussion on the government server seems to be among consultants interested in gaining IT contracts.

Business process engineering and the re-invention of government will just not be able to go far enough. However, the technology has made much of it possible, so whether individual professionals will draw organizational and political conclusions from their experience or not seems open to question.

Transport

In case everything heretofore is too generalized and abstract, there follows a little worked example following the publication of a consultative document on developing an integrated transport strategy. At the time of writing the document itself is available at the **open.gov.uk** site. As I have become increasingly interested in public transport as a policy issue (I have become convinced that the private motor car is not a sustainable transport medium), I wrote a note on transport information planning and set up a list on the mailbase list server.[11] I received no reply to my electronic despatch.

Transport seems an eminently appropriate topic to consider for open government. After all, there is a large range of policy issues on which regulation, standards, education and training, employment, health and safety, taxation and prices all depend. This is a political process in which government is the major actor, and that if we are to have open government in the information age then it provides an appropriate case.

For the government to produce a consultative document and subsequently a White Paper requesting contributions may or may not show that traditional interests are being displaced. For integrated transport to be considered indicates that there is enough of a shift from the previous government's rhetoric of the 'freedom of the market' being put into place, that change is happening, and that there is the possibility of influencing it.

The private motor car has an advantage over the public transport system in that the driver has a degree of control over the journey. Once committed to a public transport journey events have to be processed in a certain order and change is difficult purely and simply because of the absence of information.

Yet the whole of the road system and all of its land use economics and planning, in fact most of the public transport system, is organized and provided through Government, through taxation (a large part of the price of petrol and motor cars) and insurance, and also through legislation and subsidy. This seems primarily, therefore, a political system and one in which my resources are taken away from me (through taxation) in order to build something which makes my world significantly worse through wasting my time, costing me resources, polluting my environment and endangering me.

It also seems to be a system in which open government must be amenable to influence. And in addition, given my suggestion that it is through the changing of information that the reality can come to be changed, it seems particularly appropriate to a consideration for information systems engineering.

Private companies compete in marketplaces in part through prices and information. But the public transport system is above all determined by its integration. Routes, interchanges, timetables and through ticketing must be preconditions.

The framework constructed by the previous administration seems manifestly to have failed, while the increased congestion and pollution from motor cars seem incontestable. Is this where information planning can come to the rescue? But does it require legislation? Does it require the input of resources? What is the role of government that since at least 1934 has created the problem by encouraging road transport?

Information about transport also has to be information about 'whereness'. Yet the statutory mapping agency, the Ordnance Survey, has failed to provide the public service at a price we can afford, but for which we are taxed. In addition, its methods create specific information problems such as the inability to tell whether one has a right to walk on a road or the right of access to land. In the United States information that is organized by public agencies with public money is in the public domain. This goes a long way beyond public transport but the role of this policy in generating new business opportunities seems significant.

In order to organize 'whereness', definitions of space using Post Office post-codes, or of boundaries or centroids of enumeration districts defined by the Office of National Statistics, are datasets that should also be publicly available and accessible. (At least we achieved getting the national catalogue of the British Library online without having to pay for access – that was one small victory in a world of insanity!) These new area-definition data alone will not take us all that far, but their availability would serve us better than what we have at the moment. Add in the Land Registry records and we are touching very sensitive politics. Yet when I asked Surrey County Council whether the footpath database would be made accessible through a common gateway interface (it is after all on the definitive map on paper), I was told this would have to be a 'member-level decision'.

What is best done at the local level? Can councils influence the shape of the system by policies on road marking, speed limitation or park and ride schemes; and can these policies be brought to bear through involvement in Agenda 21, environment-friendly initiatives that allow activists a framework that is different from the traditional role of political parties? Do green transport plans allow workplace activists the opportunity to influence investment policies, and are guidelines from the ministry enough? This is a type of politics at the local level in which popular participation could make a real difference to the environment. It is a politics where the availability of structured information, communication and interaction could make an impact and where professionals who understand information-processing skills are particularly involved.

There are enormous variations in the quality of public transport information provided by councils, even more than the variation in the provision of public transport. This variation in standards and quality impairs the functioning of the system as a whole, as users cannot anticipate with any reliability. The only thing about which they can be certain is that there will be uncertainty! Scaling up from a local bus stop to a major rail interchange or airport, the chain from local government to central policy, planning and projects produces a framework in which the professional skills of information systems engineering has a special role to play. This will be the testing environment for open government.

Knowledge engineering

What conclusions may we draw from all this for open government in the electronic age?

My argument starts from an extension of Negroponte's 'moving bits is cheaper than moving atoms' to suggest that changing information is cheaper than changing reality.[12] Librarians used to argue that they provided information. What they provided were documents organized in particular ways, even though it was argued for a long time that this was a neutral, values-free and objective process. *Libraries and social change* tried to argue the opposite: that it was a social construction of reality. Now the capacity to change information by its digital and virtual organization, to turn information into a verb, a process, a relation between the conscious knowing subject and the world of objects from which information will be constructed, is unavoidably greater.

I wrote a position paper for the British Computer Society Working Party on the Information and Communication Technology Issues Surrounding Pornography. This was later given in similar form to the International Group of The Library Association. In it I suggested some quite major shifts in what we can do with digital technology and its significance for the changing meanings of words, their enactment in laws, the behaviour of police and courts, and therefore, quite fundamentally, government.

I considered the following issues.

* *Knowledge*
  Whenever any data are digitized, they are converted into a string of 0s and 1s. Some sort of machine is needed to convert the data back into something a human being can comprehend, during which process all sorts of transformations might be executed. What the data started off as might bear no relationship to the way they end up. What they were understood to mean by their originator might have no relationship with the recipient's understanding. The originator might not know who the recipient is and vice versa.
* *Publishing*
  Historically the process of publishing was understood to involve the investment of a considerable amount of capital on typesetting, galleying and printing with hot metal presses. Then came the photocopier and the tape recorder. Now anyone with the most basic technology may be a publisher. Historically

the publisher had a relationship with a consumer, even if indirectly; now anyone may receive, either by an action, or by no action.

* *Images*

    When there were cameras and light sensitive paper, there were realities on which transformations were made. There were drawings, which were made in a different way and had different relationships between the drawer, the drawer's mind, and a subject. Now there are images. They might have started as anything and have changed into anything, and may continue to change.

* *Groups*

    Once upon a time, for a group to exist, people had to move in time and space and know one another. Even with telephone chat lines, something was known about the parties involved. Now groups form in interactions over space and time with people involved who are unknown to each other; some participants may be machines.

* *Reasonableness*

    Courts use a measure of a 'reasonable man' for deciding whether something is illegal. The problem is that for something to become reasonable it must first be unreasonable. Lawrence on *Lady Chatterley* might be one rupture point, the *Oz* trial another. Those discussions seem utterly trivial now. A professional society must be more dynamic than society at large as it is the space where the unreasonable begins to become reason.

* *Misuse*

    This will need broad elaboration in each of the categories indicated by other chapters in this book, as laws become more tortuous. To stay legal in the information age when the concept of misuse is introduced into law is to presume we know what appropriate use is to be. Through their contracts, workers have had defined for them what *their* proper use is. Trade unions have not yet established a set of defences and neither have professional societies. It is fortunate that so far neither have employers. The Computer Misuse Act seems a special quagmire. With political good fortune it will disappear into the dustbin of history but it is equally likely to become part of the mechanism for ensuring that people are prohibited from getting things done. This leads to economic and social regression.

* *Guilty*

    There will need to be a lot more court cases. The 20% conviction rate of pornography trials when the plea is not guilty suggests that people have to be supported in pleading not guilty! If the courts come to be used increasingly in matters of contention then the strength of the defence will become determinant in fixing the political process.

* *Public good*

This is suggested as a special condition that lifts an action out of one legal category and into another. It will have wide significance for members of The Library Association, the British Computer Society and other professional societies that we are dealing with a general class of actions in this chapter on the whole process of open government, the responsibilities of professionals and our code of ethics.

- *Indecency, obscenity and offensiveness*
  Definitions of these are constantly evolving. 'Indecent' is not the same as 'obscene' (legally) or 'offensive' (socially). What is currently legal in acts from 1959 or earlier? But 'offensive' is much too broad: some people will be offended by almost anything. This nucleus is specific to the project on pornography but I suspect that almost every area of professional work will point to similar problem areas.
- *Fantasy*
  This is where I am likely to go out on a limb. Unfashionable as it is in a postmodernist, post-industrial rhetoric, I think there is a difference between someone being present and doing something and something that is purely the inventive creation of someone's imagination. In the first case the crucial issue is consent and coercion. This is for me the fracture line of the moral. Someone else might find the result offensive: that is a different question.
- *Reality*
  Once information and communication technology is involved the borderlines between fantasy and reality are even more difficult to judge than historically in photomontage or text.

These points were made specifically in the context of a consideration of pornography but they seem to me to illustrate issues in which our conception of information must change.

Information sharing

The Library Association has nailed its colours to the mast of a democratic society and an informed citizenry capable of playing its part. Through its code of ethics it requires its membership to support this position. The British Computer Society has something along the same lines. This means that when it comes to freedom of information against the leverage of the power of defence of intellectual property one should support the former.

When policies of economic development, a sustainable environment and social inclusion reach contradiction, as they invariably will, the methods of information systems engineering ought to be capable of raising argument to higher levels of rationality. It seems that the involvement of professionals in this process has to go beyond the limitations historically constructed.

But it also seems clear that the limit to information is organizational form and its link to power. This is where I see a new role for professional associations, though one that they will probably prove reluctant to play.

There is also an increased role for information planning. The work of the Library and Information Cooperation Council (LINC), the National Forum for Information Planning and similar bodies has been excessively concerned with the organization of document collections, almost to the exclusion of databases of bibliographic records. When it comes to the regional or sectoral level there has been nothing like enough attention given to the definition of the protocols by which other types of information may be given the social construction that historically was given to 'books'. Given the number of forums being put forward by the Labour government on development policy, creativity in education, and so forth, I think there is a role for an information policy forum, which would take as its starting point the sorts of issues that have been discussed here.

However, I am not naïve. The development of new productive forces always creates a tension with existing social relations. While the technologies are maturing we have difficulty in understanding their consequences. If the technologies are to mature then society has to change. If the social relations survive then new technological capacities are destroyed and consequently so is society. The fault line between intellectual property rights and freedom of information is one that society must let fracture. Information planning is new growth.

These constructs exist in a larger framework of dissolving paradigms. Market and plan, competition and cooperation, state and capital, quantity and quality, system and environment are all components of the larger picture that the professions need to address. Techniques such as structured systems analysis and design methodology (SSADM), project management methods such as PRojects IN Controlled Environments (PRINCE), Logical Frameworks, a shelf-long set of volumes from the CCTA and John Wiley on information systems design, and something similar from the Information Management Group of the National Health Service all point to the insolubility of the problem created by changing quantity to quality. The machinery imposes a structure and formality onto processes that are the result of alienation and reification and the struggle of classes over the exploitation and expropriation of resources. There can be no panacea.

When I was first training as a reference librarian much was made of the boundary between advice and information that I did not then understand. To this now is added organization. When lawmakers do not understand the technology and make foolish laws, we have a responsibility to campaign against them. But here is the point where I suspect I will differ from many of my colleagues: we also have a responsibility not to obey them, and to expect our associations to defend us.

Information is clearly not free, but it does not behave like groceries. Competitive markets might be the most effective mechanism for organizing depletable and excludable resources (groceries etc.) but they are definitely not the mechanism for organizing non-depletable and non-excludable ones (information). The organizing of information can only be done by general taxation (I owe this formulation of the information economy to McClark), although history tells us that the beneficiaries of taxation will conspire to the disadvantage of the taxed.[13]

No matter how we formulate a question on the role of information in open government we come back to a moral dimension in which there is a role for the professional associations.

The rest of this book is addressing the state of the law. Its title is *Staying legal*. I would suggest there are more important issues for professionals. If I may quote Marx on Feuerbach, 'The philosophers have only interpreted the world in various ways; the point is to change it'.[14] There is now a discussion list called Policing the Internet where the issues I've outlined here are open for discussion.[15]

References

1 Berger, P. L. and Luckmann, T., *The social construction of reality: a treatise in the sociology of knowledge*, Garden City, NY, Doubleday, 1966.

2 Branscomb, A. W., *Who owns information? From privacy to public access*, New York, Basic Books, 1994.

3 Lindsay, J., 'Policing the Internet', *Focus: journal of the International Group of the Library Association*, 23 (8), 1997. Policing the Internet ListServe: subscribe at pin@mailbase.ac.uk.

4 Rogers, E., *Libraries accessible via the Joint Academic Network*, Brighton, University of Sussex Library, 1985.

5 Government Information Service: http://www.open.gov.uk [visited 02/07/1998].

6 Standing Conference On Official Publications (SCOOP): http://www.la-hq.org.uk/scoop2.htm [visited 02/07/1998].

7 Dempsey, L., Government Information LIS-Link Archive: http://www.mailbase.ac.uk/lists/lis-link/1998-02/0075.html [visited 08/02/1999].

8 The United Kingdom Committee on Online Democracy (UKCOD): http://www.foi.democracy.org.uk [visited 02/07/1998].

9 Research Assessment Exercise in 2001: http://www.niss.ac.uk/education/hefc/rae2001/ [visited 08/02/1999].

10 *New library: the people's network*, Documentation and full text:

http://www.ukoln.ac.uk/services/lic/ [visited 02/07/1998].

11   Transport Information Planning (the role of information systems design in the development of integrated transport policies and strategies): subscribe at trip@mailbase.ac.uk.

12   Negroponte, N., *Being digital,* London, Hodder & Stoughton, 1995.

13   McClark, J., Private communication, 22 August 1995.

14   Marx, K. and Engels, F., *The German ideology*, London, Lawrence & Wishart, 1970.

15   Lindsay, op.cit.

Further readings

Barrett, N., *State of the cybernation*, London, Kogan Page, 1997.

Castells, M., *The rise of the network society, vol. 1 of The information age: economy, society and culture*, Cambridge, MA, Blackwell, 1997.

Dutton, W. *et. al., Electronic service delivery themes and issues in the public sector,* Policy Research paper 28, PICT, ESRC, London, Brunel Univesity, 1994.

European Union, *Europe and the global information society: recommendations to the European Council*, Brussels, EU, 1994.

Loader, B. D., *The Governance of cyberspace.* London, Routledge, 1997.

Manchester City Council, *Manchester: the information city: promoting economic development through the use of telematics*, Manchester, The Council, 1994.

Miller, S., *Civilizing, and cyberspace: policy, power, and the information superhighway*, London, Addison Wesley, 1996.

Tsagarousianou, R. *et al., Cyberdemocracy: technology, cities and civic networks*, London, Routledge, 1997.

Zuboff, S., *In the age of the smart machine: the future of work and power*, New York, Basic Books, 1988.

3

Legal information – the rich and the poor

John Williams

Introduction

One of the better-known legal maxims is *ignorantia legis neminem excusat*, or ignorance of the law is no excuse. This general principle is normally used in the context of people being punished or found responsible for acts that they did not know were contrary to the law. It imposes a general duty on the public to be aware of what the law says and to adjust their behaviour accordingly. This paints a somewhat simplistic view of the law. For example, the public are aware that theft is a criminal offence. However, are they fully aware of the intricacies of the law of theft and the highly legalistic definition of theft found in s. 1 of the Theft Act 1968? Even those countries that have their own 'pocket-size' civil code recognize that it is impossible for the public to know with any degree of precision what activity a particular legal rule permits or prevents them from doing. Nevertheless the law still adheres to the principle that ignorance does not provide a defence.

Accessing the law

The maxim raises the question as to whether the State is under any general obligation to inform the public of the content of the law. In common law systems, such as that of the United Kingdom, this presents difficult problems. How do we inform the public what the judges have decided the law should be? Very often the judges themselves disagree on the *ratio decidendi* (or the reason for the decision) of a particular case. They arrive at the same conclusion, but adopt different reasoning. It is impossible to provide any degree of certainty as to the content of judge-made law. Similarly the British approach to the drafting of statutes does not make the content of the law easily accessible for the lay person. Legislation such as the Children Act 1989 was intended to be user-friendly and intended to be read and understood by non-lawyers. It was a brave attempt, but one that sadly failed. Only the lawyer can fully understand with the necessary degree of precision the weight of the evidence required to prove 'significant harm' under s. 31 of the Children Act 1989. Thus access is provided to the letter of the law either through a copy of the law report or the statute, but access to the world of 'lawyers' law' is denied. Only by understanding what the lawyers make of a particular case or statute are lay people fully aware of what is expected of them.

The problem becomes more complex when the discussion moves from modifying behaviour in order to avoid transgressing a rule of criminal or civil law to identifying the personal rights and privileges that the law creates. The same duty of being aware of the content of the law applies in such situations. For a society that complains of 'information overload' it still appears that large sections are alienated by virtue of the fact that they do not have access to up-to-date information on their legal entitlements. Such complaints are not new. One of the grievances of the Plebeians in Roman times was not for the reform of the law, but for its publication and dissemination.[1]

The ability to access the law has two aspects, namely physical and intellectual. Physical and intellectual barriers to accessing law create a class of information-deprived citizens. There is a considerable imbalance between the amount of legal information accessible by commercial undertakings, the public sector, the Government and professionals on the one hand and ordinary citizens on the other. The former group has the resources to achieve both physical access and, often through the involvement of a professional lawyer, intellectual access to the content of the law. Citizens may very often give up any claim they think they have because of an inability to obtain basic information on their rights, a very common scenario in the area of consumer complaints. Thus in many cases legal safeguards are redundant because people are unaware of their rights. In short, the 'big guys' get away with it.

Physical access

Very few people have access to a law library or similar collections of legal material. They probably have easy access to general libraries that may have a limited collection of legal material. Generalist guides to the law are often to be found in local lending libraries. The media also play a part in disseminating information on the law. There are many ways in which physical access can be improved. Consumer programmes are regular providers of informative entertainment, especially in the area of consumer rights. In addition radio programmes such as '*In touch*' and '*Does he take sugar*' concentrate on disability issues and seek to inform potential service users of their entitlement. The World Wide Web is more and more being used as a source of legal information. Age Concern is one of the many groups that has its own website[2] which allows access to some 40 factsheets on topics such as making wills, legal aid, local authority charging provisions and dental care in retirement. Once accessed the site is easily navigated and provides up-to-date and easily assimilated information.

The amount of legal information available on the Web is growing at an impressive rate. Welcome as such developments are, the evidence is that not all sections of society use the Web. Georgia Institute of Technology's Graphics, Visualization and Usability Center's (GVU) ninth Internet Survey[3] found that the respondents with the most online experience tend to be in the 21–30 age range. Although the average education level of Web users has been declining and is now more representative of the general population, users are still quite highly educated, with 80.9% having at least some college experience and 50.1% having obtained at least one degree. Respondents who have been online for four years or more are much more likely to have higher degrees than newer users. Females represent 38.7% of the respondents. Europe is considerably less gender-balanced than the USA, with females accounting for only 16.3% of respondents as compared with 30.5% for the rest of the world. Younger respondents are more likely to be female – 43.8% of those aged 11–20 compared to 33.9% of those aged 50 and over. Users who have been online for less than a year represent the only category where females outnumber males (51.7% female, 48.3% male).

In America the National Telecommunications and Information Administration found that people living in rural areas with low income levels are those least likely to have access to the Web: they have a mere 2.3% online access rate. Single-parent households are much less likely to have online access than two-parent families – 25% as opposed to 57.2% for the latter.[4] The findings of a *Guardian* telephone survey in January 1999 found that 29% of UK adults have Internet access, with another 14% planning to get it before the end of the year. This shows a rate of expansion of 1% every two months, more than double that of the previous year. The survey found a direct relationship between income and online access. One in three of those in social class AB is reported to be online at home, compared with 16% of the C1 white collar workers and only 2% of the DE semi-skilled and unemployed.[5]

These findings suggest that significant sections of society do not have access to online facilities. Any idea that technology will resolve the problem of information poverty is mistaken. Greater access for some members of society is welcome and will increase the number of the information rich by including more members of the middle class. However, one consequence of this will be to create a group of people who for economic, educational and social reasons are denied the benefits of technology. This may well be the group of people who are in greatest need of legal information. However, the response to this should not be one of rejecting technology as the way forward. Information technology has many advantages over other forms of dissemination, not least the ability to update at regular intervals. The answer must be to ensure that more people are able to take advantage of the technology. One way of doing this is to ensure that more advice-giving agencies within the voluntary sector are equipped with online provision so that they can act as the gateway to these resources for those denied access. Organizations such as Citizens' Advice Bureaux and welfare rights advisors are already developing such services, although lack of funding is an inevitable problem. Public libraries also have a role to play. However, they may not have much impact as those denied access to the Web might not be regular users of public libraries.

Widening access to information technology is a key challenge for schools and colleges. Only one in five teachers has been trained to use computers, and inspectors' reports suggest that many schools are struggling to meet the demands of information technology. The Government has launched a number of initiatives, including the National Grid for Learning (NGfL). One of the objectives of the NGfL is 'to remove barriers to learning to ensure quality of access for all, including those in isolated rural areas, those with special educational needs or those in areas of urban deprivation'.[6]

Funding is being made available to provide for networking infrastructure, hardware, software and training to enable UK schools to connect to the National Grid for Learning. A sum of over £700 million has been committed up to 2002 for connecting schools. A further sum of £230 million is available up to 2002 to enhance the level of competence in information technology of existing teachers. In addition, the Government has introduced a new national curriculum in initial training institutions for the use of information and communication technology (ICT) in subject teaching. From 1999, all newly qualified teachers will need to have a competence in ICT to mandatory standards in order to receive qualified teacher status. Such initiatives are welcome. However, there is a risk that they will widen the divide between information rich and poor. The schools minister, Charles Clarke, said in an address to the British Education and Training Technology exhibition on 13 January 1999 that there is a danger of an underclass of children emerging who are denied access to computers outside of school hours. He said that 'a substantial number' of children do not have access to computers at home. This prevents children from obtaining information for themselves, and also denies them the opportunity to develop their IT skills for use in later life.

Bringing law to the people through the Web poses not only technical challenges, but also requires a willingness to invest resources in ensuring that people have equal rights of access. This may require something other than the 'computer in every home' ideal. Hartley and Williams argue that

> legal information systems for lay people must be taken to the places where they will be seen and used by those people. This means that they should not be confined to

libraries and other local or central government buildings but that they should be available in Post Offices, hospitals, shopping malls, pubs, hotel foyers, community centres and garden centres.[7]

This has to be the next big step forward in the provision of legal information. The technology cannot be restricted to certain sections of society. If our society believes in equality before the law then it cannot tolerate inequality of access to its contents.

Intellectual access

This second aspect involves the ability to make use of the information that is available. Law is for lawyers and, as noted above, makes very few concessions to the lay person. It is here that those responsible for drafting legislation face a dilemma. To present a non-lawyer with a copy of the Disability Discrimination Act 1995 does not provide a clear picture of the rights of those with disabilities not to be discriminated against. For example, the definition of 'disability', crucial to an understanding of the Act, is found in s. 1. It states:

(1) Subject to the provisions of Schedule 1, a person has a disability for the purposes of this Act if he has a physical or mental impairment which has a substantial and long-term adverse effect on his ability to carry out normal day-to-day activities.

(2) In this Act 'disabled person' means a person who has a disability.

Thus a section in the Act that purports to provide a definition of 'disability' and 'disabled' simply provides a starting point for an excursion around the legislation. What does Schedule 1 say? It supplements s. 1 by attempting to further define 'impairment', 'long-term effects', 'normal day-to-day activities' and other terms. It also makes provision for the Secretary of State to make regulations for including or excluding certain conditions from the definition of impairment. The definition of 'disability' is not, therefore, confined to one self-contained section of the Act. In order to get a comprehensive and accurate picture the user must consult the Act in its entirety, plus any regulations that the secretary of state may make. This may be further complicated by the interpretation that the courts may place on the wording of the Act. The ability to navigate the law is a skill that is central to legal training. Lawyers know where to find the law, how to make sense of it and how to use it to the best advantage of their clients. Those who lack such training may find it difficult to obtain an accurate picture of the law.

This intellectual difficulty in accessing the law is mitigated partially by the publication of official and unofficial guides to legislation. With reference to the Disability Discrimination Act 1995, the Department for Education and

Employment and the Department of Social Security have published, *Guidance on matters to be taken into account in determining the questions relating to the definition of disability*,[8] in which the definition in s. 1 of the Act is explained in a clearer style. Although it is primarily designed for courts and tribunals, it is 'likely to be of value to a range of people and organizations' (see paragraph 1). The layout of this publication makes the Act more readily understood, as it is written in an easier style and contains many cross-references. However, the extent to which this is a definitive statement of the law is in doubt: 'This guidance does not impose any legal obligation in itself, nor is it an authoritative statement of the law. However, s. 3 (3) of the Act requires that an industrial tribunal or a court . . . must take into account any of this guidance that appears to it to be relevant.' This is not a definitive statement of the law, but it is indicative of how the courts may interpret it. Its usefulness is limited in this way. In addition to the *Guidance*, the Minister for Disabled People has also published a booklet, *The Disability Discrimination Act: definition of disability*.[9] This is a more general explanation of the Act designed for the general public. Again the booklet warns that it 'gives general guidance only and should not be treated as a complete and authoritative statement of the law.' This publication is also available in Braille and in audiocassette. Such official attempts to make the law accessible are to be commended. However, some degree of caution must be exercised as oversimplification may lead to the reader's being misled.

A number of voluntary and commercial organizations have produced guides for the general public. For example, an objective of the Child Poverty Action Group is to work ' . . . to ensure that those on low incomes get their full entitlement to welfare benefits through their casework, publications and training, aiming to eradicate the injustice of poverty.'[10] The CPAG publishes a number of guides to enable people to discover their rights (e.g. their booklet on Job Seeker's Allowance). Other voluntary organizations have similar objectives. Commercial publishers and pressure groups also produce guides to various aspects of the law. Perhaps the best-known publisher in this area is the Consumers' Association, which produces a number of *Which? guides* designed to take the reader through the intricacies of topics such as making a will, selling a house and consumer matters. The Consumers' Association also produces *TaxCalc*, software that enables users to complete their self-assessment tax forms and works out the liability to tax. The tax form generated by this programme, and its calculation of tax liability, has been recognized by the Inland Revenue as an acceptable tax return. This is interesting example of how the private sector and government can cooperate to facilitate greater use and understanding of the law by lay people.

Intellectual access to the law presents a greater problem than physical access. Whereas many people will be able to access the law through technology or some other means, it does not mean that they will be able to make use of that information. British law has been described as impenetrable: however, legislators should have a duty to ensure that, so far as it is possible, law should be drafted in a way that is intelligible to lay people. This will not be possible in all situations, but those who draft the law need to move away from the mentality of complexity for the sake of complexity. It will be interesting to observe whether the Scottish Parliament and the Welsh Assembly follow the Westminster model of complex drafting, or take the opportunity to adopt a more user-friendly style. Where clearer drafting is not possible then it is beholden on government to seek to explain its legislation through codes of practice and explanatory leaflets. Technology can also play its part. The development of packages such as *TaxCalc* illustrates how computer programs can be devised to take lay people through complex areas of law without the need to resort to professional lawyers or accountants. If such developments are linked to improvements in physical accessibility we will be well on the way to eradicating information poverty.

Duty to provide information

There are some instances in which the law imposes a duty upon statutory bodies to provide information to the public. Two areas illustrate the limitations of these duties. They are firstly children, and secondly adults in need of assistance through age or disability.

Children

The international dimension

Children represent a group in society having a need for information to enable them to participate in decision-making concerning their lives. The United Nations adopted the Convention on the Rights of the Child on 20 November 1989. Over 150 countries are signatories to this Convention, which was ratified by the United Kingdom in 1991. Article 12 of the Convention gives children capable of forming their own views the right to express them freely and for those views to be given due weight in accordance with age and maturity. This is similar to, but not as extensive as, the *Gillick* principle, which will be considered below. Before benefiting from the exercise of the Article 12 right children will need to be aware of its existence. In part this is provided for in Article 13, which states:

1. The child shall have the right to freedom of expression; this right shall include freedom to seek, receive and impart information and ideas of all kinds, regardless of frontiers, either orally, in writing or in print, in the form of art, or through any other media of the child's choice.

2. The exercise of this right may be subject to certain restrictions, but these shall only
be such as are provided by law and are necessary:

(a) For respect of the rights or reputations of others; or

(b) For the protection of national security or of public order (ordre public), or of
public health or morals.

Although the Convention is not a part of United Kingdom law, it represents
recognition by this country that it will adhere to its principles. A number of signatories have entered reservations to Article 13, which means that the provision
does not apply to them or applies in some modified form. The Holy See inter-
prets the articles of the Convention in a way that safeguards the primary and
inalienable rights of parents, especially in relation to Article 13. The Malaysian
Government has declared that Article 13 shall be applicable only if it is in conformity with the constitution, national laws and national policies of the
Government of Malaysia. The State of Qatar entered a general reservation concerning provisions incompatible with Islamic law. These reservations are an indication of how difficult it is to identify a universal right on the part of a child to
information. Similarly, different views on the parent/child relationship may well
temper a country's commitment to the principle. The right of a child to information may well be thought to be an interference with parental rights and thus
something to be discouraged.

Article 13 (1) creates a broad right for children. Firstly it recognizes that freedom to receive information is a necessary component of the right of freedom of
expression. Subject to the exceptions envisaged in Article 13 (2) it extends to
'information of all kinds'. Not only will this include information relating to rights
within the health and education services, but also religious and political information. The Article also recognizes that the right exists 'regardless of frontiers'.
Children wishing to discover information about other cultures and religions will
be covered by this provision. This raises some very sensitive issues and is likely to
bring into conflict the provisions of the Article and the social, religious and political mores of signatories, especially in multicultural societies such as the United
Kingdom. The exceptions envisaged in Article 13 (2) are an attempt to leave
some discretion to individual signatories to impose restrictions, albeit within
specified boundaries. The wording of Article 13 (2) leaves much to subjective
judgment. It is sensible that the right contained in the Article should not be used
to sanction the dissemination of defamatory material. However, does the public
health and morals provision exclude or include information on illegal drugs or
sex advice for schoolchildren? Some may argue that such advice promotes health
and represents a moral duty on society; others argue with equal conviction that it
encourages children to engage in activities that are harmful to health and clearly
immoral. Such disagreement on two of the main issues facing young people is a

cause for concern. Clearly there is considerable leeway for the UK Government to compromise children's basic rights to information by resorting to the provisions of Article 13 (2). It is interesting to speculate whether the right of certain children to give a valid consent to contraception is one that all children should be made aware of as part of the general right imposed by Article 13 (see the *Gillick* case below). Those responsible for sex education in schools appear to adopt a varied and pragmatic approach to this issue.

The child's right to make decisions

In the case of *Gillick* v. *West Norfolk and Wisbech AHA*[11] the courts were asked to rule unlawful a DHSS circular stating that doctors and family planning clinics could give contraceptive advice to girls under the age of 16 years. The House of Lords held that it was not unlawful. Lord Scarman said, '. . . parental rights yield to the child's right to make his own decisions when he reaches a sufficient understanding and intelligence to be capable of making up his own mind on the matter requiring decision.' This right for children to decide for themselves extends beyond the area of medical treatment. It also goes beyond what is envisaged in the United Nations Convention on the Rights of the Child. Article 12 (1) provides for 'the views of the child being given due weight in accordance with the age and maturity of the child'. Gillick says that the child's views should prevail. Giving children the right in some situations to determine their future imposes on them considerable responsibility. It is also regarded as a pragmatic response to the rising number of teenage pregnancies. By encouraging children to be responsible and to seek contraceptive advice in confidence may help to reverse the trend. However, not all children are made aware of the existence of the *Gillick* principle. They believe that no matter how mature and responsible they may be, a visit to the doctor to discuss contraception will result in their parents' being told. That is often the last thing that they want. The existence of the *Gillick* principle should not be a well kept secret: the House of Lords was brave enough to provide children with this right and it is wrong that children should not be made aware of it. In making decisions children should have access to appropriate sources of information to enable them to make an informed choice.

One important source of information is the professional legal advisor. The Children Act 1989 recognizes that children have the right to separate legal representation in care and related proceedings (s. 41 (3) CA and r. 4.12 Family Proceedings Rules 1991). What the law does not do is give the child access to general legal advice prior to the need for care or other proceedings' arising. For example, there is no legal duty to tell children the implications for them of their parent's divorce.

Duty to promote the welfare of children

The Children Act 1989 imposes on local authorities a general duty to 'safeguard and promote the welfare of children within their area who are in need'. 'In need' is defined in s. 17 (10) of the Act as a child:

- who is unlikely to achieve or maintain a reasonable standard of health or development without the provision of services by the local authority
- whose health and development is likely to be significantly impaired without the provision of services by the local authority, or
- who is disabled.

The Act outlines the type of services that local authorities may provide for children who are in need. These include welfare services, day care, accommodation, and advice and assistance. The provision of such services is a key component of the reforms brought about by the Act: the emphasis was on prevention of abuse and neglect rather than responding to it. The services envisaged by the Act include clubs and societies, transport, help in the home, home adaptations, holidays, and advice and counselling. The Act includes a specific duty to provide information about such services. Under Schedule 2 of the Act local authorities are under a duty to publish information about the services they provide and also any appropriate provision made by the voluntary sector. They are also under a duty to 'take such steps as are reasonably practicable to ensure that those who might benefit from the services receive the information relevant to them' (para. 1 (2) (b) Schedule 2, Children Act 1989). The wording of this provision is typical of a rather begrudging recognition by Parliament that potential beneficiaries of social services should be informed of their availability. It falls far short of an absolute duty as the ubiquitous wording 'as are reasonably practicable' imposes considerable restrictions on its application.

Education

Education is arguably one of the biggest influences on the lives of children. They spend a significant amount of time at school at a particularly formative period of their lives. To what extent does the law ensure that children receive adequate information about different schools and the opportunities that they offer? The simple answer to this question is that the law fails to recognize the child as a consumer and therefore does not impose any legal duty on education authorities to provide the child with information. The so-called league tables of school performance are published in national newspapers that are designed for, and read predominantly by, adults. Yet it is children who are the actual service users. Why should they be denied information that directly affects their development? The explanation for this is that education law is designed to promote the right of parents rather than children. Jane Fortin points out that children are prevented from becoming school governors, as the qualifying age is eighteen years. Attempts during the debates on the Education Act 1993 to give children the right to be consulted were rejected on the grounds that parents had representation on governing bodies.[12]

Nowhere is the power of parents more apparent than in the area of religious education. Are children, in particular mature children, entitled to receive information on alternative religions or do parents have a right of veto? Under s. 386 of the Education Reform Act 1988 state schools must hold a daily assembly of pupils that is 'wholly or mainly of a broadly Christian character'. The law also requires that state schools provide a form of religious education as part of the basic curriculum. In both cases parents may exercise the right to withdraw their children from such religious activity. From the point of view of the provision of information this law may deny the child the right to receive information about religions other than Christianity; it may also deny some children the right to learn about the Christian religion. Under Article 29 (d) of the United Nations Convention on the Rights of the Child, a child's education must be directed to the 'preparation of the child for responsible life in a free society, in the spirit of understanding, peace, tolerance, equality of sexes, and friendship among all peoples, ethnic, national and religious groups and persons of indigenous origin'.

It is difficult to see how this objective can be achieved when children may be denied basic information on alternative religions and beliefs. However, the European Convention on Human Rights, which becomes part of United Kingdom law by virtue of the Human Rights Act 1998, gives support to the parental right to decide. The European Court in the case of *Kjeldsen, Busk Madsen and Pedersen* v. *Denmark*[13] had to consider whether sex education in Denmark contravened Article 2 of Protocol 1 of the Convention. This states that 'No person shall be denied the right to education. In the exercise of any functions which it assumes in relation to education and to teaching, the State shall respect the right of parents to ensure such education and teaching are in conformity with their own religious and philosophical convictions.' In the *Kjeldsen* case the Court emphasized that the State 'must take care that information or knowledge included in the curriculum is conveyed in an objective, critical and pluralistic manner'. Taken out of context these words support the idea that children are entitled to sufficient information with which to enable them to make their own decisions. However, the Court continues that the State 'is forbidden to pursue an aim of indoctrination that might be considered as not respecting the parent's religious and philosophical convictions'. Thus by law information provided by the State through the educational system may be affected by the beliefs of the parents.

Adults

The vulnerable adult

In 1995 the Law Commission published its *Report on mental incapacity*.[14] The report arose out of concern that, with more people living in the community following implementation of the National Health Service and Community Care Act 1990, the philosophy of this act was to ensure that vulnerable adults should be helped to live in their own home rather than entering residential care there was a risk that these people would be subjected to abuse and neglect. A number of recommendations were made concerning the 'vulnerable person at risk'. For the purposes of the report such a person is defined as 'any person aged 16 or over who (1) is or may be in need of community care services by reason of mental or other disability, age or illness and who (2) is or may be unable to take care of himself or herself, or unable to protect himself or herself against significant harm or serious exploitation'.

The issues surrounding vulnerable adults are complex. As adults they have the right to exercise their own free will and to accept or refuse services that a local authority may offer them under the community care legislation. It is essential that an individual's right to autonomy be respected. However, if the person is vulnerable because he or she lacks capacity through mental disorder, then there is a strong argument for saying that the need to protect the vulnerable adult overrides his or her right to autonomy. For the present purposes the proposals for reform are of little relevance. What is important is that by raising awareness of the plight of the vulnerable adult the Law Commission has identified the wide range of people who fall into that category. 'Vulnerability' may also include the person who has a physical disability that prevents his or her visiting the local library or advice-giving agency. Physical access to the law may present a problem. Thus people may be denied essential information concerning the services to which they may be entitled under, for example, the Chronically Sick and Disabled Persons Act 1970. Other vulnerable adults may lack capacity to make an informed decision or give valid consent.

Legal definitions of capacity are vague and varied. Nevertheless it is essential that any judgment on a person's capacity to make a decision that the law will respect is based on that person's being given relevant information presented in an appropriate manner. Consent to medical treatment illustrates this point. Before giving valid consent a patient must be informed in broad terms of the procedures involved in the treatment. Bristow J said in *Chatterton* v. *Gerson*[15] 'the duty of the doctor is to explain what he intends to do, and its implications, in the way a careful and responsible doctor in similar circumstances would have done'. The General Medical Council in *Good medical practice*[16] requires doctors to 'give information to patients in a way they can understand'. The provision of inadequate information, or more importantly information communicated in an inappropriate manner, may lead to a person's capacity to make a decision not being recognized by professionals. Regard must be had to the need for information to be communicated in a way that maximizes the recipient's ability to comprehend. There is a need to embrace the idea of total communication rather than relying solely on the spoken or printed word. The University of Edinburgh's Institute for the Study of Education and Society has highlighted the various ways in which communication can take place between people who have communication difficulties and others:

> An augmentative communication system means the whole 'package' of specific techniques and technologies making up 'total communication' for a specific individual. Typically, an individual might use their facial expressions, body postures and gestures, eye pointing, vocalisations with different pitch and tone, and speech attempts. They might also use a more specialized system such as manual signing, pointing to pictures or symbols, and/or operating a computer with message storage, rate enhancement features and synthetic voice output.[17]

A failure to consider alternative forms of communicating information can lead to the patient's being denied the basic right to refuse or give valid consent to treatment.

The provision of community care services

Difficulties also arise for people who are seeking community care services under the National Health Service and Community Care Act 1990. The local authorities and health authorities have duties in relation to vulnerable adults to assist them to live in the community. Public awareness of the community care philosophy is probably higher than ever. Often this awareness is raised by adverse publicity surrounding isolated incidents of mentally ill people living in the community committing acts of violence. Nevertheless, awareness is also raised by the work of disability groups, advice agencies and others who publicize the idea of community care. Whether this public awareness goes beyond the philosophy and extends to specific rights and duties under the legislation is debatable. Local authority social services departments have a duty under the Chronically Sick and Disabled Persons Act 1970 to publicize their community care services. Section 1 states:

> (1) It shall be the duty of every local authority having functions under section 29 of the National Assistance Act 1948 to inform themselves of the number of persons to whom

that section applies within their area and of the need for the making by the authority of arrangements under that section for such persons.

(2) Every such local authority

(*a*) shall cause to be published general information as to the services provided under arrangements made by the authority under section 29 which are for the time being available in their area; and

(*b*) shall ensure that any such person as aforesaid who uses any of those services is informed of any other service provided by the authority (whether under any such arrangements or not) which in the opinion of the authority is relevant to his needs and of any service provided by any other authority or organization which in the opinion of the authority is so relevant and of which particulars are in the authority's possession.

As with the duty under the Children Act 1989 this section adopts a minimalist approach to the duty to provide information to potential service users. In 1970 the s. 1 duty was probably state of the art; since then society's awareness of the need for information, plus the development of new technology, calls for that duty to be updated. It is time for the law to recognize the much higher profile that information provision has now acquired.

Social services departments must also publish their community care plans (s. 46 of the National Health Service and Community Care Act 1990). Such documents are not designed to be a user's guide to services and do not, as a general rule, seek to make people aware of their rights. Perhaps the talk of rights in this context is a little misleading. The law is such that it imposes very few duties on social services and thus gives the potential user very few rights. Much of the legislation in this area of law gives social services departments 'powers' rather than 'duties' – the department 'may' rather than 'must' provide a particular service to an individual.

Even where the legislation appears to be more prescriptive and imposes duties on the social services departments to provide services, the courts have taken the view that resources can be taken into account and used as a reason to deny the individual the service. A good example of this is the *Gloucestershire* case[18] in which the apparent duty under s. 2 of the Chronically Sick and Disabled Persons Act 1970 was in effect converted into a discretionary power. By taking their lack of resources into consideration in determining whether or not the duty under the Act existed, the social services department could effectively prevent the duty arising. In short a department can argue that a person does not have a 'need' (the prerequisite for the duty) because it would not have the resources to meet that need if it were legally identified as such. This decision has led to local authority social services departments formulating eligibility criteria for services for those with a disability. There is some discussion as to whether the eligibility criteria should be within the public domain. They are highly relevant for those who feel they may be in need of services, as they are an indication of how social services rate their chances of getting the services. However, social services departments may fear that publication will only lead to yet greater demands on their overstretched budgets. All too often the lack of resources provides public bodies with reasons for reducing information to a minimum. The more people are made aware of their rights the more demand they will place on the system.

Information in the wider context of public body provision

Public bodies must ensure that they exercise their powers and duties fairly and in accordance with the rules of natural justice. They have a duty to act reasonably when fulfilling their statutory duties. They must avoid unfair bias and must be prepared to provide reasons for their decisions. A public body that can be shown to have acted illegally, irrationally, or with procedural impropriety may have its decisions challenged through a procedure known as judicial review. This involves the court's reviewing the procedures adopted by the body rather than looking at the merits of the decision. In the case of *R. v. North Yorkshire County Council, ex parte Hargreaves*[19] the use of a discretionary power by a local authority to contribute towards holidays for people with disabilities was challenged. The authority had been prepared to meet the additional costs of a holiday that were the results of the disability, for example the extra costs of transport for the disabled person and the costs of a carer to travel with and look after the disabled person. However, the authority's policy was to refuse to consider contributing toward the cost of the holiday itself. Their blanket policy was only to contribute towards costs that were attributable to special equipment or special accommodation necessitated by the disabilities. This policy was the subject of judicial review and the court found that it amounted to an unlawful fettering of the department's discretion.

If the court finds that the procedure was flawed it may require the body to go through the process again. Judicial review is a very expensive and complex process and it is unlikely that many people could afford to use it. However, the principles that underlie it are important, and it is essential that the public are aware of them and enabled to challenge any public body that chooses to ignore them. Challenges may be made through the courts, the complaints procedures or through the use of the relevant ombudsman. Providing potential users of community care services with information of what is available does not present them with the full picture. They also need to be made aware of the restraints imposed on public bodies as to the way in which they operate. For example, they need to know that if a social services department fails to provide reasons for a refusal of services, or unlawfully fetters any discretionary power it has, then it will have offended one of the principles behind judicial review. A challenge, or at least a protest, should be considered. Information is only of use to the recipient if it is comprehensive and placed in its proper context, a fact not recognized by the duty in the 1970 Act. In addition to information on rights and duties within the system it is essential to be aware of the context within which it operates.

Conclusion

Social exclusion is a theme actively pursued by the current Labour Government. Within the new devolved United Kingdom it is expected that the regional Parliament and Assemblies will also address the issue. There are many reasons why people feel socially excluded. Education, poverty, gender, race, disability, unemployment and age can all lead to people feeling as though they do not belong to society. To this list we can add those who are unable to access information, especially information concerning their legal rights. The socially included can either directly or indirectly obtain legal advice and information, albeit at a cost. They have the physical, intellectual and financial wherewithal to access the system. For many this is not possible. Political initiatives such as open government and freedom of information do not really impact on the lives of such people, especially when such initiatives see technology as the primary vehicle for wider dissemination. Unless people can access the technology they will not be able to access the information. Initiatives such as the National Grid for Learning may in the longer term help to resolve this problem, but only if all children have an equal ability to access computers outside of traditional school hours. There is always the risk that the NGfL will simply compound the problem.

Where the law imposes a duty on the public sector to provide information it is essential that the extent of that duty is clearly defined and in many cases extended to take account of our greater awareness of the importance of information. As noted above, the duties under the Children Act 1989 and the Chronically Sick and Disabled Persons Act 1970 do not impose too great a burden on social services departments. Nor do they demand that the information is placed in a context – only by doing that will service users be able to fully understand their rights vis-à-vis the department.

The Disability Discrimination Act 1995 may provide some impetus for change. This Act applies to the provision of services. If, for reasons relating to disability, a person is treated less favourably than others and it cannot be shown that this different treatment was justified, it will be unlawful discrimination under the Act. An obvious example would be a failure to provide information on services for visually impaired people in Braille or some other suitable format. The appropriateness of the language used may also be relevant. If an information pack or website is designed to cover services for those with learning disabilities, it is essential that it be written in a style that can be understood by its target audience. Failure to do so may amount to discrimination.

The rights of the citizen are gradually gaining greater recognition by our law. Under the Human Rights Act 1998 the provisions of the European Convention on Human Rights are made part of the law of the United Kingdom. The rights under the Convention are extensive and include rights to privacy, family life, freedom of speech, freedom from unlawful detention and a right to due process. The *Gillick* and the Children Act 1989 case gave children greater rights of self-determination in crucial areas such as health care. The law now needs to address how it makes people more aware of these rights and, especially in relation to children, how citizens get sufficient information from professionals to enable them to exercise the rights they possess. There is little sign that this is being done.

For the lawyer the big challenge is how to make the law more intellectually accessible. In part this may be achieved by a simpler approach to the drafting of statutes especially when dealing with the rights of the citizen. With the reforms to the UK constitution the opportunity is there to adopt a more European approach to drafting and concentrate on setting down general principles rather than complex rules. Where simpler drafting is not possible due to the technicality of the subject matter, then codes of practice and official guides to the legislation should be published. Thought should also be given to employing technology to help lay people understand their rights and duties under the legislation. The Consumers' Association's *TaxCalc* is a good example of how this may be approached.

Citizens' ignorance of their rights is no excuse for Government to deny them the exercise of those rights. There is some responsibility on the citizen to seek out information, but this only makes sense if the information provided is physically and intellectually accessible and comprehensive. The information technology revolution may be under way. However, for many members of society this revolution has had little if any impact on their lives. Unless this is addressed as a matter of urgency the legal system will have failed in one of its principle objectives, namely the equality of all citizens before the law.

References

1   Nicholas, B., *An introduction to Roman law*, Oxford, Clarendon, 1962, 14–16.
2   http://www.ace.org.uk/info/
3   http://www.gvu.gatech.edu/user_surveys/survey-198-04/#exec
4   http://www.cyberatlas.com/big_picture/demographics/least.html
5   Travis, A., 'Poll points to lift off for Internet', *Guardian* (11 January,1999).
6   *Education and Training Development Agenda 1997–98: Technology in Education*, London, Department for Education and Employment, 1998.

7   Hartley, R. J. and Williams, J., 'Legal information for living: the role of information technology', in Meadows, J. (ed.), *Information technology and the individual*, London, Pinter, 1991, 51.

8   *Guidance on matters to be taken into account in determining the questions relating to the definition of disability*, London, HMSO, 1996.

9   *The Disability Discrimination Act: definition of disability*, London, HMSO, DL60.

10   Child Poverty Action Group [webpages], **http://www.namass.org.uk/cpag.htm** [visited 12/02/1999].

11   *Gillick v. West Norfolk and Wisbech AHA* [1985] 3 All ER 402.

12   Fortin, J., *Children's rights and the developing law*, London, Butterworths, 1998.

13   *Kjeldsen, Busk Madsen and Pedersen v. Denmark* (1976) 1 EHRR 711.

14   Law Commission, *Report on mental incapacity* (1995) Law Com No 231.

15   *Chatterton v. Gerson* [1981] 1 All ER 257.

16   General Medical Council, *Good medical practice*, London, GMC, 1998.

17   'Introduction to augmentative and alternative communication (AAC)', **http://call-centre.cogsci.ed.ac.uk/CALLResearch/AAC/AACIntro**.

18   [1997] 2 All ER 1.

19   *R. v. North Yorkshire County Council, ex parte Hargreaves, The Times*, 12 June, 1997.

4

Copyright and intellectual property rights

Charles Oppenheim

Introduction

Copyright and other related intellectual property rights are of critical importance to librarians and information scientists working with networked information: these legal ideas largely regulate how library staff carry out their professional duties when dealing with such materials. Copyright is just one example of a broader legal idea known as 'intellectual property', which comprises all those things that come from the human intellect, whether they are ideas, inventions, words (fact and fiction), music, theatre or art.

Lawyers view 'intellectual property' more precisely. There are certain clearly defined types of intellectual property, enshrined in different pieces of legislation, such as patents acts, trade marks acts, copyright acts and so on. In this chapter, four types of intellectual property will be considered – copyright, moral rights, performers' rights and trade marks. Librarians may come across other types, such as patents, in their day-to-day work. In many regards, moral rights are unlike other intellectual property rights, and these differences will be highlighted.

Intellectual property, as with real (physical) property, can be mortgaged, sold (the legal term is *assigned*), rented (the legal term is *licensed*), and passed on to one's heirs and successors upon death; also, as with other property where you have certain rights to prevent others from making use of your property without your permission, if you own a piece of intellectual property you are given certain rights (they vary according to the type of intellectual property) preventing third parties from making use of your intellectual property without your permission. If a third party *does* make, use or copy your intellectual property without permission, this is known as *infringement*.

Contracts

A particular characteristic of intellectual property is the existence of contracts for the exploitation of that material. This is particularly true in the case of electronic information. Such contracts are usually known as *licences*. A licence permits one or more third parties to use the property on payment of a fee, perhaps a licence fee based upon the amount of usage. Such a licence does not pass the ownership of the property to the third party. It simply gives the third party rights to enjoy the fruits of the owner's labour. Licences are negotiated between the intellectual property owner (the *licensor*) and the organization or person that wishes to exploit the material (the *licensee*).

Copyright, as its name implies, concerns rights to copy items. Copyright protects the labour, skill and judgment that someone – author, artist or some other creator – expends in the creation of an original piece of work, whether it is a so-called literary work, a piece of music, a painting, a photograph, a TV programme or whatever. Different countries in the world apply different tests in order for copyright to be enjoyed: in countries with the Anglo-Saxon tradition, the emphasis is on 'the sweat of the brow' – in other words, sheer hard work should be rewarded even if what is created is nothing very intellectually profound (although it must still be *new*). In contrast, in countries with a continental European tradition of law, the emphasis is on the intellectual creativity and mere hard work is not enough to justify copyright. This can lead to certain works enjoying copyright in some countries, and not in others.

In virtually every country of the world, copyright is an automatic right – you do not have to register with some central authority, and indeed even using the © symbol is not essential, though it is desirable especially in cases of copyright infringement heard in countries that have not yet signed or ratified international agreements on copyright. Remarks at the start of books along the lines of 'All rights reserved. No part of this publication may be photocopied recorded or otherwise reproduced, stored in any retrieval system . . . ' are not necessary to gain copyright protection, and indeed in general have no validity in law. The local copyright law (in the case of the UK, the 1988 Copyright, Designs and Patents Act) decides what may or may not be reproduced or photocopied, not some statement at the start of a book. However, such statements may have use if the publication is exported to countries that have not signed an international copyright convention.

Who can own copyright?

In UK law, the owner of copyright can be an individual or an organization. An employee who creates something as part of the course of his or her normal duties passes ownership of the copyright to his or her employer. It makes no difference where or when the material was created – it could have been created at home at a weekend, it still belongs to the employer. Many other countries have similar legal concepts, often called 'work for hire'.

This idea of employee copyright raises interesting questions in the case of people who are not employees, such as freelance journalists, consultants and photographers working for newspapers. Typically, unless there is a contract to the contrary, the freelancer owns the copyright even if he or she was paid by the commissioner to create the material. If the employee creates something that is outside his or her normal duties, then the employee owns the copyright.

Copyright can only change hands by assignment. A novelist or an author of a learned article typically assigns to a publisher the right to reproduce copies of his or her work. This is different from a licence, where the original author retains the copyright. In assignment, the copyright is sold.

In some countries, such as the UK, the law gives rights of protection not only to originators but also to those who create particular physical formats for general distribution or sale, such as publishers, producers of audiovisual media, and providers of particular public services such as broadcasting. Certain rights are also given to performers of plays and other works. Some of these issues will be considered later.

In this chapter, I concentrate primarily upon text and images, as these are the types of material most commonly found on the Internet. There are of course other important areas of copyright, such as music, films, TV and radio broadcasts and so on.

Copyright is the right to authorize copying by others. The author or creator and his or her heirs (or anyone who has been assigned the copyright) is granted a monopoly for a finite period. After the period, copyright ends and the materials can be said to 'fall into the public domain' and are then usable without restriction by third parties.

Although a particular piece of text such as that written by Shakespeare, may no longer be subject to copyright, a particular typographical layout may have appeared only recently and therefore that layout and typography may not be copied. With this important exception, materials out of their copyright lifetime can be copied without permission and even republished. The period of protection for authors who are originators of works is related to lifetime. This is normally life plus 70 years.

Under most legal regimes, copyright is said to 'subsist' in something. This is because copyright can only occur provided a work is 'fixed' or recorded in some form. In the case of material in machine-readable form, copyright is deemed to subsist in the machine readable data held on disk or tape. In other words, the recording of the bits on the magnetic or other medium is enough to qualify for that material to be a copyright work.

Originality

A work must be *original* to be regarded as copyrightable. There seems to be no satisfactory way to define 'original' except through the courts regarding specific items and circumstances. It certainly implies 'new' or 'not copied'. In some countries, such as the UK, this is typically the primary requirement for originality, but in other countries some evidence of intellectual creativity is also required. Originality is not the only criterion to obtain copyright, however. In order to be copyright, the material must be more than mere recitation of a fact. This is because there is no copyright in a fact. If this were not to be the case, anyone might otherwise claim monopoly rights on a statement about the closing share price for a company, the temperature today, the capital of a country, or the titles and bibliographic citations to articles. Therefore, there is no copyright in a single bibliographic citation. There can, however, be copyright in a *collection* of facts, such as a collection of bibliographic citations. I will return to that matter later.

Ideas and copyright

Copyright lawyers say that there is no copyright in ideas, only in the form in which they are expressed. Thus an author writing a book about an imaginary secret agent called 'James Bond', with a boss called 'M', a secretary called 'Miss Moneypenny' and an arch enemy called 'Blofeld' would not infringe any copyright. However, it is worth pointing out that such popular ideas are often protected by other forms of intellectual property, such as unfair competition, passing-off or trade marks.

The rights enjoyed by a copyright owner – restricted acts

The owner of the copyright has the right to prevent others from selling, hiring out or renting it, copying it in any form, performing the work in public, broadcasting the work on radio or TV, or amending ('adapting') it. These are the so-called *restricted acts*.

However, just because someone owns copyright doesn't necessarily mean that copies may be produced at will – for example, if the work breaks national security laws, or if the work infringes someone else's copyright, then the copyright owner does not have complete liberty to do what he or she likes with the work.

It is perfectly possible for a work to be original copyright and yet infringe someone else's copyright. To give an example, a word for word translation into

English of a German book, being new, is copyright; but being adapted from someone else's copyright work, it is also the German author's copyright. This sort of situation is not uncommon in intellectual property law.

International copyright treaties

Copyright law is governed by international treaties, the most important of which are the Berne Convention and the Universal Copyright Convention first established in 1886 and 1952, respectively. These allow for basic minimum laws in all countries that are party to the particular treaty, and allow for reciprocal protection for nationals from different countries. These conventions also mean that if there is some question about copyright, it is the local law that applies. To download some records from a French database loaded on a British host you simply need to know the laws of the country you are in when you carry out the acts.

Rights related to copyright

The term 'related rights' is used to cover rights that, whilst not concerned with copying, apply to copyright materials and are linked to the duration of copyright. These rights include rental or hire, public lending, moral rights, and so-called neighbouring rights, such as performing and broadcasting rights, recording rights and film distribution rights. Moral rights are particularly relevant, and I will return to them in a little while.

The legal basis of copyright

Copyright is controlled by local laws. Often, these acts are ambiguous in many places. In some cases, this is to encourage recourse to contract between parties. In other cases, the ambiguity is supposedly deliberate to allow for flexibility to take into account changes in technology. In other cases still, the ambiguity appears to have derived from ignorance of current practice or because the issues were subject to strongly opposed views. The result is a set of national laws that requires users of copyright materials to exercise great caution: in effect, they are being ask to second-guess what a court may decide.

The Copyright, Designs and Patents Act is not the only legislation that affects copyright law in the UK. European Union directives in the field have been issued, and will continue to be issued. An EU directive, once passed by the Council of Ministers, has two years to take effect in each of the countries of the EU. Each country has two choices. Either it rewrites its own laws to conform to the directive, or the text of the directive becomes the text of the national law after two years.

The EU directives of relevance in recent years have been those on the lifetime of copyright, on copyright in software, on rental and lending, and on copyright in databases. All of these directives should have been implemented by the national legislations in the member states by now, and in the case of the UK all have been implemented by means of statutory instruments. The legal environment they impose is reflected in the description of the law in this chapter.

Lifetime

Copyright duration varies according to the particular type of copyright under consideration. Duration of copyright is always calculated from a particular event. For example, the duration of copyright in literary works where the personal author is known is 70 years beyond the calendar year of the author's death, so the event is the end of his or her year of death. The calculation is based on the death of the author even when rights have been assigned to someone else. In the case of joint authorship of a literary, dramatic, musical or artistic work, calculation of the duration of copyright is dependent upon the latest death of all the known authors. If a book was co-authored with separate chapters by different authors, each chapter is typically handled separately from the point of view of expiry date.

If there is no personal author on a title page or in a © notice, or a pseudonym is used instead, the work is treated as 'anonymous or pseudonymous' and its copyright duration lasts for 70 years after the end of the year of first publication. Unpublished works – that is, ones where copies of the work have not been issued to the public – are particularly complex but are not often encountered on the Internet as, by definition, placing something on the Internet *is* issuing a work to the public, and so are not considered further here.

Literary works

Much material on the Internet is text and numbers – the so-called literary works. These need to be considered in more detail than some of the other forms. Virtually anything that is written, printed or recorded in some other way can be the subject of such copyright protection. The term covers handwritten documents, books, pamphlets, magazines, song lyrics, poetry, learned journals, tabular material such as statistical tables or railway timetables, as well as computer programs and data in machine-readable form. There is no implication that this is quality literature.

Compilations

There is a special type of literary work called 'compilations'. This is a collection of works, *each of which may or may not be subject to individual copyright*. The compilation enjoys its own copyright if skill and effort were expended selecting and organizing the collection. Directories, encyclopaedias, anthologies and databases, whether in written, printed or electronic form, are all compilations. Those that involve intellectual creativity in their selection or arrangement enjoy copyright protection; those that do not are given a special database protection right instead. This leads to a somewhat confusing set of rights in databases. Basically, these can be divided into four groups:

- a compilation of items, each of which is copyright, where the compilation itself involves skill and creativity – for example, an issue of a newspaper
- a compilation of items, each of which is copyright, but there is no skill or creativity in the compilation itself – for example, a collection of the latest annual reports of every publicly quoted company in a country
- a compilation of non-copyright items in which there is skill and creativity in creating the compilation – for example a yellow pages directory, or a compilation of old poetry, and
- a compilation of non-copyright items in which there is no skill or creativity in the compilation, such as a simple telephone directory or TV listings.

In the first case, the newspaper issue, there is double copyright protection – each item is protected, and the compilation as a whole is further protected. In practice, users should respect the copyright of each item individually, and this will ensure they will not infringe the compilation copyright either. In the second case, the annual reports listing, each annual report is copyright, and in addition there is the special 15-year database protection for the compilation as a whole. Because the special database protection right can be renewed if there is significant investment in updating the database, in practice the database right could last longer than the copyright! Time will tell if the courts do allow such regular renewals of database copyright. In the third case where there is skill and effort in compiling out-of-copyright materials, the compilation enjoys copyright. In the final case, such as simple telephone directories, the compilation enjoys database rights only.

These database rules came into effect in January 1998, and it is too early to be sure what the implications are. Readers are warned to be careful in their use of database materials and to watch for reports of relevant court cases.

Infringement and exceptions to copyright

If anyone copies, adapts, broadcasts, etc. a copyright work without permission, he or she has committed an infringement. Either the whole work, or what is called a substantial part of the work, must have been copied, adapted, etc. 'Substantial' means substantial in quality as well as quantity. So how should one judge 'substantial'? Look at it from a negative point of view. What if the material copied were *missing* from the book? How much would that reduce the book's value?

If it would reduce it a lot, then the material copied is substantial. If not, then it is not substantial. Another way to look at it is to consider substitutability. If the material copied would act as a useful substitute for the original, then it is substantial. If it would be an inadequate or useless substitute, then it is not substantial.

If someone is prosecuted and convicted for infringement, he or she may have to pay damages or face criminal penalties. The damages are *either* the monetary damage done to the copyright owner's business *or* the profits (or reduction in costs) gained from the copying. Damages are the usual penalties, but in severe cases, such as piracy (making copies and selling them deliberately), the infringer can be sent to prison as well. Note, too, that people can be sued either for infringing, for authorizing infringement, or for permitting infringement to take place. These range from a manager telling a member of staff to carry out illegal copying to having such a slack approach to copyright throughout an organization that there is no respect for the law. Just having photocopiers available for people to use is *not* an offence so long as suitable warnings about copyright infringement are also posted.

It is probable that most copying carried out is substantial. People are allowed to make such copies because there are two very important so-called exceptions to copyright that provide people with a defence against an infringement action. These are fair dealing (sometimes known as 'fair use' or 'private copying') and library privileges. Fair dealing and library privileges are different things.

What is fair dealing? It means that an individual may make a single copy, or multiple copies of a substantial part of or all of a literary work as long as two things apply:

- the copying is fair, that is, it does not damage the legitimate interests of the copyright owner
- the copying is for the person him- or herself (or for a colleague) and is for one of the purposes permitted in local law. These local exceptions to copyright vary from country to country, but typically include permission:
  - for research (sometimes only non-commercial research)
  - for private study

– for the purposes of criticism or review
– for reporting current events, and
– for educational purposes.

Note that in principle one can make a fair dealing copy by means of a photocopy or by means of making an electronic copy – the law does not prevent the latter.

The copy is permitted only if it does not damage the copyright owner's legitimate commercial interests. Courts would have to decide this issue for themselves. It is difficult for an individual to judge what may or may not damage a commercial company's interests. However, making a single copy obviously will have far less impact than making multiple copies.

Readers should carefully examine the wording of their local laws to decide whether the types of copying they plan to carry out do indeed fall within the exceptions permitted by law. Fair dealing applies to most literary works – to books, journal articles, databases equally. However, it does *not* appear to apply to computer software.

Certain types of libraries have an alternative defence to fair dealing. In some countries, they are given a guaranteed immunity against being prosecuted for making copies for patrons, or are entitled to deliver interlibrary loans, so long as certain administrative rules are followed. The copyright owner cannot even start an infringement action against such a library in the first place. Librarians are in a unique position in the law with this guaranteed immunity, but with this immunity comes certain responsibilities: in particular the ground rules specified in law must be respected. In principle, the library privileges apply equally to printed and electronic materials.

Artistic works

The term typically includes photographs; microfilms – a type of photograph; films; paintings and drawings; models of buildings; sculptures; diagrams; maps; slides, including overhead projector transparencies; engravings; etchings. Generally, copyright is owned by the person who created the work. If a work, such as a photograph, is commissioned, the copyright is still in the hands of the person who made the work unless there is a contract making it clear that copyright is assigned to the commissioning person.

If the work is made in the course of employment, then the copyright is owned by the employer. If the material is made on the employer's premises, using the employer's equipment, but the employee was doing it outside his or her normal duties, the copyright then belongs to the employee.

In general, the ground rules regarding ownership and lifetime of copyright in artistic works is as for literary works. There may, however, be important differences in terms of exceptions to copyright, and the reader is advised to consult either the relevant local Act or textbooks for guidance on these matters. The current UK legislation is the Copyright, Designs and Patents Act 1988 (1988 c.48). However, because this Act has been amended several times by statutory instruments because of EU directives, readers should not rely on the original act as printed, but should consult a textbook that incorporates the latest changes, for example *Butterworths intellectual property law handbook*.[1]

Moral rights

Moral rights legislation varies considerably between countries. Some countries have stringent regulations, some are more relaxed, and in some countries the concept of moral rights is not enshrined in law at all, but the principles may appear under other legal guises. In general, though, there are three types of moral rights that apply to virtually all copyright works, including literary and artistic works, in many countries. The first is the right to be identified as an author. The second is the right to object to derogatory treatment of your work. The third is the right to object to your name being associated with something that you did not create.

The first, the right to be identified as the author, must in some cases be *asserted* – in other words, it may not be automatic. Once you have asserted the right, it remains with you. This is the so-called paternity right, and lasts as long as copyright does. As with all moral rights, this right cannot be assigned to anyone else, and so remains with the creator even if copyright itself is assigned.

The second right, the right to object to derogatory treatment, is perhaps the most important. Its lifetime is the copyright of the work, and derogatory treatment is any amendment to the work that impugns the reputation of the creator. This potentially includes quoting out of context, making a frivolous pastiche of the work, or any other change that is, in effect, defamatory. This is an important right, because it is potentially so wide ranging – even actions such as copying a portion of someone's work could infringe this moral right if the copy gives a misleading impression of what the creator was trying to say.

The third right, the right not to suffer false attribution of a work, could be used, for example, to sue a newspaper that claimed someone had said something that he or she had not. This right, unlike the other two, applies to everyone, and not just authors or creators.

That said, in some countries the law somewhat restricts who is entitled to moral rights: for example, it might not apply to works that have appeared in newspapers, magazines or learned journals, or to employee-created materials.

Moral rights cannot be assigned, but in some countries they can be waived – in other words, you can be asked to disclaim the moral rights you have. Moral rights are especially important in the electronic information environment; this matter is discussed further below.

Electronic copyright

'Electronic copyright' is a convenient label, not much used by lawyers, to embrace electronic databases and other machine-readable data, and copyright law as applied to their usage. Thus offline electronic databases such as diskettes or CD-ROMs, online electronic databases and Internet materials are covered by the term. Whilst it is true that there is no such thing as 'electronic copyright' as a separate legal idea, it is also true that because of the ease and low cost of copying materials in machine-readable form (such as downloading) or of converting print documents into electronic form (so-called electrocopying), the ease of disseminating such digitized materials over the Internet, the perfect quality of any copies made and the difficulties of policing such activities, the question of copyright in machine-readable records does pose some problems that do not routinely turn up with (say) print products. For this reason, it is worth considering some particular aspects of copyright that are relevant to such types of materials.

Electrocopying

This is a major concern for the publishing industry. The term covers any or all of the following activities:

(a) keying-in or machine-scanning of publications to make or augment a database (this is the most common use of the term)
(b) downloading from an online or offline database to form or augment another database
(c) transfer of data from one database to another
(d) manipulation of data to make different files and/or publications
(e) print-out or publication, either reproducing original input or manipulated information
(f) networking of materials created by any of the above methods.

These can at present be done only under specific contract with a copyright owner such as a database producer or publisher. Any electrotyping, transmission down a telecommunications network or transfer to a remote site of a copyright work is *prima facie* infringement. A defence of 'fair dealing' is unlikely to be successful if the full texts of documents have been transferred.

The problems are exacerbated by the developments in telecommunications such as the Internet. Such networks permit for the first time routine and inexpensive transfer of large volumes of data between organizations many miles apart. Such developments make more difficult the already tense relationships between owners of copyright materials and the users of such materials.

This is an important issue, and one that librarians and information scientists should be actively interested in. The most likely outcome is licences issued by publishers, consortia of publishers or maybe collecting societies, such as the Copyright Licensing Agency in the UK, giving permission to digitize materials that they own or that they are entitled to act for. These licences may well be negotiated by one-stop-shop type organizations set up with the express purpose of negotiating deals on behalf of consortia of libraries. However, it will be a few years before a clear pattern emerges. At present (May 1999), each library has to approach individual publishers for permission to digitize copyright materials if that is what it wants to do, and indeed, even if one-stop-shops do emerge, non-standard requests will still have to be negotiated on a one-to-one basis.

Software copyright

Software is quite clearly a 'literary work' in law, but it has certain special rules associated with it. Thus, standard rules, such as the lifetime, the need to be original, and so on, apply. The special rules are as follows:

1   In practice it seems one cannot 'fair deal' in software. This means users may not make a copy of part of computer code for the purposes of research, private study or any other reason. I use the phrase 'in practice' because it would be difficult to reproduce a portion or all of a piece of software code and to be able to argue that this is 'fair'.
2   On the other hand, users are explicitly permitted in law (in EU countries) to make a single back-up copy of the software. If that back-up copy fails, they can then make another back-up copy. They may not make multiple copies in law; they must get a licence permitting this.
3   Again in EU countries, users are permitted in law to reverse engineer, that is, take portions of some software code in order to ensure that software being developed is fully compatible with the other software.

Software publishers are in general more aggressive in defending their copyrights than are other types of publishers. Therefore, whilst engendering respect for copyright is *always* important, it is particularly important for organizations to have rigorous rules to prevent staff creating unauthorized copies of software. Thus, it should be a disciplinary offence for staff to have illegal software held on machines owned by their employers.

Internet copyright

There is a common fallacy that the Internet is like the Wild West – unregulated and lawless. This is incorrect. Laws do apply to the Internet. However, what is often not clear is whose laws apply (if, say, data is transferred from one country to another), or who is responsible for a particular act (particularly if the act in question has been carried out by someone using an anonymous remailer, or if the act has been carried out with the 'assistance', say, of an Internet service provider that may claim it was ignorant of what was going on. There are further problems because of difficulties in policing illegal activities, and because what is lawful in one country may be illegal in another – or, in a more extreme case, what is lawful in one state in the USA is illegal in the neighbouring State. These problems are compounded by the fact that many of the relevant laws were formulated using words appropriate to traditional media, such as print, and it is difficult to see how exactly they can be applied to Internet materials. Finally, it is worth noting that there is relatively little case law, and such case law that exists is rarely applicable to any specific query because either the facts are different or the case was decided in a different country.

Despite these difficulties, certain broad principles that are generally applicable worldwide can be enunciated, and these are shown below. Firstly, e-mail messages, material loaded onto ftp (file transfer protocol) sites or Web servers, and anything else put up on the Internet are copyright. Just because the material is widely available free of charge does not change the situation. There is *no* implied licence to copy. The fact that most authors of such materials are only too happy for their work to be reproduced and disseminated is irrelevant to the strict legal position. The material is still copyright and should be respected as such. Therefore one should be careful about any copying of such material, for example forwarding it to someone else. That may sound alarming, but it need not be. Such copying is only a real problem if the person who owns the copyright loses income or the infringer gains income (or reduces costs) as a result of the infringement. Therefore, typically, e-mail messages can be copied and forwarded without too much concern. Furthermore, individual URLs (uniform resource locators), e-mail addresses and so on are facts, and can be copied as they are not protected by copyright. Compilations of URLs or e-mail addresses are, however, protected by copyright, just as are Internet indexes such as those created by Yahoo, AltaVista, FAQ (frequently asked question) collections on UseNet newsgroups. Some people have spent considerable time and effort to create subject gateways that include a careful selection of appropriate URLs, perhaps with commentary about the content. Such collections should never be copied and forwarded.

A question that is often asked is whether listing URLs is an invitation to infringe because people may choose to visit the sites in question and download the material they find there. Logic suggests that this is no more an invitation to infringe copyright than a library catalogue is an invitation to users to photocopy the books referred to, but anyone preparing such lists should be careful not to imply (or state explicitly) that users should feel free to download or copy the materials they find at the recommended addresses.

To download someone's World Wide Web homepage and use it as the basis of one's own homepage is clearly copyright infringement, and may involve infringement of trade mark rights (another form of intellectual property – see below) if the page included some device or logo that is a registered trade mark (a not uncommon feature). Amending someone's copyright material is 'adaptation' in copyright law, and is infringement.

In the context of forwarding and copying messages, copyright is not the only consideration: moral rights also apply, and this implies that a message should only be forwarded in its entirety. If someone copies and forwards a portion, or adds material implying it was written by the individual, this might be deemed to be derogatory treatment and therefore an infringement of the creator's moral rights.

Despite the fact that the law clearly does protect material loaded on the Internet, the fact remains that policing what goes on, and pursuing a successful infringement action perhaps in some foreign court, is problematic. The best advice, therefore, for any individual or organization greatly concerned about having material copied illegally on the Internet is simple: don't put the material up on the Internet! This does not prevent someone from scanning text, say, and offering it on the Internet, but it does make the process of Internet infringement a little more laborious for would-be infringers.

Some Internet copyright cases

There have been several notable Internet copyright cases, mostly in the USA. These have primarily concerned the liability of Internet service providers (ISPs) for the actions of their subscribers. In general, bulletin board suppliers and ISPs have been found guilty of copyright infringement when their users downloaded, and then passed over the bulletin board, copyright material when particular circumstances prevailed. These are that the ISP either knew, or had good reason to know, that copyright infringement was taking place. This provides a good general rule of thumb, not just for ISPs but also for employers worried about whether they will be prosecuted for infringements carried out by staff, or universities worried about the activities of their students. In order to avoid liability, three criteria must be in place. Firstly, the employer could not have known, or had no reason to know, that infringement had taken place. A good reason for knowing would be if someone with a track record of infringement was using the system, or if suspiciously large volumes of data were being transferred. Secondly, the employer should have publicly stated rules warning that anyone caught infringing copyright would be subject to disciplinary procedures, and perhaps advising on good practice. Finally, the employer should have a track record of genuinely carrying out the threat to discipline anyone caught infringing. Only if all three are established can an employer be reasonably certain of avoiding liability.

In addition, there has been an interesting case in the New York courts (*Tasini et al. v. New York Times*), where a number of freelance authors have been suing online hosts. They wrote articles for the *New York Times* and other newspapers in the 1960s onwards. When they did so, they assigned the copyright to the newspaper. However, they believe that they did not assign electronic rights, because such rights did not exist in those days and thus it would have been impossible to assign them. The response from the defendants has been that electronic rights were included in the copyright assignment. In May 1999 the case remained at appeal stage. In future, it is likely that many authors will only assign print publishing rights to publishers and will reserve electronic rights to themselves – which they are perfectly entitled to do.

There have also been a number of copyright cases regarding the development of links or of frames linking to another site. In the case of *Shetland Times* versus *Shetland News*, the question was whether one service could copy headlines from the other service onto its website, whilst at the same time providing links to the other service. Unfortunately (from the point of view of clarification of the law), the matter was settled out of court, and therefore no definitive conclusions can be drawn. The *TotalNews* case in the USA was similarly settled out of court, but there was a clear implication in the case that the use of frames to pass off someone else's webpage as one's own website could lead to a successful court action against the user of such frames. The topic of passing off is discussed further below under trade marks.

At this stage, with technology developing fast and the law trying to catch up with these changes, the best advice that can be given is as follows: any organization wishing to use (i.e. copy or adapt) third-party copyright material on the Internet (whether its website, in e-mail or whatever, and whether the material is text, image or sound) *when the organization makes money from the material, or when it could be plausibly argued that it saved money by incorporating such material on its site* should ensure that it has the requisite licence to do so. The fact that the material is available free is irrelevant. It would be just as much copyright infringement to reproduce large chunks of text from a newspaper that is provided free of charge as it is to copy text from a newspaper that costs money. The analogy holds good for the Internet.

The second piece of advice is for anyone who is an Internet service provider, or who provides computer facilities for others to create Internet materials (such as a university for its staff and students). The provider is just as likely as the originator to be sued *if the provider knew, or had good reason to know, that infringing material was being placed on the service.*

There is, however, a strong argument that placing material on the Internet is giving an implied licence to browse, notwithstanding the fact that browsing involves copying material onto the user's computer memory, and this is technically infringement. Downloading and/or making a single printout of material found on the Internet for one's own private use would almost certainly be considered 'fair dealing', and I would advise that, in general, copyright owners would not object to such activities, but readers are advised that this is by no means certain.

Electronic copyright management systems (ECMS)

Publishers have concerns when agreeing to a licence for the distribution in electronic form of material for which they hold the copyright. There are two major reasons stated for their concern. The first is the worry that the material will be copied and/or re-disseminated in an unauthorized manner, and therefore, by implication, the publishers will lose sales. The second concern is that material will be amended, which leads to two further issues. Firstly, there is the danger that the amended material, although not 'authentic', may be passed off with the original publisher's imprimatur, thereby potentially damaging the reputation of the publisher. Secondly, there is a danger that the copied (and perhaps also amended) material will then be passed off as new material, and it will be difficult to demonstrate that the material had originated from that to which the publisher owned rights. Such copying and amendment are, if carried out without the permission of the copyright owner, *prima facie* copyright infringement.

There is a need, therefore, for the development of robust, reliable, economical and tamper-proof mechanisms to identify, or tag, copyright material and/or to control the usage of such material. The existence of such mechanisms would give publishers the reassurance that they require to more readily give permission for the release of their material in machine readable form, or for the digitization by clients of print material that they own.

Electronic copyright management systems address these issues. These include, for example, the addition of visible or invisible data identifying the rights owner, ways of identifying who had made any amendments to the document, and software used solely to govern or control distribution of the work in electronic form. This can be used to limit what can be done with the original or a copy of the file containing the work. It can limit the use of the file to view only. It can also limit the number of times the work can be retrieved, opened, duplicated or printed.

Such systems will serve the functions of tracking and monitoring uses of copy-righted works as well as licensing of rights and indicating attribution, creation and ownership interests. Such measures must not only effectively protect the owner's interests in the works but also not unduly burden use of the work by readers or compromise their privacy.

ECMSs will also provide copyright management information to inform the user about authorship, copyright ownership, date of creation or last modification, and terms and conditions of authorized uses. Once information such as this is affiliated with a particular work, users will be able to easily address questions over licensing and use of the work. No well-established electronic copyright management system currently exists, but they can be expected on the market soon.

At the time of writing, no country's law protects such systems. However, there are moves in many countries to pass laws to prohibit the importation, manufacture or distribution of any device, or the provision of any service, the primary purpose or effect of which is to avoid, remove, deactivate, or otherwise circumvent, without authority of the copyright owner, any ECMS for the purpose of infringing copyright. These moves would also prohibit the provision, distribution, or importation for distribution, of copyright management information known to be false, and the unauthorized removal or alteration of copyright management information.

ECMSs will not solve all problems, but they will put up barriers, both financial and in terms of user-unfriendly systems with hurdles to overcome before information can be accessed. The track record of similar devices (copy-protected software, dongles, etc.) in the PC software industry shows that users will often boycott products of this type. There are also privacy problems raised by ECMSs. There is little point in developing an ECMS that is impractical to use because of too complex a password or charging mechanism, or one that is so expensive that people are tempted to bypass it or ignore it. Whilst many would regard legal protection for ECMSs as desirable, there is great concern that such devices should be sufficiently 'intelligent' to recognize activities that are permitted in law, and that they should protect moral rights, e.g. to ensure an author's name can never be deleted from a text or amended.

Trade marks and passing off

In the pre-Internet age, the law of trade marks and of passing off was relatively straightforward. In order to acquire a trade mark, one must trade within the country in question, and acquire a reputation or goodwill associated with that mark. One could then obtain a registered trade mark by paying certain fees and applying to the local trade mark registry, and this would give the owner monopoly rights over the use of that mark for a fixed period of time; unlike copyright and other forms of intellectual property, registered trade marks can be renewed *ad infinitum*, so long as the renewal fees are paid. Alternatively, one did not bother with the registration procedure, but relied on protecting the unregistered trade mark by means of a 'passing off' action. 'Passing off' is the UK term, but there are equivalent rights in most countries under unfair competition laws. In effect, these rights are that you can sue for loss of reputation if someone deliberately passes off their product or service as if it was yours. In the case of registered trade marks, one can sue even if the mark was used without permission accidentally or non-maliciously; in the case of unregistered marks, one must prove the intention was to deceive, and that the trade-mark owner does enjoy a reputation in the country in question. In addition to these protections, most countries of the world have rules stopping an organization or individual from using a trade name that is confusingly similar to or identical to an existing company name, or from creating a company with a name too similar to another company registered in that country.

Unfortunately, these comfortable rules have caused intense difficulties on the Internet. The problem has been brought into sharp focus in the area of domain names for e-mail addresses and URLs (domain names identify information provider network addresses). Previously it was not uncommon for companies in different countries to own rights to effectively the same name or mark in different countries. Generally, unless one company chose to expand into the home market of another, there were no problems, and even if problems did arise, the first owner of the trade mark generally won and the newcomer lost. However, the global nature of the Internet means that two companies, both with well-established trade names, may be advertising their services or products in the same territory even though their histories and geographic bases are different.

Readers will be aware that as a result a number of organizations have sprung up offering a service to register domain names, and there has at times been an unseemly race to be the first or unique owner of a particularly useful domain name. In some cases, the race and competition are legitimate, in the sense that both organizations genuinely have the same name. In others, people have registered opportunistically to sell the domain name at a high price to the well-known organization that wishes to use that name. In others still, people have registered domain names with the express purpose of setting up unofficial fan clubs or hate sites. Two good examples of the latter are **http://www.britishtelecom.co.uk** and **http://www.britishpetroleum.co.uk,** which were set up by disgruntled customers of the two high-profile companies.

By definition, a domain name has to be unique. There have been court cases that have stripped individuals of a domain name when they have offered to resell it to a large organization that was likely to need it, but the problems remain. Trade-mark and passing-off law is territorial, and domain names are international. A classic case was that of Prince plc, a UK training company with world-wide sales. The company had a website incorporating the term **prince.com** and found itself sued in both the UK and US courts by a US company, Prince Sports Group, for infringement of the latter's US registered trade mark. Prince Sports Group had not at that stage applied for a domain name, and demanded the transfer of the **prince.com** name. In the UK, Prince Sports Group's case was rejected, and following this Prince Sports Group withdrew its action in the US courts. The main conclusion from the case seems to be that the existence of a registered trade mark does not prevent a *bona fide* organization from using a similar or identical name in its domain name.

Thus the law at present is in the rather unsatisfactory situation of stating that whoever gets a domain name first wins, unless it can be shown they obtained the name for the 'non-legitimate' reason of acquiring it for the purpose of reselling to a likely purchaser. Also it does not protect the organization with a number of trade marks that thought it had a monopoly on those marks in all areas of commerce, including the Internet, and does not appear to protect a company from an aggrieved customer that sets up a site with a name similar to its own. It also does not stop someone acquiring a domain name for a name that is not uniquely associated with one company (for example *swan*) and then in effect auctioning the name to the highest bidder (in this case, a kettle manufacturer or a producer of safety matches might be interested in bidding for this domain name).

The only realistic way forward is a global trade-mark law, combined with a comprehensive database of all trade marks and domain names, and a large increase in the number of ways of ending a domain name from the current **com**, **org** and **co** categories to permit many more similar names to coexist. In addition, certain global 'famous names' must be given defensive protection (obvious examples include *Coca-Cola, McDonald's, Rolls-Royce* and *Marks and Spencer*), so that no one other than the owner of the mark under any circumstances can use such names within any domain name anywhere in the world. Even in such a new system, it would be difficult to avoid the idea that the first one to register is then the winner. It is therefore strongly advised that employers register relevant domain names and/or trade marks sooner rather than later. Library and information staff should also regularly search the Internet to identify other organizations or individuals using domain names similar to names important to their employer.

Finally

This chapter is intended as a general description of the law. It is not intended to give legal advice: in the area of copyright and trade marks, so much depends upon individual circumstances that it is virtually impossible to generalize, and this is particularly true when dealing with the Internet. Readers are strongly urged to take legal advice and/or take any necessary insurance before making decisions in this area. I regret I can accept no responsibility for any consequences of people taking action based upon the wording of this article.

Because copyright and trade-mark law differ subtly, but in important respects, from country to country, there has been little or no reference to specific laws, court cases or regulations in this chapter. Readers requiring further guidance are advised to consult a standard text on intellectual property that applies to their country. Readers in the UK are directed to either *The Aslib guide to copyright* or *The legal and regulatory environment for electronic information*.[2, 3]

References

1   Phillips, J., *Butterworths intellectual property law handbook*, London, Butterworth, 1997.
2   Phillips, J., Wall, R. A. and Oppenheim, C., *The Aslib guide to copyright*, London, Aslib, 1994–.
3   Oppenheim, C., *The legal and regulatory environment for electronic information*, Calne, Infonortics, 3rd edn, 1999.

5

Legal deposit

F. W. Ratcliffe

> You have only to ramble round the Internet to realise that copyright is doomed. Many
> literary texts still in copyright are freely available to all ... Books are no longer the best
> way to store and disseminate such data. But for copyright holders to try to block the
> new Websites would be like closing public libraries in the hope that people would buy
> more books: it would be seen as unacceptable interference in the diffusion of infor-
> mation.

J. McCue was certainly not alone in thinking that copyright is doomed, when he
wrote this in the *Times* on 4 September 1997.[1] He clearly attached little importance to the law of intellectual property of which copyright is one important part:
'Instead of trying to uphold Queen Anne's law of copyright, we should be working out new rewards for authors'. The historical development of copyright and
the, at times, hotly contested issue of legal deposit could hardly have been in his
mind. Yet the growth of copyright law and the development of the deposit principle have been instrumental in promoting and preserving the published record
of the nation's history and culture for almost the last half millennium. They are
likely to be no less important in securing the record of the future.

Whilst the necessity of copyright or something very much like it has never seriously been in doubt during that time, the significance of the archival and cultural
role of legal deposit was only fully grasped when the fragility of the record began
to be appreciated. The concept of an archive of the nation's published output,
which is today generally acknowledged as essential to the nation's heritage, is in
fact of comparatively recent origin. To scholars and the library world it validates
the importance of legal deposit. Without the latter there would be great gaps in
the fabric of the nation's history.

The creation and preservation of the record in the future are likely to be much
more difficult. Identifying and saving it in the context of the new technology,
whether statistical, historical, literary or whatever, share all too many of those
imponderables that copyright law itself is experiencing. The recognition that the
rapid growth of publishing via non-print media is threatening the published

record has provoked urgent concern beyond librarians and archivists at national, governmental and international levels. The discussions so far confirm the view that the future record will not merely be different from the legal deposit of printed materials, it will be more difficult to achieve comprehensively if, indeed, it is achievable at all.

The transition from manuscript to printed book transformed, in a way created, the intellectual property rights of the author and printer as the single laboriously produced manuscript copy was replaced by many at very little extra cost. It marked the beginning of the publishing trade as it is recognized today. Yet, in this country, over a century elapsed after the use of moveable type by Gutenberg before the Stationers' Company was granted a charter in 1556. This was despite the fact that the potential of printing technology to undermine the rights of the author and the printer must have long been apparent from the rapid spread of printing through Europe.

It appears as though much the same may be said in the years ahead about the new technology and its relationship to printing. Computers have now been with us for over half a century and are at the heart of today's information revolution. Although the technology's potential as a competitor to, let alone substitute for, the printed text may initially have been less obvious – because of its more complicated technology with so many applications in other fields and its very high costs – a full realization of its impact on copyright and legal deposit seems only to have registered in the last decade. That it was recognized owes much to that hitherto much neglected aspect of library science, preservation. The realization in the USA that much of the country's recorded history was preserved on highly acidic paper and would eventually disappear stimulated a concern that has since become worldwide.

Just how serious this issue was has only been revealed relatively recently, when a report from the US House of Representatives Committee on Government Operations was published in 1990.[2] It disclosed that the data of the US 1960 census had been held on tapes which proved vulnerable to rapid obsolescence and were almost lost, along with a number of other virtually irreplaceable, not to say vital records. This not only underlined the vulnerability of the type of new media used for storage preservation, it also warned pointedly of the problems that the developing new media might bring with them. The 1990s saw a series of publications in the USA addressing these issues. Of these, an article of J. Rothenberg is especially relevant to the problems of legal deposit: 'Ensuring the longevity of digital documents'.[3] Virtually all of his observations are applicable to legal deposit. 'Because digital information can be copied and recopied perfectly, it is often extolled for its supposed longevity. The truth, however, is that because of changing hardware and software . . . [little or nothing] will be immediately intelligible 50 years from now'.

In Britain, the government consultation paper, *Legal deposit of publications*[4] appeared somewhat belatedly in February 1997, issued by the Department of National Heritage, the Scottish Office, the Welsh Office and the Department of Education Northern Ireland. It drew in part on the *Proposal for the legal deposit of non-print publications*[5] submitted to the Department of National Heritage by the British Library which was endorsed by the five other legal deposit libraries and the British Film Institute. This typescript document incorporated in addition to the main text the individual submissions of all seven bodies. The *Proposal* itself followed the report *The management and development of the legal deposit collections*[6] produced by the librarians of the deposit libraries in 1994.

Legal deposit is firmly linked in the mind with copyright. Until very recently it was more generally referred to as copyright deposit. This is hardly surprising since it has featured in all the copyright acts since 1709. The current law governing legal deposit is contained in Section 15 of the Copyright Act of 1911, which represented a milestone in copyright legislation. It remained untouched in the Copyright Act of 1956 and in the Copyright, Designs and Patents Act of 1988, despite the views of the Gregory Committee of 1951 and the Whitford Committee of 1977. Whitford observed that 'there no longer seems to be any good reason why the legislation for the maintenance of libraries of deposit should form part of the Law of Copyright'.[7] The consultative document on the *Reform of the law relating to copyright, designs and performers' protection*[8] of 1981 in its chapter on legal deposit made no reference to this recommendation. That notwithstanding, the Office of Arts and Libraries and the Department of National Heritage were subsequently much involved with questions of legal deposit.

Nevertheless, to judge from some of the questions posed by the 1997 consultation paper, it seems appropriate that legal deposit has remained with the law of copyright. Many of the questions asked are clearly of immediate relevance to legal deposit, for example, those seeking precise definitions of 'publication' and 'publisher' or views on 'intellectual property rights'. That apart, the paper's purpose was not solely to find solutions to the problems raised by the new technology. Its remit also encompassed the existing arrangements for printed materials. Since the paper's publication there have been changes in copyright law that will be important to legal deposit. For example, the European Commission's Directive (96/9/EC 11 March 1996) on 'the protection of databases in both electronic and non-electronic (i.e. paper) form' came into force in the UK on 1 January 1998. It aimed to harmonize the laws of the member states, and the Copyright, Designs and Patents Act 1988 has been amended accordingly by these regulations.

An association of three and a half centuries dies hard. The deposit libraries are still often referred to as 'copyright libraries' and are likely to remain so for the foreseeable future. Of the six the British Library still claims its copies through its

Copyright Receipt Office, the other five through their Copyright Licensing Agency in London. In its earliest manifestation in England deposit was an essential in establishing copyright. It came into being in Europe not so much at the instigation of authors but of printers and publishers on whom production costs fell. The earliest example of deposit came as a result of the Montpelier Ordinance of 28 December 1537, introduced by Francis I in France. This recognized the power of the printing presses and ensured that a copy of any work 'worthy to be seen' entered the royal library.

In England the Letters Patent issued by Henry VIII and Elizabeth I showed that the commercial potential of the copyright principle was appreciated but the Letters involved no such official element of deposit. This first appeared tentatively in England half a century later, when an agreement between Sir Thomas Bodley and the Stationers' Company was made in 1610 under which a copy of each book registered at Stationers' Hall was deposited in Sir Thomas's new library in Oxford, the Bodleian (founded 1598). It was in fact an archival copy that could be produced, in theory at least, as evidence of the registered copyright. This arrangement had all the marks of a 'gentleman's agreement' and was of limited success. It was succeeded, this time at an official level, by what is sometimes referred to as the first copyright act, the Press Licensing Act of 1662. Introduced by parliament, it obligated printers to deposit three copies on the best and largest paper in the royal library and the university libraries of Oxford and Cambridge.

Legal deposit in Britain did not arise as a result of a deliberate attempt to create an archival record of published materials nor even as a desire à la française to preserve copies of books 'worthy to be seen'. It may be that Sir Thomas Bodley was influenced by the French example but his motive was clearly to provide a supply of free books for his new library and in so doing contribute to the Stationers' control of publications, which was, in essence, an exercise in copyright, or as some may think, monopoly. Exactly how this agreement was achieved is unknown but it seems certain that the presentation by the Stationers of 'one perfect book' of every newly registered title 'towards the furnishing and increase of the said Librarie' was not made solely 'out of their zeale to the advancement of good learning' or as an altruistic 'benefit to the generall state of the Realme'. What is certain is that it laid the basis for future deposit in the country and did so with an eye to a cultural or educational benefit in mind.

The Copyright Act of 1709, the Statute of Queen Anne, is the first of the many acts to be referred to officially as a copyright act, although the word did not appear in the title of the act itself, which became law on 4 April 1710. It marked the real beginning of copyright law as practised today. It made clear once and for all that the 'sole rights and liberty of printing books' belonged to authors and their representatives or agents. It still did not include the so-called moral rights and it was not until the Copyright, Designs and Patents Act of 1988, which endorsed the proposal of the consultation paper of 1981, that these came formally into force, despite the fact that Britain subscribed to the Berne Convention on Copyright of 1886 which prescribed such rights.

Like the Licensing Act of 1662, the 1709 Act made provision for deposit, establishing the principle of deposit as it is known today, despite the resistance of publishers. However, it increased the number of deposit libraries from three to nine. This was to rise to eleven after the Acts of Union with Scotland and Ireland, arousing fiercely the opposition of publishers then and during the nineteenth and much of the twentieth centuries, although the number was later reduced to the present six. Much of the activity in respect of legal deposit in the nineteenth century was directed at compelling publishers to deposit their publications. Whilst this has been much less in evidence in this century there have been a few valiant attempts in Parliament to eliminate deposit altogether. With regard to the costs of the deposit to publishers the observations of the Whitford Committee were thought to have contained, if not resolved, this contentious issue, but it was raised again in the 1997 consultation paper.

The deposit libraries, anxious though they are to retain and expand the principle of legal deposit, will most likely in the context of the new technology interpret deposit in the flexible way they do now, as far, that is, as they are able. Deposit libraries have not been concerned, for example, to secure by deposit examples of typographical arrangements, not because of failure to claim but simply because the deposit libraries have been, and will remain, interested essentially in the contents of the document. Similarly, it seems certain that many of those areas of the new technology that attract copyright protection, such as computer programs, will be of no intrinsic interest to the deposit libraries, whose interest rather lies in the database itself that the programs facilitate. However, the problems are not only different and more numerous, they are much more complicated. Tangibility, for example, is a major aspect of copyright law. The opportunities in the new technology to update or change text go far beyond those of the new edition or new impression in a printed work. It is the ephemeral or fugitive nature of much electronic publishing, the essence of intangibility, that poses major problems for the deposit.

The comments of D. I. Bainbridge on the Internet point to some of these very difficult and different problems now facing legislators and the librarians of the deposit libraries:

The Internet is made up of interlinked public telecommunications networks to which computers are connected. Anyone can gain access by use of an appropriate modem . . . Material can be accessed, viewed, retrieved, printed and downloaded from all over the world and a vast and growing amount of information is available. Virtually any kind of work can be made available via the Internet. At the present time, there is no one person who is in overall control of the Internet; it could be described as information technological communications anarchy. [9]

McCue puts flesh on this statement, indicating what is probably the widely held view of the general public:

> One can download tapes from concerts – and for all I know videos too. And that is the future: free, unpoliceable, immediate, utmost access to all words, sounds, pictures and ideas that are worth having. Instead of going to the record shop, we will be ordering CDs by e-mail so that we can copy those old Beatles tracks or the *DNB* at home. The technology has a short way to go, but there's no stopping it.[10]

Directives on the protection of databases are one thing: achieving the protection is quite another. This is of special importance to British suppliers who are estimated to have more than a 50% share of the European market.

It would be a mistake to believe that the deposit of printed materials was currently without problems for the deposit libraries. The publication in 1987 by the British Library's Bibliographic Services Division (BLBSD) of the *Consultative paper: currency with coverage*[11] and the appearance the following year of the British Library report *Selection for survival: a review of acquisition and retention policies*,[12] were clear indications that 'anarchy' of a kind was already evident in the handling of printed publications, that the library could no longer contain the proliferation of traditional publications by established means. The disclosure by BLBSD that not all deposited new titles were finding their way into the *British national bibliography* (*BNB*) came as a shock even to the librarians of the other five deposit libraries. The creation of a national bibliography was facilitated by legal deposit and to some extent justified it in terms recognizable to the trade. The *BNB*, which came into being in 1950, had often been seen as of major importance to and by publishers and it was at risk. To some extent a degree of anarchy was also evident in the processing backlogs in some of the other five deposit libraries despite the fact that they, unlike the BL, were modestly selective in their acquisitions.

In referring to the present legislation the 1997 consultation paper raised many issues that have been pursued in the past. These include the vexed question of microform, which the deposit libraries have long urged should be subject to deposit. The individual submissions of all six libraries contained in the BL Proposal endorsed the statement that 'the rights owners of microforms should be obliged to deposit up to six negatives of archival quality for indefinite storage'. Indeed, Oxford and Cambridge were 'anxious and willing to become libraries of deposit for such materials'. This format is self-evidently a logical extension of print and was identified as such in the Copyright Act of 1956, by Whitford in

1977 and in the consultative document of 1981. A significant proportion of these publications derive from printed sources, as, for example, in the texts of *The nineteenth century*.[13] Many of the original texts are based on the holdings of the deposit libraries. The BL Proposal conceded that where microforms were simply duplicates of items already held in printed form deposit would not be required.

The 1997 consultation paper, in discussing this, recognized that microform publications are analogous to printed works but also observed that they are 'a much more specialised and limited medium for publication than print'. They have 'high costs and low subscription runs' and, moreover, there are few publishers (it cites the figure 27) at work in the field. The remarks could almost be construed as speaking against the proposal to deposit, or at least of modifying deposit by establishing powers to prescribe exceptions. Since the deposit libraries are the main customers of these publishers, deposit could effectively put most of the latter out of business and it might seem perverse to pursue it. Although microform publishing activity is unlikely to decline in the immediate future it is also unlikely to expand, given the search and access facilities offered by digital publications. Since no legislation is likely to be retrospective, deposit would today be of questionable value since it is doubtful, given the advances and the potential of the new technology, whether the future output of these publishers will equal that already produced.

Although microform publication falls into the category of non-print it is certainly 'tangible', and as such should present no difficulties of deposit, were Parliament so minded. However, the case for compulsory deposit, even at only one of the six libraries, is less than compelling. Microforms resemble in this respect expensive subscription printed books and among the deposit libraries Cambridge, at least, and probably others, has rarely pressed for the deposit of very expensive, short-run print publications. To do so would usually threaten a financial loss for the publisher who more often than not was aiming at a tight subscription market, comparable to that of the private printer. Copy, when acquired, was often bought at cost and was far more acceptable than deposit, which could impose such a burden on the publisher as to discourage publication.

The consultation paper suggested either voluntary deposit with one or more of the deposit libraries or deposit in a single repository, the British Library or, if the content relates to Wales or Scotland, with their national libraries. Whilst this would be possible for the few large microform producers it would still impose a significant burden on the rest. Moreover, as the paper noted, much microform output often has a primary archival or conservation role as well as a research purpose. In these circumstances it would seem preferable to seek voluntary deposit but, where that fails, to seek purchase on advantageous terms as with the example of expensive short-run print publications. Legal deposit has among its aims the provision of access to information and a heavy handed approach to such publishers might well, as already noted, deter publication, at least in the UK.

However, given the copyright issues involved in the new technology, it is a matter of no real surprise that microforms, in essence 'old' new technology and easily its least complicated area, should be accorded a comparatively low level of priority in the paper. At around the time that the BL's *Currency with coverage* and *Selection for survival* appeared, desktop publishing (DTP) began to make an impact on the deposit libraries. Since desktop publications derive from personal computers they are strictly 'electronic publications', although not in the sense in which such publications are generally regarded today. Although not recognized at the time, their growing frequency was a disturbing warning of what lay ahead in the field of electronic publishing.

Selection for survival, in its chapter 'Implications of new technology', devoted a considerable amount of space to DTP. It noted that 'a commercial publisher has commented that DTP is beginning to have an impact on the publishing process'[14] and proposed that acceptance and retention of such materials 'might be modelled on present guidelines in the Department of Manuscripts'. It had virtually nothing to say about the impact of the new technology as a publishing agent but restricted its comments to its use in preservation as 'alternative storage media'. In a report of major importance to legal deposit, as yet barely eight years old, publication *via* the new technology was clearly not seen as being particularly significant. By implication it underlines the extraordinary rate of progress made by the new technology in the publishing field since 1989.

DTP documents that are identified by ISBNs (international standard book numbers) can be difficult to distinguish from trade publications, since text will have been set electronically. Often such publications arrive unsolicited in the deposit libraries, which are faced with decisions whether to take them all or to practise selection, whether to include desktop publications in their catalogued stock or not. Some undoubtedly merit inclusion but many do not. When they first started to arrive they were received by processing staff whose responsibility might not extend to decisions on acceptance or rejection. When the problem eventually came to light it created a new task for the legal deposit department.

Since an ISBN, obviously, can give no indication of whether a publication has been refereed or not, acceptance in the case of academic works could easily prove misleading to readers, since its presence in a deposit library might suggest that it is a normal refereed product of the publishing industry. In a distant way the depositing of such works resembles the original registration and deposit of books with the Stationers' Company which in itself established copyright and status. It is important for readers to know that an academic publication has been refereed and, as far as that process will allow, been deemed worthy of publication. It is, therefore, in the interests of scholarship that some means of establishing this should be found. Securing an ISBN is simply a matter of application. If ISBNs could be equated somehow with refereed work they would be welcome. In any event they are an ominous pointer to the potential problems on the Internet of such random publishing exercises alongside refereed publications. However, like microform, desktop publications represent a minor element in the deposit problems posed by the new technology and receive no mention at all in the 1997 consultation paper.

The BL's *Selection for survival* had obvious implications for all the deposit libraries and a Copyright Libraries' Working Group representative of all six was established. It met first in 1990 and produced in 1994 their report, the main thrust of which was the proposal to create a new level of cooperation between the British Library and the other five not only in terms of the cataloguing of deposited materials but also in regard to their holdings. It was concerned with the questions of retention and discarding as well as the acquisition of deposited materials. With regard to the impact of new technology the report also stated that the Working Group expected 'to contribute fully to the wider discussions which must take place in the near future on the development of legal deposit for electronic texts and other non-print media'.[15]

The deliberations of the Working Group and of its successor, the Standing Committee on Legal Deposit, took place in the context of the Follett Report.[16] This echoed the concern of the deposit librarians about 'the scope and growth of primary publications . . . as a result of the application of the new technology' (p.13) but expressed no views on their legal deposit or their significance for the archive of published materials. It recognized that 'the availability of extensive collections accumulated over several centuries' by Oxford and Cambridge under the legal deposit legislation was an important asset that was legitimate for the Higher Education Funding Council for England to support through non-formula funding, but with the proviso that the collections were accessible 'to all bona fide research staff and research students from within the UK'. The report was more concerned lest 'publishers will not permit copying into electronic formats', 'that licensing agreements should be effectively policed', about fair dealing and the like. It noted, however, that 'the vast majority of journals used by academics in British universities originate overseas' and commented on 'the impact of actions taken in the UK on the development of electronic journals worldwide'. These remarks approached some of those deeper concerns about deposit exercising the librarians of the deposit libraries.

It is axiomatic that laws are subject to constant change: copyright law is no exception. From the time of the Queen Anne act its range has been steadily extended from property rights in books to engravings, lithographs, prints and so on. Whilst the 1911 Act determined British law for most of this century, it did so in the context of later amendments and acts, not all of which added to the responsibilities of the deposit libraries. The British Museum Acts of 1915 and 1932 reduced these responsibilities by removing certain labour-intensive categories from compulsory deposit, although, if the library considered an item in these categories important, it could still claim deposit. Others, like the Theatres Act of 1968, added to the BL's responsibilities, but not necessarily to those of all the deposit libraries. Again, the Berne Convention of 1886 introduced a new element in copyright which in theory at least affected the laws of all the subscribing countries but which not all those subscribing, including the UK, necessarily implemented. A major change in the BL's responsibilities, which excited little comment at the time but which in retrospect was significant for future legal deposit, took place in 1983 with the inclusion of the National Sound Archive in the British Library. It affected legal deposit in the principal deposit library in a fundamental way by introducing a virtually new element of deposit for non-print media alongside the predominantly printed.

The Commission of the European Communities stated in July 1994: 'The information society is on its way. A "digital revolution" is triggering structural changes comparable to last century's industrial revolution with the corresponding high economic stakes. The process cannot be stopped and will lead eventually to a knowledge-based economy'.[17] It was clearly not concerned with microform or desktop publishing. The securing of the knowledge base, the record of civilization now and in the years ahead, poses problems that are utterly different from anything experienced before. The speed of communication, the relative ease of publication, the potential for changes to the 'record', the obsolescence built into equipment of a technology that never seems to stand still – these are just a few of the factors that are challenging the principle and even the concept of legal deposit. Securing the record will be difficult enough: finding the machines to read it several generations of computer machines on simply adds to the difficulties.

The growth in desktop publishing coincided roughly with the appearance of that clearly recognizable product of the new technology, the CD-ROM, which is clearly electronic and a part of the 'digital revolution'. The 1997 consultation paper described compact discs as 'tangible electronic formats' and it easy to see why. They resemble printed works in comprising a finite or finished 'text' and can be processed and handled in libraries in much the same way. They are, in effect, books that can only be read on a screen – hence the expression 'glass books' – but are capable of being manipulated electronically. Since many printed works are set by electronic or digital means the relationship is closer than may generally be thought. A major difference is that books cannot be 'networked', not without resorting to some form of mass copying, which under present and presumably any future legislation is illegal without the publisher's permission. In the BL *Proposal* the deposit libraries use the term 'hand-held' for such publications, emphasizing their tangible form.

The consultation paper plotted the growth in annual output of CD-ROMs worldwide from 48 titles in 1987 to 9691 in 1995, and concluded that this has become, and will increasingly be, a 'substantial sector of the publication industry'. An increase over 1994–5 of almost 50% underlines the point strikingly. By comparison with the 80,200 monographs published in 1995–6 CD-ROM output may seem small, but even if the rate of growth remained at the 1995 level it means that serious losses to the published record will have been incurred by the end of the millennium unless some form of deposit is put in place. Although much of the output so far has been based on printed works, CD-ROMs contain an element of originality that is now virtually lost to the archive of published work.

In libraries there are at present two main uses of CD-ROMs. There are those that reproduce well-established printed works, usually of major scholarly importance, such as the *Patrologia latina,* the *Bible* or the *Oxford English dictionary*. These are usually based on the 'definitive' edition of the work produced, sometimes on the only edition. Their main attraction, apart from making available a text that may have been long out of print, is the searching facility that the computer brings to the text. This is such a valuable innovation that it is likely to deter scholars from consulting the printed text, except in rare cases. The disadvantage to the deposit library is that the CD-ROM, unlike the gratis printed version, is only available by purchase. If in the course of time the electronic version were to supersede the printed such publications would under present legislation escape the archive of published materials.

There are also CD-ROMs that, though tangibly fixed in format, represent live or dynamic databases that are subject to updating. These resemble new editions in printed works and would be equally easy to recognize. Deposit in these two cases could compare directly with that of the printed book. Capturing the 'first edition', or succeeding ones would present few real problems or at least no greater ones than those currently posed by print. Of much greater importance is the fact that in the present state of the technology both kinds of CD-ROM will probably be unreadable by 2025 either because of the limited life of the medium or because of the unavailability of appropriate hardware, unless action being taken now to remedy this is successful.

Following the comparison with printed works the solution would seem to suggest deposit of a similar order. The cost of manufacturing the necessary copies, even more so than for printed books, is marginal. However, since CD-ROMs are rarely cheap to purchase and may involve both licensing and networking conditions, cost is a factor in the publishers' profits. CD-ROMs differ from books in their networking accessibility, which is clearly bound up with their profitability. Where production costs are likely to be very high and profits are directly related to use it is hard to pursue the comparison with the printed work. When a printed copy of the *Patrologia latina* was bought it could not be made available at various locations except by the laborious processes of borrowing or licensed photocopying, and certainly not simultaneously. The CD-ROM version changed that.

For subjects that by their nature entail the publication of large quantities of printed text the CD-ROM has become a benefit of immeasurable proportions. Primary source materials, such as *All England law reports,* the law reports produced by the Incorporated Council of Law Reporting, *Electronic law reports,* or the database of European treaties and other legislation *Eurolaw,* demonstrate the strength of the medium. Cases and citations can be summoned up and printed out in a way that makes manual searching and the once much prized 'knowledge of the literature' redundant. Much secondary legal material is also appearing in CD-ROM format, including indexes to legal journals, daily law reports, financial journals and the like. Licensing enables institutions to network such CD-ROMs so that to the user access is immediate and, as far as the individual is concerned, 'free'. Significantly, many CD-ROMs are now also available on the Web. The costs to publishers of depositing such products with six libraries are not significantly higher than for the printed work: it is in their use that losses could be incurred. Nevertheless, the BL *Proposal* requested that 'rights owners should be obliged to deposit up to six copies' provided that these are consulted only in the 'reading rooms [of the deposit libraries] at one stand-alone workstation'.

The consultation paper also suggested three options for deposit, none of which is likely to be welcome to the trade. Of the three, the suggestion that one copy be deposited with the British Library and that the other five libraries claim as desired, presumably through the Copyright Licensing Agency, conforms entirely with present practice for print and reflects the BL *Proposal* recommendation. In practice it would almost certainly mean that each deposit library would request a copy. The second option, voluntary deposit at one or more of the deposit libraries, would depart from existing practices both in its voluntary nature and in the reduced number of libraries involved. Experience of voluntary deposit or deposit not backed by legislation does not suggest that publishers will willingly hand over such items to the deposit libraries. Previous attempts to reduce the number of libraries have also been strongly resisted in the past. The third option, deposit of one or two copies in one repository for networking to the other deposit libraries as necessary could put the host library under some strain since the organizational problems and costs would seem to involve complications that the libraries could do without. In each option the condition confining use to one standalone workstation applies. In terms of simply preserving the record, publishers could argue justifiably that deposit in certain instances should not take place until the information was no longer current in order to protect their profit.

It is convenient before discussing the deposit of other electronic publications to consider at this point such important issues as the number and location of legal deposit libraries that the country maintains and should maintain in the future specifically for printed work and their impact on trade sales. The 1997 consultation paper stated that 'the objective of legal deposit is to maintain an archival record of the nation's published output and preserve it for future generations'; it continues, somewhat ingenuously, 'limited access is provided for academic and business users but it is not a means of providing wider access in competition with publishers' business'. Unintentional though it may be, legal deposit undoubtedly provides a degree of 'wider access'. During the last two decades at least, external users at Cambridge University Library have been the predominant group of readers at certain times of the year, simply because the literature that they needed was there and they or their home institution would not or could not buy it. Against this, it was equally true that the weekly display of current deposit materials undoubtedly promoted sales of such items in local bookshops.

The costs to the publishers in the production of the six printed deposit copies and their impact on potential sales were assessed in the paper, as were those of the libraries in the claiming, processing and storing of the materials. No reference was made to the comments of Whitford on publishers' costs, which were much more realistic, or to the observations of the librarians, were they to lose the deposit. The latter would doubtless make clear that the costs of purchasing the huge range of materials now deposited 'free' and the costs to scholarship in general would far outweigh those currently incurred by the public purse. As already noted, the costs to the publishers of running off the extra copies for deposit are so small as to merit little or no consideration, being estimated at between 0.06% and 0.31% of the turnover of the industry. Their competitive impact on sales is another matter but it does not seem to have harmed the trade in any real sense over the last two centuries.

The geographical distribution of the six deposit libraries was not planned but is an accident of history. It has been and still is to many of those resident furthest away from such a library a source of discontent. The scholars among the 12.5 million people living within a 50-mile radius of Manchester, for example, can derive little satisfaction from the fact that the National Library of Wales and the Library of Trinity College Dublin (TCD) are deposit libraries. To add to their discontent, the library of TCD serves the scholarship of a population of some 3.5 million in a foreign country. The Whitford Committee recognized this anomaly when it recommended that the John Rylands University Library of Manchester should become an additional deposit library, but this proposal was rejected in the consultative document of 1981 and was not implemented in the 1988 Act. Although the locating of the British Library's Document Supply Centre (BLDSC) at Boston Spa in Yorkshire appears to have improved the situation marginally, few living in the north of England would agree with the consultation paper that 'the geographical distribution of the libraries enhances their value to users'.

The benefits of legal deposit status are more than just the cumulative growth of stock received in this way from British publishers. The access to current foreign – especially European – literature which is purchased in quantity with money that would otherwise be spent on deposited materials is a major benefit. The size and quality of the resources of the two English university deposit libraries are largely attributable to their long history of deposit. The paper emphasizes that the current output of published material is 'used extensively by members of the academic community throughout the country, by business and industry, and by the professions'. It should be added, not easily from places like Manchester which, after London, has the largest concentration of university students in Britain. The paper is concerned with the possibility of establishing a further deposit library in Northern Ireland not with meeting the needs of major population centres in England. Such concern can only be justified in political terms, as indeed are the libraries of TCD and the National Library of Wales.

The deposit of publications in electronic format is certain to raise the question of the number of deposit libraries again. This is already apparent in the discussion of CD-ROMs. It will be difficult to consider the new situation created by such formats without reference to the current deposit arrangements for printed works. Having listed the benefits arising from the present arrangements (paragraphs 2.17-2.22), the paper commented that, 'while the Government has no present plan to change the basis of legal deposit for printed publications', it seeks views on whether voluntary deposit might be substituted for legal deposit and 'whether the national published archive could be maintained effectively . . . by reducing the requirement to the deposit of one or two copies of each print publication at a single legal deposit library'. This must be of concern to the university deposit libraries that have the longest history of deposit among the six and predate all three national libraries.

It is particularly unfortunate that the debate on Oxbridge college fees and the statements about the wealth of the two ancient universities is taking place at the time of the discussions on legal deposit. It is unlikely to help their libraries' case for continued deposit status. There are sure to be calls for it to be transferred to some other more needy institutions. This would damage seriously the archival and scholarly purposes of the deposit. The rich resources of these two libraries are already today more easily accessible to scholars outside Oxbridge than they have ever been before and, following the Follett recommendation on their funding, this access can only improve. They have played a leading part in establishing cooperation among the six deposit libraries and, in the founding of the Consortium of University Research Libraries (CURL), were instrumental in the creation of a bibliographical database that has the making of a national network and was promoted as such by the Follett Report. Whether two university deposit libraries can meet all the demand from other institutions for printed deposit materials in the way Follett suggested is highly questionable. The answer lies not in a reduction in the number of libraries or in seeking to redistribute them but in increasing them in the way proposed by Whitford in 1977.[18]

Tangible works of the kind considered so far pose the same problems of deposit both as to 'how many' and 'where'. It will almost certainly be argued that given the gradual digitization of publication only one deposited and one back-up copy are necessary, since the transmission of such texts renders more than two superfluous. Equally, it could be argued that rapid as the growth in electronic publication seems to be there are no signs yet that printed publications are diminishing; on the contrary, the number of titles recorded year by year in the *BNB* continues to increase, and the consultation paper quoted the *Bookseller*'s projection that publishers' annual output would top 100,000 titles in 1996. The paper's further suggestion that publishers might, in addition to the printed text, deposit the digital format prepared in the production of the print publication requires much more thought. Printers used to keep standing type in case new issues or editions were required: the potential of the digitized text in this context is even greater.

The paper pointed to gaps in the national published archive 'as a result of migration to new media away from print as a publishing medium' but the *Bookseller*'s data suggest that these publications must be largely additional to the printed output. Again, despite all the statements to the contrary, the electronic journal has not yet superseded the printed publication, and there are no obvious signs to many practising librarians that it will in the near future. The Follett Report recognized that 'most libraries will continue to combine traditional media with electronic media for the foreseeable future and the purely electronic or "virtual library" will be rare'. The *Apt review*,[19] sponsored by LINC, pointed out that 'few respondents forecast the very early mass adoption of the new electronic systems of storing, distributing and accessing information; yet most of the required technology is already available'. Nevertheless, the BL *Proposal* stated firmly that eventually 'the electronic versions' of journals in electronic form 'will drive the hard-copy serials off the market'. It did so on the basis of evidence which is dauntingly convincing:

> On-line databases emerged in the 1960s and have enabled publishers to transmit data directly to the customer's own computer. By 1994 there were 8776 online databases produced world-wide, and 1454 in the UK. There is a great variety of material published in this way. There are cumulating online services analogous to traditional bibliographic, cataloguing, indexing and abstracting services. There are content and alerting services where greater emphasis is placed on currency and there are real-time

transactional services such as financial databases, which are updated from moment to moment . . . It has been estimated that, world-wide, there are already 14,000 electronic texts, including electronic journals, available over networks, and there will be 16,000 in 1996 and 21,000 in 1997. There are also many informal bulletin boards and discussion lists and other services which are readily available on the Internet since the expansion of the World Wide Web.

It is essential to bear in mind the international, not merely British, dimension of the problems. The very title of the World Wide Web should be a sufficient reminder. Electronic publications can be easily sent across national boundaries and it is on these publications, for which no deposit mechanism exists, that attention has to be focused In the consultation paper's chapter 'Extending legal deposit to new publication media' little space was devoted to its section 'On-line publications', and the reasons for this are clear: 'There remain a number of very substantial and complex issues to be resolved before any system of legal deposit could be introduced for such publications'. By November 1996 only Norway, a non-European-Union country, had legislated for the deposit of such publications, and that legislation leaves much unsaid. British legislation, like that of other European Union countries, will be much influenced, if not determined, by the directives of the European Commission. The new 'database right' following Directive 96/9/EC is one such development. However, although the Commission's Green Paper *Copyright and related rights in the information society*[20] in July 1995 and the *Follow-up to the Green Paper*[21] in November 1996 expressed much concern about the 'cultural dimension', no reference was made to legal deposit in either publication.

Among the many problems facing legislators not the least is the very accessibility of the Internet. Bainbridge referred to a common misapprehension: 'there is a view held by some that placing material on the Internet is equivalent to placing it in the public domain. Nothing, could be further from the truth'.[22] The HMSO webpage now makes statutes available free. If statutory instruments are on the Internet and free to copy, why electronic journals should not be similarly accessible may not be clear to the public. It does not help that many see copyright as simply 'something to do with books'. Moreover, much information on the Internet, though undoubtedly copyrighted, is offered free to anyone who shows an interest. Many webpages are a form of advertisement that owners would be very sorry to see ignored. Much superficial published material was excluded from legal deposit by the British Museum and other Acts, and there is similar material on the Internet that will also be excluded. It is also true that not all information is worth knowing and that will undoubtedly affect decisions on archiving.

In the deposit of publications that appear on the Internet or elsewhere online, much depends, as with CD-ROMs, on whether they are complete or finished, live or dynamic – that is, subject to frequent, irregular or constant updating. An electronic journal on the Internet issued in regularly updated parts forms a finite whole that could be captured and deposited like a normal CD-ROM at specified intervals, if an appropriate mechanism could be put in place. A publisher might even welcome unloading an expensive storage problem of long runs onto a legal depository to which, as now, access would be afforded. This presupposes access to issues as they appear to maintain the degree of currency at present offered by printed journals, but this should not be a problem if properly policed. Of much greater importance, it presupposes commitment by the publisher to the principle of legal deposit in online publishing, and this is far from clear in either the national or international setting, since profits are tied to access and use.

There are now a considerable number of electronic journals available in British universities. In many instances they appear alongside the printed version and are described as 'free' to subscribers of the printed form. Some require an additional payment, but this is most likely accounted for in the subscriptions of those offered 'free'. These journals are more often found at present in the sciences and medicine and certain publishers like Springer and Highwire Press, Stanford, are especially active in promoting them. In the humanities the SuperJournal research project based at Loughborough University involves 20 publishers, 12 universities, including the two deposit libraries, and some 42 journals. It is still very much at an experimental stage. Publishing interest is all directed at access. As far as legal deposit is concerned both the BL *Proposal* and the consultation paper pointed to the many problems that have to be resolved before consideration can be given to deposit of such publications. They are unlikely to be delivered in 'tangible' form unless provided specially by the publisher or, failing that, created by the deposit library.

Publishers are rightly concerned about policing online access documents but there is already considerable experience in controlled access to datasets *via* such data service providers as Bath Information Data Services (BIDS), Edinburgh Data and Information Access (EDINA), National Information Services and Systems (NISS) and Manchester Information Dataset and Associated Services (MIDAS). The experience of the licensing of reprographic reproduction *via* the Copyright Licensing Agency may also prove useful. It should, in theory at least, be possible to control electronic copying of text and other materials held online in electronic form by inserting some sort of instruction that might render illegally copied text illegible. The very vulnerability of such online publications may influence some trade publishers to adopt measures that will be advantageous to the deposit libraries. The issue of 'fair dealing', so controversial in the past and assumed by many librarians and scholars to be an automatic right also in elec-tronic publication, may prove no less difficult to establish than it was in print, unless safeguards can be built into use. The legislators in consultation with the trade, information brokers and the users each have a vested interest in resolving such issues.

The reactions of the great institutional publishers, with their global dimensions, are yet another unknown. Authorship is international in so many scientific and medical online journals and it is suggested may add to the problems of their legal deposit. The 'globalization' of information may turn out to be a very mixed blessing. To make matters worse, passwords to protect databases are unfortunately often seen as a challenge to hackers, as the Pentagon discovered a short time ago, and rights owners cannot be guaranteed immunity from attacks at the national or international level. Piracy in publishing has always been a problem and not only at the hands of those countries not subscribing to the Berne Convention. It will be far more difficult to police on the Internet.

Electronic journals are only one problem area in online publishing. The online publication that falls outside that category and is in a constant state of flux, through additions or deletions – annuals, gazetteers, almanacs, directories, indexes, bibliographies and the like – will require unprecedented decisions. Back numbers of the *BNB* or *Books in print*, for example, are as important as the current ones. Moreover, it will be so much easier to introduce textual changes on screen, to update information, and so much more difficult to keep track of them. No printed work can be changed in a comparable way: in legal literature, which is regularly updated, a cumulative volume recording such changes is usually issued periodically. The Cambridge Crystallographic Unit has long operated online but it publishes its annual index in printed form. In scholarly publications such termini have been as important to the publisher as to the librarian and scholar. It is a sobering thought that had the *Domesday book* been subjected in its production to the same technology as the Ordnance Survey is today a vital part of our recorded history would have been lost.

The possibility of taking 'snapshots' for archival purposes has been frequently put forward and is repeated again in the consultation paper, but these are no substitute for the complete record. Few librarians or users would welcome the record in the form of a series of changes rather like a list of errata. Libraries are not equipped at present to make or store such snapshots nor is it their responsibility. It is a publishing matter and, as far as the published archive is concerned, the onus should rest with the publisher to provide cumulative records available for deposit in archival form.

Decisions on legal deposit cannot be made until the many legal issues in copyright itself have been settled. These are for others to decide and the BL *Proposal* gave a good idea of their complexity:

> With on-line publications, it is not clear as yet where the responsibility for deposit would lie. Would it be with the originator, a print publisher, a producer, a host or a

gateway/network operator? No single entity controls the whole process and intellectual property rights are created at several points in the chain . . . In the case of works available online, there are problems in establishing the definitive form of publication, and in some case perhaps no such thing exists . . . Many on-line databases are not national in character, but are compilations of material whose rights owners are spread throughout the world.

It made other equally relevant observations. Its conclusion almost predictably is that:

it is not possible for the legal deposit libraries to accept the permanent exclusion of online publication from the realm of legal deposit . . . there are kinds of material which are at the very heart of the legal deposit libraries' collections and these may in future be published only online. Scientific and medical journals, for instance, may cease to appear as print on paper.

The *Proposal's* recommendations, no less predictably, were open-ended: '(i) that the new legal deposit legislation should be framed in such a way as to permit the eventual extension of it to online publications; (ii) but that at present time no regulations should be drawn up to give immediate effect to this possibility'.

The past failure to secure legal deposit of microform has in a way sharpened the determination of the deposit librarians to ensure that deposit of the potentially much more prolific 'new' new media is comprehensively achieved. This catch-all recommendation seems the only way forward given all the uncertainties in the present legislation. The copyright position of sound recordings and films, video recordings and related material was also considered in the *Proposal*, but this involves, fortunately, none of the extreme problems entailed in online access. It seems clear from the *Proposal* that the present voluntary arrangements with the National Sound Archive, the BBC and the Independent Sound Broadcasts are barely adequate and statutory arrangements, extending also to cable and satellite broadcast material, would appear to be essential. The BL currently receives around 80% of all sound recordings published in the UK *via* voluntary deposit. This secures about 80% of all such recordings published in the UK, and the paper pointed out that the statutory deposit of two copies would represent at the most about 0.013% of total turnover of the industry. The question here is whether the BL is the appropriate place to have responsibility for such deposits. It would seem more appropriate to archive them with the British Film Institute's National Film and Television Archive (NFTVA), which also incorporates the entire output of all BBC television channels. Along with the output of cable and satellite broadcasts this arrangement would simplify existing provision for both the archival bodies and the users. Since this will eventually become a very large archive with many of the problems of obsolescence of equipment, it would seem sensible to concentrate the expertise required in one place.

The consultation paper, despite the very real difficulties surrounding online texts, raises certain issues that can be settled, at least, as far as this chapter is concerned. Printed publications should continue to be deposited in the way they are at present; microforms might reasonably attract voluntary deposit and failing that be purchased on advantageous terms; CD-ROMs could for the most part be treated like printed publications; and sound recordings could profitably be merged with broadcasting, in its various manifestations, under one new authority, separate from the British Library. The problems with online publications suggest that the 'wait and see' recommendation of the BL *Proposal* is the only one possible, and the consultation paper's presentation of this issue endorsed that. However, it may be that the European Commission, the members of which have had hitherto no uniform practice in regard to the legal deposit of printed publications, will turn its attention to this issue, which is no less important to the cultural history of Europe than it is to that of individual member states. For the librarian of the deposit library the crucial question is how far all deposit libraries need to be involved in the archiving and transmission of electronic texts, given the speed and ease of information transfer. The case for the deposit of 'tangible', 'hand-held' materials seems clear; that for material published directly online will be the subject of much debate.

Although there can be no doubt that electronic publications will be critically important in the future, it would be unwise to ignore the views of the users. The fact that screen presentations often exist alongside a printed version could suggest that they are as unwieldy for a sustained piece of reading as they have proved to be in microform. Reference work is one thing: continuous reading or, for that matter, composing on a screen, lacks the contextual perspective of the printed book, apart from imposing eye strain, which in office conditions is now attracting the attention of health and safety legislation in the UK.

It is also important to remember that to many established trade and academic publishers in the UK the archival benefits provided by legal deposit are now more likely to be regarded as useful than they were in the past, for practical economic reasons, and it is to their advantage that solutions to the copyright problems in the using of information technology be found quickly. It is the small publisher, whose output may be important but sporadic, possibly a minor part of the business, who may feel disadvantaged. Desktop-type publishing on the Internet may suggest a possible way forward in such cases. In the way that desktop publications have secured ISBNs perhaps an ISEN could become available for those online publications that the deposit libraries would wish to secure.

Postscript

On 17 December 1998, in a written answer to a question on the *Report of the Working Party on Legal Deposit* chaired by Sir Anthony Kenney, the Secretary of State for Culture, Media and Sport, endorsed its findings as follows:

The report recommends that there should be a single national published archive of non-print material. It proposes that a code of practice for voluntary deposit of electronic publications should be drawn up, but suggests that, in the longer term, only statutory deposit can secure a comprehensive national published archive.

The report proposes that the following should be deposited with the national published archive:

- CD-ROMS to be deposited in a single copy only after 12 UK sales. The group has put forward alternative options for access:
  - accessibility on a stand alone basis at a single site (the preference of the publishers); or
  - dissemination among the legal deposit libraries using a secure ring fenced network (the preference of the libraries)
- Microfilms to be deposited in a single copy only after six UK sales.
- For British films, a mint print to be deposited, plus a negative or equivalent after three years; for other films released in the UK, a best copy; for British videos, a mint condition duplicate; for other videos, a new condition reference copy.
- For sound recordings, two copies to be deposited.

The uncertainly about dealing with online publications and databases remains unresolved – 'It would not be feasible to include them at present.' These still constitute the principal potential gap in the national archive and the Minister agrees with the Report's 'convincing case for moving towards legislation for the legal deposit of non-print publication'. However, much work needs to be done and the Chairman of the Working Party has been asked to investigate the issues further. There is to be no change in the number of deposit libraries but 'if an acceptable way can be found to allow secure networking of deposited electronic material, an access point in Northern Ireland could be included in a secure network'.

References

1   'Oysters in the Net', London, *Times,* 4 September 1997, 35.
2   United States, House of Representatives, Committee on Government Operations, Washington, [untitled] 1990.

3   Rothenberg, J., 'Ensuring the longevity of digital documents', *Scientific American,* **272** (1), 1995, 24–7.

4   Department of National Heritage, the Scottish Office, the Welsh Office and the Department of Education Northern Ireland, *Legal deposit of publications: a consultation paper,* [London], Department of National Heritage, 1997.

5   British Library, *Proposal for the legal deposit of non-print publications to the Department of National Heritage* [typescript], London, British Library Board, January 1996.

6   *The management and development of the legal deposit collections: a report by the librarians of the six legal deposit libraries,* [London], 1994 [unpublished].

7   Committee to Consider the Law on Copyright and Designs, *Copyright and designs law: report of the Committee to consider the law on copyright and designs chaired by the Hon. Mr. Justice Whitford,* London, HMSO, 1977 (Cmnd. 6732).

8   Department of Trade, *Reform of the Law relating to Copyright. Designs and Performers' Protection: a Consultative Document,* London, HMSO, 1981 (Cmnd. 8302).

9   Bainbridge, D. I., *Intellectual property,* 3rd edn, London, Pitman, 1996, 210.

10   McCue, op. cit.

11   BLBSD, *Currency with coverage,* London, British Library Board, 1987.

12   Enright, B., Hellinga, L., Leigh, B. and Corrall, S., *Selection for survival: a review of acquisition and retention policies,* London, British Library, 1989. [the Enright Report].

13   *The nineteenth century,* Cambridge, Chadwyck-Healey, 1987–.

14   Enright et al., op.cit., 70.

15   Ibid., 16.

16   *Joint Funding Councils' Libraries Review Group, Report for the HEFCE. SHEFC, HEFCW and DENI,* Chairman Sir Brian Follett, Bristol, HEFCE, 1993.

17   commission of the european communities, *report to the council: europe's way to the information society, an action plan,* Brussels, European Commission, 1994 [quoted from *The Apt Review,* p.4.1].

18   Committee to Consider the Law on Copyright and Designs, op. cit.

19   Apt Partnership, *The APT review: a review of library and information cooperation in the UK and Republic of Ireland for the Library and Information Cooperation Council (LINC)* (British Library R&D Report 6212), Sheffield, LINC,1995.

20   Commission of the European Communities, *Green paper: copyright and related rights in the information society,* Brussels, European Commission, 1995.

21   Communication from the Commission. *Follow-up to the green paper on copyright and related rights in the information society,* Brussels, European Commission. 1996.

22   Bainbridge, op. cit.

6

The Data Protection Acts 1984 and 1998

Angus Hamilton

At the time of writing (July 1998) the law relating to data protection in the United Kingdom is in a state of flux. The 1984 Data Protection Act was in force for almost 12 years but is being replaced by the 1998 Data Protection Act.

The 1998 Act (the text of which can be found at **http://www. hmso.gov.uk/acts/acts1998/19980029.htm**) received royal assent in July 1998. Under the EU Data Protection Directive (95/46/EC) the new law was to be in force by 24 October 1998, although in the case of the UK the law came into force in April 1999. The new Act does not sweep away the old legislation but seeks to retain familiar concepts and to build on the system that the earlier legislation established. There is also a substantial transitional period (running at least until 2001) during which both the 1984 and 1998 regimes will have relevance. This chapter therefore looks back to the old legislation and how it was implemented and enforced as well as forward to the new regime.

The 1984 Act

According to research conducted by the Office of the Data Protection Registrar (ODPR) approximately 60% of the British public have heard of the Data Protection Act 1984. Of this proportion, however, less than one fifth think that they know what the legislation is designed to tackle. In all likelihood that small proportion is aware only of the civil rights aspect of the legislation that empowers individuals to check what information is held about them on computer and to amend it if it is incorrect.

Certainly this would seem to be the message that the Office of the Data Protection Registrar currently wishes to convey about the legislation. At the beginning of 1997 the ODPR spent over £100,000 of its inadequate budget on an advertising campaign to promote awareness of the Act. Owing to budgetary restrictions the campaign ran only in the north of England. The advertisement consisted of a series of aggrieved faces complaining 'But your records are *wrong*!' This rather Orwellian vision of unregulated computerized bureaucracy running amok was reinforced by the (presumably) ironic helpline number which made use of the numbers 1, 9, 8 and 4 – in that order.

Elizabeth France, the second incumbent in the post of registrar, also sought to promote the civil rights aspect of the legislation. At her instigation the ODPR adopted a mission statement that now appears on all of the office's literature and which reads: 'We shall promote respect for the private lives of individuals and in particular for the privacy of their information'. This is an interesting emphasis, particularly as the concept of 'privacy' does not actually appear in the original legislation.

In fact the legislation did not just bequeath rights to individual British citizens but it also imposed obligations on anyone holding information about living individuals on computer and created considerable financial penalties for breaches of those obligations (*see* Figure 6.1). Given that so many computer users use their hardware to store information about others – customers, clients, contacts, etc. – these obligations have had a potential impact on millions of people. Yet there was a frighteningly high incidence of ignorance about these obligations amongst computer users. The most typical explanation given when such a user was brought before a criminal court for breaching the terms of the Act is that he or she either simply did not know of the existence of the legislation or assumed, erroneously, that it only applied to large-scale data handlers and those who traded in or sold personal information.

The Data Protection Act 1984 originally came into force in 1986 and it regulated for the first time the storage and use of information about living individuals that is recorded on computer. The legislation could in fact apply to information not held on computer but its principal thrust was towards computerized data. It was not necessary for someone to own a computer to be defined as a data user. A person may still be regarded as a data user even if he or she used an external agency (a computer bureau) to handle his or her data, providing he or she actually controlled or owned the data. Thus, a person running a small business whose clients submit orders on written applications forms and who then passes those forms on to a computer bureau for the recording and processing of the data would be regarded as a data user. This is not an insignificant point – people investigated and prosecuted under the Act for breaching its terms have been known to plead, 'But I don't even own a computer!' Nor was it possible to avoid the obligations imposed by the Act by identifying customers or contacts on computer by a code or reference number only and then having a separate manual list with the customer's details next to each code number.

Data users

The basic obligation under the Data Protection Act 1984 is for all *data users* to register with the Office of the Data Protection Registrar. You register by telephone (01625 545740) for a maximum of three years and at a cost of £75.

A *data user* is a person or company that *holds personal data.*

Personal data are information about living individuals (the deceased and animals are not included) which are kept on computer (or in a form capable of being processed on computer, e.g. punch cards or tape).

A person *holds* personal data if he or she controls their contents and use – you can still hold data even if you do not own a computer but use an external agency to process your data.

You must register fully and properly with the Office of the Data Protection Registrar making it clear:

- the *types* of personal data held
- the *purpose* for which they are held
- the *sources* from which they are obtained
- the persons to whom they may be *disclosed*
- the *countries* to which they may be transferred.

You must also provide a contact name and address for individuals wishing to make a subject access application.

Thereafter you must operate within the terms of your registration or amend it as necessary and you must remember to renew your registration in three years' time.

Am I exempt?

There are a number of exemptions to the obligation to register under the 1984 Act. It must be emphasized that the exemptions are very limited and consequently need to be approached with care. The four of significance are holding data:

- to administer a payroll
- to administer accounts – but note if you use your customer data for another purpose such as marketing a new product or service you will lose your exemption
- for social and domestic purposes
- about club members providing they know and do not object.

Fig. 6.1 *Data protection: the basics under the 1984 Act*

Despite these important obligations, the Act was, avowedly, not essentially prohibitive but designed to encourage openness and good practice amongst those that kept personal data on computer.

Openness was promoted by establishing a register of all data users, which is open to inspection by members of the public. They can then apply to any data user to check if that individual or organization holds information about them and can apply, in certain circumstances, to have that information corrected or removed altogether. The Act also gave a right to compensation to individuals who have suffered damage or, sometimes, distress as a result of inaccurate, lost or wrongfully disclosed data. It has to be said, however, that the ODPR has no record of any individual citizen applying for such compensation.

The original intention was that the register of all data users would be kept at public libraries and would be available for instant inspection by members of the public. In reality the problems inherent in keeping such a sizeable register up to date when it is in printed form have rendered this original vision impractical. In practice the majority of enquirers have raised their enquiry via the Office of the Data Protection Registrar. Responding to this unexpected role, the ODPR has now set up an online searching facility. However this facility only enables a searcher to ascertain the name and enquiry address for a data user. It does not enable a check to be made on the actual information that may or may not be held on an individual by a data user. To ascertain that requires more (written) effort and expenditure (*see* Figure 6.2).

As well as imposing obligations the 1984 Act enables individuals to check on the information held about them by different institutions.

To do this you have first to identify the contact point for the data user you are concerned about. A contact point must be stated by data users in their data protection register entry so you can ascertain this either by doing an online search of the Data Protection Register at **http://www.dpr.gov.uk/search.html**, by writing to the data user and asking for the contact point, or by contacting the ODPR on 01625 545745.

Once you have identified the contact point then you can apply to ascertain what information is held about you. You invariably have to pay a fee (the maximum permitted fee is at present £10) and you will also have to provide proof that you are who you say you are, just in case you are trying to get hold of information about another person's bank balance, for example. The data user must reply to your request within 40 days.

One of the applications that can be made, and that is often a cause of surprise, is to the police to ascertain what information is held about you on the Police National Computer. This will not disclose if you are currently under police surveillance or if the police know about that multi-million pound fraud you are plotting, as criminal intelligence data are exempt, but it will show up any past misdeeds and misbehaviour.

If any information held about you is wrong you can ask for it to be amended. If the data user fails to amend the information then you can complain to the ODPR and ultimately apply for a court order for its amendment or erasure. There is nothing special about making a complaint to the ODPR – the office tries to be as user-friendly as possible. A simple letter setting out the essence of your grievance will suffice. If the office believes that a criminal offence has been committed then an investigator will usually be appointed to look into the matter.

Fig. 6.2 *Exercising your rights*

The 1984 Act encouraged good practice amongst data users by establishing a set of eight data protection principles that set out guidelines for the fair obtaining and the fair and secure handling of individuals' personal information. It was a breach of the principles rather than the Act itself that usually provoked a complaint from a data subject (see Figure 6.3). The most commonly breached was the first principle, which required that data users obtain and process personal data fairly and lawfully.

One of the most frequent complaints to the registrar related to large-scale data users passing – or more commonly selling – their data on to another data user so the data subject is inundated with marketing offers (junk mail) from other organizations. The registrar has intervened to restrain this practice by requiring all data users to make clear, when they gather information, all the uses to which that information may be put. If you fill in an order form for a special offer in a Sunday newspaper for a collection of garden gnomes you are providing the advertiser with your personal data (at the minimum your name and address). It is clear that Garden Gnome Enterprises is going to use that information to process your order ('customer/client administration' in data-speak). That is the obvious use which the data user would not have to make explicit. However, Garden Gnome Enterprises may also wish to sell on all the data it has carefully gathered to another organization that believes that there may be a high take-up for their product amongst garden gnome purchasers.

This selling-on of personal data is the 'non-obvious' purpose that the data user is now required to make explicit at the time the data are gathered. In practice, in the case of mail-order businesses, this takes the form of putting an 'opt out' box on the order form. This will have wording to the effect of 'Garden Gnome Enterprises may wish to pass your details on to other organizations manufacturing products that you may be interested in. If you do not want to receive details of such offers please tick here'. The same principle applies, however, whatever the original purpose of the data gathering. The language training company Linguaphone and the direct-mail company Innovations have both been the subject of action by the ODPR to prevent them selling, without prior notification, their customer lists.

It would also be a breach of the data protection principles to continue to send junk mail to a recipient who had asked to be removed from a mailing list. It was not an offence under the 1984 Act to breach one of the principles, but such a breach could lead to the registrar's issuing an enforcement notice under the Act requiring a data user to comply with the principles. A subsequent breach of the enforcement notice could result in a prosecution. On this basis the Church of Scientology was prosecuted, in the late 1980s, for failing to remove an individual from their mailing list when he objected to receiving what he saw to be the church's propaganda.

In the late 1980s and early 1990s various police forces began developing the practice of recording an individual's known or suspected HIV status on the Police National Computer (PNC). This practice was the subject of a complaint in 1992 to the Data Protection Registrar by, amongst others, the leading HIV and AIDS charity the Terrence Higgins Trust. The basis of the complaint was that the information was excessive and irrelevant and was therefore held in breach of the fourth data protection principle.

The registrar, at that time the first incumbent Eric Howe, was initially reluctant to intervene, indicating that he was persuaded 'that there is a small, but foreseeable, risk of infection with HIV/AIDS which could arise in connection with policing activities'. Accordingly, he felt that, 'in general the holding of a factual warning signal, including an indication of HIV/AIDS status in the PNC conviction records, was neither excessive nor irrelevant to policing purposes.'

In practice an individual's HIV status should have no relevance at all to their arrest or detention since the police should already have in place procedures to reduce the risk of contracting infections during arrest and detention without such procedures being dependent upon ascertaining the detainee's health status. Furthermore, even if such procedures are not implemented the information that an individual is HIV positive becomes available invariably after a 'risk' situation has passed. For example, if the police are dealing with someone injured and bleeding after a fight or car accident, it is very unlikely that personal details sufficient to carry out a PNC check and ascertain health details will be obtained until after the immediate emergency has passed.

For these reasons further representations were made to the DPR against permitting the police to record an individual's HIV status on the PNC. These further representations were instrumental in achieving a change of view on the part of the registrar, so that in 1993 he determined that the recording of HIV status on the PNC was both excessive and irrelevant.

Fig. 6.3 *Principles in practice*

However, the registrar could only enforce the principles against *registered* data users. Members of the public could carry out a successful subject access application only in respect of *registered* data users. It therefore follows that the key to the successful operation of the 1984 Act was registration. The Act placed an obligation to register on all those (whether individuals or companies) that hold personal data. The obligation is so fundamental that failure to register was made a criminal offence of what is called 'strict liability'. This means that it was not necessary for the offending data user to know or even suspect that he or she should have been registered for an offence to be committed. All that has to be shown for a criminal offence to be established is that the person held personal data and that he or she was not registered. Strict liability offences are fairly rare in criminal law because their consequences can be draconian. The adoption of the concept here is a reflection of the importance of registration to the proper operation of the 1984 Act.

Prosecutions for failing to register were by far the most common type of prosecution under the 1984 Act. They were also the most successful types of prosecution. This is unsurprising given that the concept of strict liability made it almost impossible to defend such a case (unless the data user could claim one of the exemptions). The penalty for a failure to register (and indeed for all the criminal offences under the Data Protection Act) was a fine; in England there was a maximum of £5000 in the magistrates' court (the lower tier of criminal courts) and no limit in the crown court. The actual penalty tended to depend on the size and nature of the data user and the number of individual records contained within a database. In practice the fines tended to range between £500 and £1500 for a first offence.

Non-registration offences could arise not only because a data user failed to register in the first place but also if a registration was allowed to lapse. Registrations lasted for a maximum period of three years. This limitation was adopted as a way of forcing data users to review their data use reasonably regularly. Reminders to renew were sent out by the ODPR but non-renewals still run at a very high rate – about 40%. The excuse that the failure to renew was 'merely an oversight' has tended to leave the courts thoroughly unimpressed, as did the explanation that the data user had moved and did not get any reminders. The latter is particularly unimpressive given that the 1984 Act contained an obligation to notify the ODPR of any change of address.

Data users must not only register but do so fully and properly (see Figure 6.1). Registration used to be by way of completing a rather lengthy application form (albeit one consisting principally of check boxes). Responding to criticisms of the length and complexity of the form, the ODPR adopted a far simpler telephone registration system whereby template registrations are suggested, based on the office's past experience of the varying types of data use that different kinds of business are likely to require. The need to register fully and properly also created an obligation to operate within the terms of the registration. Criminal offences were committed, for example, if data users made use of their data for an unregistered purpose, or disclosed data to an unregistered destination.

Prosecutions for failing to operate within the terms of a registration were the second most common class of prosecutions (see Figure 6.4). Unlike prosecutions for simple non-registration it was necessary for the registrar to show that failing to keep within the terms of a registration occurred either knowingly or recklessly. 'Recklessness' is one of those hideous legal concepts whose analysis can takes up chapters of text and hours of judicial time. It is perhaps best to think of recklessness as carelessness. If a decision is taken within a company to sell its personal data and those taking the decision either did not consider the implications for their registration at all or gave it a brief consideration and, wrongly, concluded

In 1995 the ODPR brought a case against a manger of the Woolwich Building Society for disclosing personal data to a person not sanctioned by the Woolwich's data protection register entry. This was a case, therefore, of the Woolwich, through one of its staff, operating outside the terms of its registration. The manager had been trying to trace a Woolwich customer who was allegedly in arrears with her Woolwich mortgage. In doing so the manager disclosed to a tenant of the customer that she was in arrears. The manager was successfully prosecuted for the unauthorized disclosure. On the basis that the manager's career had been jeopardized by the prosecution the court dealt with the matter relatively leniently by imposing a conditional discharge.

In 1996 a prosecution was brought in respect of an alleged theft of data by a disgruntled employee. This type of action is becoming increasingly common and an increasingly frequent source of complaint to the ODPR: customer or membership data gathered by a company or club can be a valuable asset and an extremely useful tool in the event of a schism in the organization. In this particular case an employee of the Black Music Industry Association (BMIA) was successfully prosecuted for taking the organization's membership data and attempting to use it to establish a rival group. The prosecution was for an unauthorized use of the data on the basis that the BMIA was not, rather obviously, registered for such a use.

Fig. 6.4 *Case studies: prosecutions in practice*

that the sale was covered by the current registration then 'recklessness' would probably be established.

The lesson to learn here is to ensure that any changes in the use of data are kept strictly under review so that new uses and disclosures can be notified to the ODPR. A registration can be altered at any time so that if new uses or disclosures of data are being considered then a protective amendment can be made to the registration ensuring that no criminal offence is committed. Larger organizations will have specific systems in place and will often have a specific trained data protection officer to keep such matters under review. For smaller enterprises it will be a matter of pausing and reviewing data protection registration before any personal data held are used for a new purpose. The need to keep registration details up to date applies not only to the uses to which data is put but also to the data user's details – it is an offence, for example, to fail to notify the registrar of a change in the data user's address. Training to ensure compliance with data protection obligations is provided by various organizations. One of the longest established is Privacy Laws and Business. Their website is at **http://www. privacylaws.co.uk**.

The original 1984 Act was amended in February 1995 by the ragbag of criminal law alterations that constitutes the Criminal Justice and Public Order Act 1994. The amendments stemmed not from any fundamental criticisms of the original statute or from proposals for streamlining from the ODPR but, apocryphally, because someone played a practical joke on the new head of British Intelligence, Stella Rimington. She was the first named head of the organization and the press decided to celebrate this limited openness by seeing what other 'confidential' information could be unearthed about her. 'Investigative' journalists therefore set about finding out details about her financial affairs by duping various data users (banks, utilities, etc.) into parting with her personal data. When a complaint was made to the ODPR it was decided that no prosecution could be brought since the duped data users had not committed any knowing or reckless breach of their register entry.

In truth it is unlikely that this incident alone sparked the alterations to the 1984 Act – rather it was symptomatic of a general concern about the ease with which private detectives and journalists were apparently able to obtain supposedly confidential personal information. Some private investigators even boasted in advertisements that they could obtain 'full financial profiles' of any named individual.

The amendments introduced three new offences:

- s. 5 (6) – a person who procures the disclosure to him of personal data the disclosure of which to him is in contravention of subsection 5 (2) or 5 (3), knowing or having reason to believe that the disclosure constitutes such a contravention shall be guilty of an offence
- s. 5 (7) – a person who sells personal data shall be guilty of an offence if (in contravention of subsection 6) he has procured the disclosure of the data to him
- s. 5 (8) – a person who offers to sell personal data shall be guilty of an offence if (in contravention of subsection 6) he has procured or subsequently procures the disclosure of the data to him

The amendments were fundamentally well intentioned but in reality were not very well drafted and were consequently fraught with potential difficulties. Since subsections 7 and 8 are wholly dependent on an s. 5 (6) offence's being committed it is sensible to concentrate on the elements of that offence.

The subsection suggested that an offence was committed only if the procurer obtained a disclosure to himself. This is in marked contrast to, for example, s. 16 of the Theft Act, which makes it an offence for a person by any deception to dishonestly obtain *for himself or another* any pecuniary advantage (my emphasis).

This might seem a minor point but it is an apparent loophole that appeared ready for exploitation. For example, a private detective agency procuring the disclosure of confidential financial information may be able to arrange for the data to be disclosed direct to their client rather than to the original procurer of the information. It might be argued that the client, by employing the agency, is also a 'procurer' but the mental elements of the offence are going to be nigh on impossible to establish in respect of a client. Such a person is probably going to be unaware of which data users the agency is going to approach let alone the methods to be used to extract information – if the client had known all of that, then he or she would hardly be paying an agent in the first place. The problem could have been avoided simply by the insertion of the words 'or another' after the phrase 'the disclosure to him' in the subsection.

The implicit problems caused by this apparent oversight were made explicit in a prosecution brought by the Office of the Data Protection Registrar against a mortgage broker in February 1997. The allegation, under s. 5 (6) of the 1984 Act, that the broker had attempted to obtain a disclosure of personal financial information from a credit reference agency foundered on the fact that the arranged disclosure was not the original procurer.

It was a requirement of the offence that the procurement resulted in a breach of s. 5 (2) or 5 (3) of the 1984 Act – these were the provisions that obliged a data user to operate within the terms of the user's data protection register entry. Given that the emphasis in s. 5 (6) was on procuring a *disclosure* it might be presumed that the only possible relevant breach of s. 5 (2) would be under subsection (d), which prohibits disclosures to persons not mentioned in a register entry.

However, the wording of s. 5 (6), possibly unintentionally, does not refer to s. 5 (2) (*d*) alone but to the entirety of s. 5 (2), which seems to admit the possibility of an s. 5 (6) prosecution's being founded on a consequential unauthorized *use* of personal data (that is, s. 5 (2) (*b*) of the 1984 Act) or an unauthorized overseas transfer (that is, s. 5 (2) (*e*)) and not just an unauthorized disclosure. This is important because arguably it is going to be easier to establish an unauthorized use of personal data in an s. 5 (6) scenario than an unauthorized disclosure. This is because data users (especially large-scale ones) are quite conservative in defining their actual or potential uses of data, but seem to adopt a very open ended approach in defining classes of disclosees. Thus a journalist conning a large utility into disclosing personal financial information may be able to argue that he or she is a 'person making an enquiry' (a commonly chosen category of disclosee) but would be in difficulty in squeezing the purpose of 'investigative journalism' into one of, for example, British Gas's registered purposes.

The problem of data procurers' claiming that they fall into a category of disclosee in the data user's register entry (and thus that no s. 5 (2) breach has occurred) may also be countered by contending that if a procurer pretends to be one category of data user (a very common ploy with detective agencies and journalists) then the benefit of being, in reality, in another category cannot be claimed. Thus, if a journalist obtained confidential financial information from British Gas by pretending to be a data subject then he or she would be lumbered with the definition 'person pretending to be a data user' (not a category to which any data user would register to disclose) and could not claim also to be a 'person making an enquiry' or any other category of disclosee.

Finally, problems arose with trying to establish the mental element in s. 5 (6) offences. The subsection required that the procurer knew or had reason to believe that a breach of s. 5 (2) resulted from their actions. In practice, knowledge would be extremely difficult to establish since it suggests a detailed knowledge of the duped data user's data protection register entry. 'Reason to believe' sounds like a familiar legal concept but in reality it is a phrase that does not appear anywhere else in the criminal law. The legislators seem, almost wilfully, to have made a rod for their own backs by choosing a new phrase rather than an equivalent concept such as 'having reasonable grounds for suspecting', which does already exist (s. 24 Police and Criminal Evidence Act 1984) and which has been the subject of judicial consideration and interpretation. In practice it would be likely that the Data Protection Registrar would invite the courts to infer 'reason to believe' whenever a deception was practised by the procurer – on the basis that no deception would have been used if the procurer believed that he or she was acting within the terms of the data user's register entry.

The Office of the Data Protection Registrar ran a number of 'test' prosecutions (*see* Figure 6.5) under the 'new' amendments, but it would be fair to say that the

---

At Harrow Magistrates' Court on 28 October 1997, Rachel Barry, a former private investigator, was convicted of a total of 12 offences of procuring the disclosure of personal data and of selling the information procured, in contravention of sections 5 (6) and 5 (7) of the Data Protection Act 1984.

Mrs Barry used deception to obtain information from BT, such as ex-directory numbers and itemized bills, relating to people in whom the media were interested. Her basic modus operandi was to contact BT's customer services department and claim that she was purchasing the home of a celebrity and had agreed to take over the telephone number. This usually led to BT disclosing even ex-directory numbers. Her clients included the proprietors of *The News of the World, The Mail on Sunday, The People,* and the *Sunday Express.* Her victims included sports personalities, soap actors and the participants in alleged sexual scandals. Mrs Barry pleaded guilty to all 12 offences. She was fined a total of £600 for the offences of procuring the information and a total of £600 for the offences of selling the information. She was also ordered to pay costs of £800.

Commenting on the case, the Data Protection Registrar, Elizabeth France, praised the cooperation BT had given her office: 'When the amendment was introduced the concern and the intention of Parliament were clear, but we said then that convictions would only be secured with the cooperation of targeted data users. We are now working with a number of them to make clear that this kind of invasion of personal privacy is unacceptable'. She added that in this case she was also particularly grateful for the cooperation of the witnesses who had suffered as a result of these offences.

Fig. 6.5 *One of the first successful prosecutions under the amended legislation*

difficulties inherent in the subsections were not greatly clarified.

Arguably, large-scale data users were unlikely to have to worry about s. 5 (6) – s. 5 (8) of the 1984 Act very much – although the development of sharp practices and corner-cutting amongst staff should always be monitored. It is far more likely that they would be victims of such offences than the perpetrators. However, even being a victim is doubly undesirable since it carries the implication of lax security within the data user's organization and may suggest a breach of principle 8 of the data protection principles, which requires data users to have appropriate security measures in place to prevent unauthorized access to or disclosure of personal data.

The reforms introduced by the Criminal Justice and Public Order Act were aimed at a clear evil but it is questionable whether they hit their target.

The 1998 Act

The 1998 Data Protection Act constitutes the implementation of the EU Data Protection Directive (95/46/EC), which seeks to unify data protection systems throughout the EU (*see* Figure 6.6). The directive is clearly a sensible step forward. It is inherent in the nature of electronic commerce that data gathered about individuals is being bounced around the globe. As the UK government has argued: 'We all want access to the benefits which the information society can offer us. But we are also entitled to expect those handling information about us to do so properly and responsibly. Data protection is about ensuring that they do.'[1]

However, without a move towards a common global regulatory system of personal data protection then problems will arise from a use of personal information being lawful in one country and unlawful in another. Without common stan-

---

The United Kingdom's existing data protection legislation, the Data Protection Act 1984, meets many of the requirements of the EU directive. However, the directive goes beyond the present law in a number of respects. In particular it:

- extends data protection controls to certain manual records
- sets detailed conditions for processing personal data
- sets tighter conditions for processing 'sensitive' data (for example, details of political affiliations or sex life)
- requires certain exemptions for the media (to ensure that 'investigative' journalism is not unduly restrained)
- strengthens individuals' rights
- strengthens the powers of the Data Protection Registrar
- sets new rules for the transfer of personal data outside the EU.

Fig. 6.6 *The EU directive: the basic changes*

dards there is a risk of what might be termed 'personal data blackspots' developing – countries where anything goes in respect of the handling of personal information and which are used by the less diligent organizations to circumvent inconvenient national legislation.

The same problem, of course, arises with some activities on the Internet. Something defined as obscene, libellous or blasphemous in one country can be hosted perfectly happily and lawfully on a server in another country, and be quite accessible from the former location. Developments in data protection may therefore establish the principles for the development of more general global Internet regulation.

As indicated at the start of this chapter the new Act does not sweep away the 1994 legislation but seeks to retain familiar concepts and to build on the system that that legislation established.

Familiar features

Table 6.1 contains a brief glossary of new terms introduced by the 1998 Act and their approximate equivalents under the 1984 Act. The 1998 Act also confirms individual rights similar to (but more extensive than) those under the 1984 Act and imposes similar (but extended) obligations on data controllers (previously data users). A significant attempt has also been made with the new data protection principles to echo (or, indeed copy) the existing eight principles from the 1984 Act.

Table 6.1 *Glossary of 1984 and 1998 Act terms*

1998 Act	1984 Act
Commissioner	Registrar
Data controller	Data user
Notification	Registration
Processing	Holding

Principle 1, which was 'fair and lawful obtaining and processing' in the 1984 Act, becomes, simply, fair and lawful processing in the 1998 Act, but is additionally qualified by the requirement that personal data cannot be processed at all unless one of the Schedule 2 conditions is fulfilled (or in the case of sensitive personal data one of the Schedule 3 conditions). These conditions are dealt with in the following section.

Principle 2, 'holding only for one or more specified and lawful purpose' in the 1984 Act, becomes 'obtaining for one or more specified and lawful purpose and not further processing in a manner incompatible with those purposes'.

The old Principle 3 (restrictions on disclosures) disappears. The new Principles 3–5 (accuracy, relevance, adequacy, etc.) effectively duplicate the old Principles 4–6. The old Principle 7 (data subject access rights) goes and is replaced by new Principle 6, which requires personal data to be processed in accordance with the rights of the data subject under the new legislation. New Principle 7 (security measures) duplicates the old Principle 8, and the new Principle 8 prohibits transfers outside the EU unless to a country with adequate data protection structures.

The new principles may mirror the old to a quite considerable extent, but the provisions on the interpretation of the principles are considerably extended and modified so as to comply with the requirements of the EU directive. A good example of the changes is the interpretation of the fair processing principle (the first principle). This states that, save in exceptional circumstance, processing will be deemed unfair unless the data subject is told of the data controller's identity and the purpose or purposes for which it is intended that the data are to be processed.

Significant changes

Manual records – defined in the 1998 Act as information recorded as part of a 'relevant filing system' – will be brought within the terms of the new data protection system. A 'relevant filing system' covers any set of information relating to individuals that is structured in such a way that specific information relating to a particular individual is readily accessible. This is legalese for a filing system where you have the name of each patient, subject, suspect, or whatever on the file. Bizarrely, the government has indicated that personnel files will not be included although it is very difficult to see why, given the breadth of the definition.

Special transitional relief applies to manual files so that the complete data protection system will not fully apply until 2007, although some aspects – for example, a subject's rights to see the data – will apply from 2001.

Whilst on the subject of transitional arrangements – the government may allow up to three years from 24 October 1998 for personal data processing already under way before that date to comply with the new regime. However, any new processing started after 24 October 1998 must comply with the new system immediately. This was the latest date that the new law is supposed be in place, but, even with the slippage to April 1999, 24 October will not alter for the purposes of transition. This conjures up the disturbing scenario of new processors having to comply with a system not yet even in place.

The definition of 'processing' is also substantially changed under the new legislation. Processing means obtaining, recording or holding data or carrying out any operation on the data including organizing, adapting, altering, retrieving, consulting, using, disclosing, disseminating, aligning, blocking, erasing or destroying the data. In short absolutely anything that you might want to do with personal data (apart from just letting it sit there) is covered by 'processing'.

Processing itself is only permissible if it is carried out:

* with the consent of the individual, or
* to perform a contract with the individual, or
* under a legal obligation (e.g. the electoral roll), or
* to protect the vital interests of the individual, or
* to carry out public functions, or
* to pursue the legitimate interests of the data controller unless prejudicial to the interests of the individual.

These are the Schedule 2 conditions referred to earlier. Furthermore, in the case of 'sensitive data', one of the following Schedule 3 conditions also has to apply:

* with the explicit consent of the individual, or
* under a legal obligation in the context of employment, or
* to protect the vital interests of the individual where consent cannot be given or is withheld, or
* by certain non-profit bodies in respect of their members, or
* where the information has been made public, or
* in legal proceedings, or
* to carry out certain public functions, or
* for medical purposes.

'Sensitive data' are data relating to:

* the racial or ethnic origin of the data subject
* political opinions
* religious or other beliefs
* trade union membership
* physical or mental health
* sexual life
* commission or alleged commission of any criminal offence
* court proceedings or disposals.

Data subjects or individuals have increased rights under the 1998 Act. At the stage that data are gathered individuals are entitled to know who is to use the data and for what purpose. The individual has similar rights in respect of any bodies to whom his or her data are passed or sold on. An individual is also entitled to be told if data about him or her are being processed and to be given a detailed description of that data and the data's usage and source.

Transfers of data to countries outside the EU are allowed only if those countries have 'adequate' data protection systems. There are also exemptions to the transfer restrictions, which allow ex-EU transfers:

- with the consent of the individual
- to make or perform a contract
- for substantial public interest
- in legal proceedings
- to protect the vital interests of the individual
- where the information is on a public register
- on terms approved by or with the authority of the data protection commissioner.

The provision prohibiting the transfer of personal data outside the EU unless the destination country has an adequate level of personal data protection is a cunning way of extending the impact of the directive beyond the borders of the EU. Effectively it is a way of Brussels ensuring that other countries have a system of regulation similar to those of the EU – if you don't play by our rules you can't have our ball.

This is all well and good – the principles for handling individuals' personal information as set out in the directive are commendable, aiming as they do at promoting privacy in an era of technological intrusion. But the attempt at extending these principles to other jurisdictions is causing considerable consternation in the US. There the 'adequate protection' provision has been interpreted as a ploy to keep US businesses out of the EU personal data market and to prevent commercial online access to the EU's 360 million consumers.

US privacy and data protection rights are unashamedly patchwork – and are often found in regulations applying only to certain sectors of industry or commerce. Whilst 'adequate protection' has not been exhaustively defined by the EU there have been broad hints that the self-regulatory frameworks so common in the US will not be considered to provide 'adequate' protection (*see* 'First orientations on transfers of personal data to third countries – possible ways forward in assessing adequacy', **http://www.bna.com/e-law**).

There is considerable resistance in the US to introducing a data protection system on a federal and legislative-basis. The reaction to the imminent implementation of the EU directive seems to be to regard it as a matter of impudence and an implicit attack on US free trade. Ira C. Magaziner, President Clinton's principal adviser on electronic commerce issues, spent 1997 going back and forth between Washington and Brussels on a mission to persuade the Eurocrats that the US is unlikely to cave in on the issue. Equally, the EU member states are unlikely to back down after a decade spent thrashing out the current content of the directive.

There seem to be two glimmers of hope in terms of finding a way out of this quandary:

- First, there are precedents for individual US based data controllers entering into an agreement with an EU-based data protection authority over the degree of data protection provided for a specific category of personal data. The best example of this is an agreement between Citibank and the German data protection authorities in respect of data gathered by the bank from German citizens applying for a Citibank credit card. Citibank wanted to administer this data from their US headquarters but were prevented from doing so by the German data protection commissioner until they entered into a quite extraordinary agreement with the commissioner, which gave the German authorities the right to visit the bank's headquarters and inspect its data protection systems.

  However, the emphasis in the EU is on individual citizens' rights and purely contractual solutions are unlikely to be considered adequate. There is, for example, the difficulty of a data subject enforcing his or her rights under a contract to which he or she is not a party.
- The other possibility is that there may be some ranking of personal data according to sensitivity, so that the 'least sensitive' data may be transferred to countries with more lax data protection regimes. Again, however, this is unlikely to provide a satisfactory solution since it is probable that personal financial information will be considered as more, rather than less, sensitive data. It is precisely this sort of data that US-based companies will want to receive, analyse and utilize.

It is very likely that the EU countries will establish a centrally maintained approved list of countries with adequate levels of protection. A common list is important since different EU states with distinct rules about overseas transfers would allow the directive's principles to be circumvented, and would also affect competition between the member States.

The US's hostile reaction to the EU directive is, of course, symptomatic of that country's desire to dominate cyber-commerce. The US already dominates the relevant software market and is in the vanguard of establishing the relevant rules for the conduct of electronic commerce – in July 1998 the US issued its policy paper on the so-called global information structure ('A framework for global electronic commerce', **http://www.iitf.nist.gov/elecomm/ecomm.htm**). This report, unsurprisingly, seeks to adopt a minimalist approach to the regulation of Internet-based commerce – allowing the market alone to set the pace. Economically this may make sense but it is likely to mean an almost total loss of control over the use of personal information in the environment of Internet commerce. The EU data protection initiative seeks to strike a sensible balance between individual and commercial rights. Arguably it is time for a firm stance to be taken against the US hegemony and to insist that individual rights are worth protecting in cyberspace.

The ODPR also wishes to take the harmonization of the laws proposed by the EU directive one step further by empowering the UK commissioner to enforce the laws of foreign jurisdictions in respect of data that is handled in more than one jurisdiction.

Enforcement of the principles – business as usual

The concept of enforcement by way of the data protection commissioner's issuing enforcement notices is retained under the 1998 Act and, indeed, the whole enforcement notice procedure is virtually identical to that under the 1984 Act.

As before, the commissioner may serve an enforcement notice on any data controller suspected of breaching one or more of the data protection principles. The notice will set out steps to be taken to rectify the breach and a timescale for rectification. The commissioner must take into account, when deciding whether to serve an enforcement notice, whether any person has or is likely to be caused damage or distress by the suspected breach.

When dealing with a breach of Principle 4 (the requirement for accurate and up-to-date data) the commissioner may require the data controller to rectify or erase inaccurate data or any expression of opinion based on inaccurate data or to incorporate an amending comment from the data subject.

A data controller has identical rights of notice and appeal as under the 1984 Act, and the commissioner may as before require urgent compliance with an enforcement notice in exceptional cases. Appeals are heard, again as before, by the Data Protection Tribunal.

Assessment and information: a new procedure – take notice!

What is new in the 1998 Act is the assessment procedure. By this a data subject (or, significantly, a person who believes him or herself to be a data subject) may ask for an assessment of whether it is likely or unlikely that data processing has been carried out by a data controller in compliance with the provisions of the 1998 Act.

The commissioner may then serve an *information notice* on the data controller, requiring the provision of information to enable the commissioner to carry out the assessment. The commissioner may also serve a *special information notice* in order to investigate suspected breaches of claimed exemptions under the 1998 Act. The relevant exemptions are those set out in the 1998 Act relating to journalistic, literary and artistic material (referred to in the legislation as the 'special purposes'). If the commissioner determines that the exemption has been wrongly claimed then a *determination notice* to this effect may be issued.

The commissioner may not issue an enforcement notice against a controller processing personal data for the special purposes without first issuing a determination notice to the effect that exemption has been wrongly claimed.

As with enforcement notices the commissioner must notify the controller of rights of appeal against information and determination notices. Again, as with enforcement notices, the commissioner may seek an urgent response (not less than seven days) to information notices in exceptional cases.

A person who fails to comply with a notice under the legislation or who knowingly or recklessly provides incorrect information in response to any information notice commits an offence punishable by a fine. It is a defence to show that all due diligence was exercised to comply with the notice. The concept of 'due diligence' is one that appeared in the 1984 Act.

Entry and inspection

The new Act preserves powers for the commissioner to obtain a warrant for his or her officers to enter and search premises and to seize evidence where a breach of the legislation (including the principles) is suspected. These powers existed under the 1984 Act although, until fairly recently, there seemed to be some reluctance on the part of the registrar to use them.

It is an offence under the 1998 Act to obstruct the execution of a warrant or, without reasonable excuse, to give assistance for the execution (an example might be the refusal to give a password to access a computer system). Unlike other offences under the 1998 Act this offence may only be dealt with in England in the magistrates' court and is punishable with a maximum fine of £5000.

Notification offences

Under the new legislation the system of registration by data users is replaced by one of notification by data controllers. This writer sees considerable shortcomings in the drafting of the supporting criminal offences that buttress the requirement of notification. No longer are the offences neatly contained in one comprehensible section of the legislation (as with s. 5 of the 1984 Act). Rather they are now scattered throughout the Act in a confusing fashion that requires continual cross-referencing to comprehend. One particular section (s. 22 – dealing with 'preliminary assessments' by the commissioner) is guaranteed not to win any awards from the Plain English Campaign.

The requirement to 'notify' the commissioner is set out in sections 16–20 of the 1998 Act. These provisions require controllers to notify the commissioner of:

- their name and address
- a description of the personal data
- the purpose(s) for which they are held
- the recipients of disclosures
- non-EU countries to which the data may be transferred
- security measures to comply with Principle 7.

The requirement to notify is buttressed by section 21, which makes it an offence to fail both to notify the commissioner of the processing of personal data and to keep the commissioner notified of relevant changes (for example, in the address of the controller, or in the intentions of the controller with respect to the processing of personal data, or in the security measures to comply with Principle 7).

As with the 1984 Act, the failure to notify can be prosecuted in the magistrates' court or the crown court in England, and is punishable with a maximum £5000 fine in the former or an unlimited fine in the latter.

The s. 21 offence is the clear equivalent of the 'old' offence of non-registration under s. 5 (1) of the 1984 Act, with an additional offence based on a failure to keep notification up to date. This latter point is an effective distillation of the offences in s. 5 (2) of the 1984 Act (operating outside the terms of one's register entry) and of the offence under s. 6 (5) of failing to notify the registrar of a change in the data user's address. Interestingly, in England the s. 6 (5) offence is a matter that may only be tried in the magistrates' court and in respect of which a prosecution must be commenced within six months of the date of the offence (that is, the date on which the data user moved). As a result very few s. 6 (5) prosecutions were brought because the offence was not discovered in time. The small change in the law introduced by the 1998 Act should overcome this problem.

Unlawful obtaining and disclosing of personal data

Section 55 of the 1998 Act radically reworks aspects of the s. 5 (2) offences in the 1984 Act and the much criticized amendments introduced by the 1994 Criminal Justice and Public Order Act (s. 5 (6)–5 (8)).

It will now be an offence:

- to obtain or disclose personal data or the information contained in personal data or
- to procure the disclosure to another person of the information contained in personal data without the consent of the data controller.

The offences may be committed knowingly or recklessly. These established legal concepts are carried over from the 1984 Act – s. 5 (2) offences had to be committed either knowingly or recklessly.

The obtaining/disclosing/procuring without the consent of the data controller will not be an offence if:

- it was for the prevention or detection of crime
- it was required by law
- the 'obtainer' acted in the reasonable belief that he or she had a right to act as he or she did, or that he or she would have had the consent of the controller if the particular circumstances were known
- it was justifiable as being in the public interest.

Aspects of s. 5 (6) to s. 5 (8) of the 1984 Act are open to criticism, and it is pleasing to see that the new section 55 provisions go a long way to removing those concerns – gone is the odd concept of 'having reason to believe' that appeared in those provisions and the lacuna whereby it did not appear to be an offence if a person duped a data user into disclosing personal data to a third party.

This is not to say that section 55 will be without problems – 'without the consent of the data controller' is going to require some careful interpretation. In the successful Rachel Barry prosecution (Figure 6.5) an enquiry agent was convicted of s. 5 (6) offences after duping BT into parting with ex-directory phone numbers. On some analyses it could be said that BT 'consented' to the disclosure – certainly it was offered willingly but only because BT was duped. Presumably the commissioner is going to be arguing that 'consent' must be interpreted as 'fully informed consent'.

It is an offence to sell or to offer to sell personal data that have been unlawfully obtained/procured/disclosed. This is an effective (and sensible) extension of the similar provisions in s. 5 (7)–(8) of the 1984 Act. These offences attract the same procedure and penalties as the non-notification offences.

Damaging and distressing data

Data that are particularly likely to cause significant damage or distress to data subjects or to prejudice their rights and freedoms significantly are subject to a special monitoring procedure by the commissioner, which is set out in s. 22. It is an offence for a controller to process such data without first complying with the monitoring procedure. Exactly what data this will protect will be the subject of an order made by the home secretary.

Data subject rights

As under the 1984 Act, a data subject's rights (which under the 1998 Act are to see their data; to prevent processing likely to cause damage or distress; to prevent direct marketing – junk mail; or to object to automated decision-making) are enforced not by way of prosecution by the commissioner but by the data subject applying for a court order. Again, as before, the data subject is given a right to compensation. In practice the commissioner is likely to play a semi-formal role in such disputes by raising any pertinent complaints with the relevant data controller.

Likely prosecutions policy

Prosecutions have had a role in promoting the 1984 Act. Their unusual nature and the implication that individual citizen's rights have in some way been compromised invariably attract publicity and thereby spread the message that the legislation not only exists but also imposes obligations to be taken seriously by data users. A prosecution brought against a Brighton-based pharmacist in 1996 for failing to register was written up in the pharmaceutical profession's journal and resulted in some 300 pharmacists' contacting the ODPR for information about the need to register and method of registering. Despite the clear benefits of bringing prosecutions, the most recent report from the ODPR shows no planned increase in the level of prosecutions for the next three years. Even with willingness on the part of the courts to award costs in successful prosecutions, the investigation and prosecution of breaches of the Act are an expensive process.

Francis Aldhouse, the current deputy registrar, believes that in the future there may be a shift away from promoting legislative obligations prosecutions (what he calls 'the punishment model') and towards a system of obliging businesses to adopt quality control systems (like ISO 9000) that would include a data protection management system. The ODPR would then reserve a general right to inspect and approve control systems at random (what Aldhouse calls the 'audit model'). This shift in strategy would still, however, require policing and sanctions for failing to adopt the necessary systems and it is something of an illusion, therefore, to see this as a shift from a punishment model.

A cynical analyst might take the view that with the ODPR inundated with enquiries regarding the implementation of the new legislation, and with data users/controllers struggling with two parallel regimes, it is likely that there is going to be much confusion and little enforcement for the next three years. Whether this scenario materializes remains to be seen.

Reference

1   Straw, Rt Hon. Jack, MP, Home Secretary, Data protection: the government's proposals, http://www.home.office.gov.uk/datap2.htm [visited 10/02/1999].

7

Criminal liability

Andrew Charlesworth

Introduction

The ability to provide information in digital form, in particular via the Internet, has massively increased the average computer-literate individual's ability to publish to national and international audiences. However, that increased ability has left would-be electronic publishers and, in some cases, their prospective audiences, potentially exposed to a wide range of national legal restraints and sanctions that they may neither be aware of nor understand. These restraints and sanctions essentially define the types of electronic information that national authorities will permit to be published, used or held. The precise nature of what is deemed to be legally acceptable electronic information is inevitably bound up in the social, political and economic norms of the rule-making jurisdiction. Thus, the laws of the US relating to permissible types of electronic information will inevitably differ in some respects from those of the UK, which in turn will differ from those of Iran or Singapore.

Whatever the jurisdiction, in the early days of the electronic dissemination of information, the efforts of both the law makers and law enforcers could be seen to be lagging significantly behind the technology curve. This resulted in a situation where, from the viewpoint of the casual observer, practical legal enforcement of national rules relating to electronic information seemed to be weak or nonexistent. As this was usually combined with a paucity of public information on the potential legal issues of electronic publication, it tended to encourage the development of the mistaken belief that the new routes of disseminating electronic information were in some way immune, or exempt, from the operation of national laws. The rapid development of the Internet in the early 1990s saw the transfer of such beliefs into wide public circulation, as the mainstream media leapt onto the Internet bandwagon, with sweeping statements by ill-informed pundits about the absolute freedom of speech, and freedom from censorship, available in cyberspace. Statements such as: 'The net exists outside of physical, geographic boundaries, and no state or nation will long succeed in utilizing its laws to restrict the net. Information wants to be free and the net treats such restrictive efforts as damage and re-routes around them'[1] are fine words, and in the long term may well be true. However, in the medium term at least, national laws will be applied to Internet use, and as former CompuServe manager Felix Somm discovered, it is all too easy for individuals to get caught up in the damage.

Somm was general manager for CompuServe in Germany until he resigned in June 1997 after being indicted on 13 counts of distributing online pornography and other illegal material. He was charged even though he had no direct role in disseminating the material on the Internet. The charges followed an investigation in 1995, when prosecutors forced CompuServe to shut down access to more than 200 Internet newsgroups, some of which were suspected of displaying child pornography. In February 1998 he was given a two-year suspended sentence by the Munich district court. The court's decision came despite the fact that Germany had passed a law since his indictment providing a degree of protection for internet service providers (ISPs) from criminal liability for carrying illegal material on their services. (The new law was the German Information and Communication Services Act 1997,[2] otherwise known as the German Multimedia Law, valid from 1 August 1997. It means that Internet service providers can be held accountable for illegal material they publish, as well as content posted on their services by customers. However, they will not be held liable for pornography or hate speech posted by third parties unless 'they have knowledge of such content and blocking its use is both technically possible and can be reasonably expected'. They are also not responsible for images that customers download from the Internet.)

Certainly, it would seem from media reports that there are a rising number of Internet related arrests and prosecutions now taking place worldwide. (For example, in May 1998, after a number of arrests, six offshore gambling companies were charged by the US Department of Justice with illegally advertising and accepting bets on sports events over the Internet; there have been further examples in the area of paedophilia.[3]) This would seem to indicate that the initial legal inertia with regard to the control of certain types of electronic information has ended. That having been said, due to patchy, unbalanced, or just plain inaccurate reporting of such arrests and prosecutions, it is extremely difficult to gauge either the appropriateness of the legislation being used, or the effectiveness of the law enforcement agencies in tackling particular forms of crime. As a result, as with computer misuse, the actual degree and nature of crime relating to electronic information are very hard to assess.

In general, however, when one examines the issue of crime and criminal liability in the context of the wider debate over the legal issues relating to publication and use of electronic information, it has thus far tended to play a fairly low-key role. From time to time the media have latched onto some aspect of criminal behaviour on the Internet, such as computer hacking, or the distribution of pornographic and racist material, but this has not yet had the galvanizing effect on lobbyists and legislators that is demonstrated with issues such as copyright and data protection. The United States Communications Decency Act (see below for further discussion) is almost certainly the highest profile piece of Internet-related criminal legislation. Yet for all the furore it provoked at the time of its passage, its major effect, following the Supreme Court's decision to strike down much of the Act for being unconstitutionally vague, has been to provide US Internet service providers with protection from liability for simply carrying illegal materials.

In the main, many countries have continued to rely upon existing criminal legislation when dealing with Internet related crimes, making only minor amendments to cover the new technologies. English law is a classic example of this process. The most recent new criminal legislation is the Computer Misuse Act 1990; obscene material is still dealt with by the Obscene Publications Act 1959, and child pornography by the Protection of Children Act 1978, as amended by the Criminal Justice and Public Order Act 1994. The Public Order Act 1986 and the Contempt of Court Act 1981 cover racial hatred and contempt of court respectively. Thus the majority of relevant legislation predates the explosion in the use of personal computers, which was in its early stages in the late 1980s, and all of it predates the arrival of the World Wide Web in 1993. This state of affairs shows no immediate signs of radical change. Indeed, it is possible that the main impetus for change will not come from UK legislators, but rather from the Commission of the EU which has taken an active interest in Internet content regulation.[4]

At present, criminal offences on the Internet can be fairly readily divided into four aspects:

- obtaining unauthorized access to data
- the provision of illegal or illicit material for display or downloading
- the display or downloading of illegal or illicit material
- the provision of illegal or illicit services.

The often heated debates over what should or should not be published, what is or is not obscene, and what the general public have or do not have the right to know will continue in most countries for the foreseeable future. Such debates will undoubtedly be increasingly influenced by cross-fertilization of cultural norms from other nations, a process aided by the medium of electronic information transfer. However, while such debates are an important part of the democratic process, a simple fact remains, and that is that most nations are determined to enforce their particular restrictions upon the dissemination and use of certain types of electronic information. For the most part, those restrictions are, and will continue to be, enforced under national criminal law.

This chapter will examine the issue of criminal liability for the provision, use or ownership of electronic information, with an overview of the relevant areas of English law. This overview will take in computer misuse, pornography, racial hatred, contempt of court, and some other less well-known offences.

Computer misuse

Key UK legislation

*   The Computer Misuse Act 1990

Background

With the increased sophistication of the information technologies, the collection, processing, and utilization of electronic data have become increasingly important aspects of a wide range of human activities. For example, in the commercial sphere, new computerized techniques, such as data mining, allow the extraction of potentially valuable commercial information from sources of data that were previously unavailable or unusable. This new, or increased, value of electronic information has created some major conceptual difficulties for the law. The perception by society that electronic information is valuable has, not unnaturally, led to the assertion of property rights in it. However, unlike most forms of property, electronic information has no tangible form, can be copied perfectly an infinite number of times, and can be created or destroyed with no obvious effect on the storage medium on which it is contained. This intangibility was to prove problematic when the UK legal system was faced with the challenge of providing a method of protecting property rights in electronic data via the criminal law.

In the 1980s the introduction of the personal computer led to a surge in the use of computer systems and computer networks. This in turn led to a rise in instances of unauthorized access to computer systems and their data. While the majority of these instances took place in the workplace, it was the stereotyped image of the teenage hacker that caught the attention of the media. The resultant media coverage raised serious concern that unauthorized access to computer systems, and theft of, or damage to, electronic information would prove to be disastrous for modern businesses.

However, when the first cases started to come to court, it rapidly became apparent that existing legislation such as the Theft Acts, and the Criminal Damage Act were simply not suited to dealing with criminal offences against intangible objects.[5-6] Several high-profile cases involving computer hackers resulted in either acquittals or in convictions based on less than convincing reasoning by the courts. The result of this lack of success, combined with pressure from business, and lobbying by some MPs, resulted in the passing of specific legislation in the form of the Computer Misuse Act 1990.

The Computer Misuse Act 1990

This Act remains the primary piece of UK legislation as regards the misuse of computer systems. It is primarily designed to protect electronic information by criminalizing unauthorized entry to computer systems, as well as unauthorized amendment or deletion of computer data. A key element of the Act is that it created three new criminal offences specific to computer misuse that were clearly designed to avoid the type of problems that had come to light in previous computer misuse cases.

Those new offences are provided for in s. 1–3 of the Act as follows:

1   (1) A person is guilty of an offence if
   (a) he causes a computer to perform any function with intent to secure access to any program or data held in any computer
   (b) the access he intends to secure is unauthorized, and
   (c) he knows at the time when he causes the computer to perform the function that that is the case.
   (2) The intent a person has to have to commit an offence under this section need not be directed at
   (a) any particular program or data
   (b) a program or data of any particular kind or
   (c) a program or data held in any particular computer.
   (3) A person guilty of an offence under this section shall be liable on summary conviction to imprisonment for a term not exceeding six months or to a fine not exceeding level 5 on the standard scale or to both.

Thus, section 1 (1) clearly makes unauthorized access (hacking) an offence, and section 1 (2) states that there need be no intention to cause harm. However, this is only a summary offence, and thus on conviction the maximum imprisonment possible is no more than six months and the maximum fine £5000. The limited penalties available under this section have been partially responsible for the problems in utilizing the Act. Sections 2 and 3 contain the more serious offences. Section 2 applies to unauthorized access with intent to commit, or aid the commission of an offence, and section 3 concerns the unauthorized modification of the contents of any computer.

2 (1) A person is guilty of an offence under this section if he commits an offence under section 1 above ('the unauthorized access offence') with intent

(*a*) to commit an offence to which this section applies, or

(*b*) to facilitate the commission of such an offence (whether by himself or by any other person)

and the offence he intends to commit or facilitate is referred to below in this section as the further offence.

(2) This section applies to offences

(*a*) for which the sentence is fixed by law, or

(*b*) for which a person of 21 years of age or over (not previously convicted) may be sentenced to imprisonment for a term of five years (or, in England and Wales, might be so sentenced but for the restrictions imposed by section 33 of the Magistrates' Courts Act 1980).

(3) It is immaterial for the purposes of this section whether the further offence is to be committed on the same occasion as the unauthorized access offence or on any future occasion.

(4) A person may be guilty of an offence under this section even though the facts are such that the commission of the further offence is impossible.

(5) A person guilty of an offence under this section shall be liable

(*a*) on summary conviction, to imprisonment for a term not exceeding six months or to a fine not exceeding the statutory maximum or to both, and

(*b*) on conviction on indictment, to imprisonment for a term not exceeding five years or to a fine or to both.

3 (1) A person is guilty of an offence if

(*a*) he does any act which causes an unauthorized modification of the contents of any computer, and

(*b*) at the time when he does the act he has the requisite intent and the requisite knowledge.

(2) For the purposes of subsection (1) (b) above the requisite intent is an intent to cause a modification of the contents of any computer and by so doing

(*a*) to impair the operation of any computer

(*b*) to prevent or hinder access to any program or data held in any computer, or

(*c*) to impair the operation of any such program or the reliability of any such data.

(3) The intent need not be directed at

(*a*) any particular computer

(*b*) any particular program or data of any particular kind, or

(*c*) any particular modification or a modification of any particular kind.

(4) For the purposes of subsection (1) (b) above the requisite knowledge is knowledge that any modification he intends to cause is unauthorized.

(5) It is immaterial for the purposes of this section whether an unauthorized modification or any intended effect of it of a kind mentioned in subsection (2) above is, or is intended to be, permanent or merely temporary.

(6) For the purposes of the Criminal Damage Act 1971 a modification of the contents of a computer shall not be regarded as damaging any computer or computer storage medium unless its effect on that computer or computer storage medium impairs its physical condition.

(7) A person guilty of an offence under this section shall be liable

(*a*) on summary conviction, to imprisonment for a term not exceeding six months or to a fine not exceeding the statutory maximum or to both; and

(*b*) on conviction on indictment, to imprisonment for a term not exceeding five years or to a fine or to both.

As can be seen, the penalties for offences under Sections 2 and 3 are considerably more severe. A conviction on indictment can lead to unlimited fines and up to five years' imprisonment. It is important, however, to note under Section 3 (1) (*b*) the different degree of intent on the part of the defendant that the prosecution has to prove.

Those who use the Internet to gather and disseminate information should also be aware that the legislation covers more than the act of unauthorized access. In addition, the publishing of material that might be used in order to breach computer security, or to facilitate unauthorized entry into computer systems, may be caught by those provisions of the Computer Misuse Act 1990 that deal with the issue of conspiracy to commit an offence under the Act. This was demonstrated by the prosecution and subsequent conviction in 1996 of the virus author Christopher Pile (also known as 'The Black Baron'). Pile admitted 11 charges under the Computer Misuse Act 1990 with regard to writing and distributing computer viruses, and one charge of inciting others to spread computer viruses; he was jailed for 18 months. As yet there is no indication as to the likely liability of an institution that carries hacker-related newsgroups such as **alt.2600** on its UseNet newsfeed, thus potentially disseminating material that could allow others to access computer and telecommunications systems without authorization.

It is interesting to note the extra-territorial aspect of the Computer Misuse Act. In the main, national legislation does not attempt to regulate the behaviour of individuals outside the immediate jurisdiction of the courts. There are both theoretical and pragmatic reasons for this.

In practical terms, national territorial borders may be historically arbitrary, but they play a large role in the way in which national legal rules develop. For legal rules to be meaningful, the body legislating requires control over the territory in which the rules are to be applied. Equally, if those rules are to be applied effectively some mechanism for law enforcement will be needed, and this will require physical control over, and the ability to impose coercive sanctions on, those who break the law. In addition, most legislators are not concerned with activities that do not directly affect the territories they legislate for, and in practice where such activities take place outside the physical boundaries of a nation, there is a diminished likelihood of their having such a direct effect.

From a more theoretical angle, in democracies at least, it is argued that national laws are legitimized by the fact that the legislators who create them have been elected by the citizens who are affected by them. If national laws are imposed on individuals who have no role in that 'consensual' process, then those laws lack that legitimizing element. Finally, national laws are rarely applied extra-territorially because, they would be being applied to individuals who might have no knowledge of their existence, nor any reason to believe that those rules might be applied to them (see Johnson and Post[7] for a more detailed analysis).

However, activities based on computer communications, such as computer misuse, can clearly have an extra-territorial effect. For example, a hacker working on a PC at his or her home in Germany can access a computer in the UK, perhaps via other computers in the US. He or she is operating outside the UK, but his or her activities can clearly have a direct effect there. Sections 4 and 5 of the Computer Misuse Act deal with this situation by stating that if either the person committing the offence, or the computer against which it was committed, are in the UK, the British courts will have jurisdiction. In practice, this is more likely to be used against the UK-based hacker who is attacking computers outside the UK, primarily because the majority of crimes that fall under the Act would not meet the criteria required to trigger extradition proceedings against an overseas hacker.

Obscene materials and pornography

Key UK legislation

- The Obscene Publications Act 1959 and 1964
- Unsolicited Goods and Services Act 1971
- The Protection of Children Act 1978 (amended by the Criminal Justice and Public Order Act 1994)
- The Telecommunications Act 1984, s. 43
- The Criminal Justice Act 1988 (amended by the Criminal Justice and Public Order Act 1994)

Background

If one is to believe the media, and some supposedly academic studies, such as Rimm,[8] the most prevalent form of activity on the Internet is the provision, distribution, and downloading, of computer pornography. (The Rimm study caused immense controversy when first published, even making the cover of *Time,* but was rapidly exposed as, at best, methodologically flawed, and at worst, fraudulent.[9]) In the main, when this is discussed, the material in question is usually assumed to be photographic, though pornography (and other forms of obscene material) on the Internet may also take the form of movie clips, sound files, and textual material. Whilst it is certainly possible to locate with relative ease material that most people would classify as pornography – by using a search engine such as Yahoo! for example[10] – statements as to its prevalence often considerably overstate the role and status of pornography on the Internet.

It is likely that pictorial pornography has been available on the Internet from the point that it became feasible to digitize pictures and compress them to a bandwidth-friendly size, and textual material was probably available before that. However, whilst public access to the Internet was limited, such developments largely took place outside the experience of the general public, legislators, and law enforcement agencies. By the early 1990s, however, the Internet was beginning to see much wider use in the academic community, and various sections of the media were beginning to pay increasing, if ill-informed, attention to its possibilities as a distribution mechanism for pornography and other illicit material. However, the available statistics for this period would not seem to demonstrate that computer pornography was yet perceived, or prosecuted, as a major problem: in the period 1991–3 it was reported that, of the 976 obscenity cases handled by the Crown Prosecution Service, only 11 involved computer pornography, and only 7 of those went to court.[11] (Those few cases however, received lurid publicity that seems disproportionate to their importance. For example, an article in the *Guardian*, somewhat unoriginally entitled 'Computer going down', noted that a University of Wales computer was put out of action for two days due to an overload caused by a student downloading pornography from the US.[12]) It is worth remembering that at this time, the Web was still in its early stages of development, it remained largely text based, and it required users to have a level of computer literacy not widely available in the general community.

Developments in the mid-1990s changed the traditional Internet demographics dramatically. As hypertext markup language (HTML), a programming language used to create websites, became a more sophisticated protocol, and commercial development of the software got underway, web browsers, programs used to view information on the Web, started to evolve into more user-friendly tools. This development played a vital part in altering the business ethos of the major online service providers like CompuServe and America Online. Customer demand led a move away from their previous tactic of locking their customers into proprietary information systems and towards offering entry into the free-for-all information explosion of the Web. This led to a massive expansion of the Internet user base, and as the user base increased, so did the viability of various new forms of Internet commerce.

Commercialization of the Internet has led to a number of interrelated developments, some based on technological developments in the wider computer market, others specifically Internet driven, all of which have played some part in driving the issue of Internet pornography onto political and legislative agendas:

1   Greater individual access to the Internet required an increase in access speed. To hook the wider consumer market into using the Internet required faster modems, better graphics cards, greater processor power, and more memory – all at lower prices. Once it became easy to download graphics at a reasonable speed, and display them in 24-bit colour, high quality digital reproductions of photographs could be displayed and printed. At this point commercial distribution of pornography started to become truly viable – Internet users could obtain high resolution pornographic material that might not be accessible in paper form locally, and could do so in relative anonymity, with little chance of discovery.

2   The low cost of publishing or distributing digital information on the Internet meant that many people worldwide saw an opportunity to enter a pornography market that was hitherto heavily nationally regulated, and in which production and distribution costs, not to mention the risk of arrest, or the seizure of material, were high. All an Internet pornographer needed was a scanner, some photographs, and a computer with Internet access, in order to publish to the world. However, initially at least, the question of how to generate revenue from those accessing the material remained problematical.

3   The increased interest from major players on the information market led to the development and encouragement of Web-based technologies that would enable the further development of electronic commerce, such as encryption, site access programs, and online payment mechanisms. These were seized upon by commercial pornographic distributors as ways of allowing them to switch their income generation from their reliance on click-through advertising income to actually selling pornography online.

4   The increased mainstream commercial interest in the Internet was based on the premise that home computer ownership, Internet access and web browsing would increase. However, mainstream commercial players were aware that the perceived prevalence of pornography and other 'undesirable' material on the Internet was having a chilling effect on the family uptake of such

facilities. It was thus clearly in their interest to be able to present the Internet, and in particular the Web, as a safe online 'shopping mall' experience, rather than an anarchic and possibly dangerous place for families. This produced a number of new initiatives, including the creations of ratings systems for web-pages, the production of software that allowed individuals to self-censor their access, and the lobbying of government to regulate the Internet.

5   Special interest groups as diverse as Christian pressure groups, law enforcement agencies, feminist authors, and politicians also took advantage of the publicity surrounding Internet pornography, and the lack of experience of the Internet in the general community to further their own religious, political, social and funding aims.

It is clear that the commercial development of the Internet has led to an increase in both webservers containing pornography, and those with web browsers who wish to access it. The technical development of the Web, the development of user friendly browsers, the expansion of the user base, and the ubiquity of the Internet in the public consciousness have all led to Internet pornography becoming an increasingly visible industry, and a publicly perceived problem.

Examination of Internet sites containing pornographic material appears to show that the majority of them fall into three main categories:

* those run by individuals, which contain small personal collections of pornography, which are accessible at no charge, and which are rarely widely advertised
* commercial websites that contain relatively small amounts of pornography to advertise paper-based products such as magazines and books[13]
* commercial websites that contain large amounts of digital pornography, and which either charge for access to all but a very small amount of it, or require users to click through advertising in order to access material.

Of these three categories, it is the last that appears to continue to be a major area of growth. In general, most bodies providing Internet access, particularly academic institutions, are keen to avoid any problems with hard- or soft-core pornography. This may be for legal reasons, or because it is thought that association with pornographic material would be damaging to the institution or business concerned, or simply because the high rate of accesses to sites containing pornography is disruptive to the operation of the computer on which the material is based. Thus a great deal of control on content is exercised by peer pressure on institutions without the aid of the law. This may even occur where the law of the country involved does not forbid the possession or distribution of such material. To take examples from the education sector, two European educational institutions, the University of Delft in the Netherlands, and the Conservatoire National des Arts et Metiers (CNAM) in France, had web servers at their institutions that carried pornographic pictures downloaded by automatic newsfeed from UseNet groups which were subsequently removed.[14] Employers can also be seen to be taking a tougher line against employees who are seen to be using computer equipment for inappropriate purposes. In June 1998, an employee at the Defence Evaluation and Research Agency (DERA), an agency of the UK Ministry of Defence, was arrested and later dismissed over the collection and distribution of 170,000 pornographic images via DERA computers.

The problem of defining 'pornography'

The question of the standard that one uses to establish whether material is, or is not, 'pornography' is a highly contentious one. It is also a debate that over the years has created some unusual alliances. An example of the type of definition that may be used is 'offensive, degrading, and threatening material of an explicitly sexual or violent nature'. However, it is clear from the debates and the caselaw over the years that one person's 'offensive, degrading, and threatening material' may well be another's great work of literature, great work of art, protected social, political, or sexual, statement, or holiday snaps.

The problems that this definitional uncertainty may sometimes cause were demonstrated in June 1998 when British police seized a book, *Mapplethorpe,* from the stock of the library at the University of Central England in Birmingham. The book contained photographs of homosexual activity and bondage scenes taken by the internationally renowned photographer and artist Robert Mapplethorpe. Despite the fact that the book was widely acknowledged as serious artistic work, the police told the university that its contents might contravene the Obscene Publications Act 1959. The book came to the attention of the police when a student at the University's Institute of Art and Design took photographs of prints contained in the book to a local chemist for developing and the chemist forwarded them to the police. Ironically, the student had taken the photographs to include them in a thesis entitled 'Fine art versus pornography'. It seems that the police, at least, had little doubt as to their interpretation.

The debate over pornography on the Internet is not helped by the fact that different jurisdictions take very different attitudes to what is and is not nationally acceptable. The Sex Museum, a tourist attraction sited on a main street in Amsterdam, contains photographic material in its displays of a type that, if one attempted to import examples of it back to the UK for distribution, would almost certainly attract the attention of the UK law enforcement authorities. These different attitudes are reflected in the wide range of material found on the Internet:

very little 'hard-core' pornography is hosted in the UK, but it can be readily found on sites in continental Europe, the USA and Australia.

From a UK legal point of view, the debate over the meaning of pornography is one that has little relevance to the law itself. Despite the constant use of the word 'pornography' in much of the literature, the term is avoided in the relevant UK legislation, which concerns itself rather with whether the material in question is 'obscene' or 'indecent'. However, while this means that the courts are not caught up in an argument as to what is or is not 'pornographic', neither 'obscene' nor 'indecent' lend themselves easily to clear definitions either, and this difficulty of definition is reflected in both the legislation and the existing caselaw.

In UK law, different types of computer pornography can be caught by different pieces of legislation. The primary pieces of legislation are the Obscene Publications Acts of 1959 and 1964 (not applicable in Scotland) and the Protection of Children Act 1978 (as amended by s. 84–87 of the Criminal Justice and Public Order Act 1994 – see s. 172 (8) for those parts of the 1994 Act applicable to Scotland), although the Telecommunications Act 1984 also contains relevant provisions.

The Obscene Publications Acts 1959 and 1964

The Obscene Publications Act 1959, section 1 (1) states that 'an article shall be deemed to be obscene if its effect . . . is, if taken as a whole, such as to *tend to deprave and corrupt* persons who are likely . . . to read, see or hear the matter contained or embodied in it.' This test bears considerable similarity to that in a nineteenth-century court decision, *R.* v. *Hicklin* (1868) [LR 3 QB 360, 371], where the judge stated that whether an article was obscene or not depended upon 'whether the tendency of the matter . . . is to deprave and corrupt those whose minds are open to such immoral influences and into whose hands a publication of this sort may fall'.[15]

It is clear that this legal definition of obscene has rather more specific meaning than would normally be attributed to the definition of obscene in non-legal usage. It is important also to remember that while the depiction of sexual acts in pictorial or textual form is the most obvious form of potentially obscene material, the caselaw demonstrates that, for example, action may also be taken against aural presentations such as music albums,[16] pamphlets advocating the use of drugs,[17] and material showing scenes of violence.[18]

The key issues to consider when assessing particular material are:

- *the possibility of the relevant material being seen as likely to deprave and corrupt.* Could an observer come to the conclusion that some of those who viewed the material might be depraved and corrupted by it?

- *the likely audience for the material, as this will form part of the assessment of its tendency to deprave and corrupt.* When deciding whether material is obscene, an important determining factor is the consideration of who its likely audience is going to be. This is because some potential audiences are regarded as being more susceptible to being depraved and corrupted than others. Children are seen as an audience that is especially vulnerable in this respect. Thus, material made available in a forum or media that is available to children will always be subject to stricter regulation than material that is not. Material on the Internet is obtainable in relatively uncontrolled circumstances, and thus the definition of what is likely to deprave and corrupt those likely to have access to the Internet will be accordingly broad.

If an article is obscene, it is an offence to publish it or to have it for publication for gain. The Obscene Publications Act 1959, section 1 (3) as amended by the Criminal Justice and Public Order Act 1994,[19] defines a publisher as one who in relation to obscene material:

(a) distributes, circulates, sells, lets on hire, gives or lends it, or who offers for sale or for letting on hire, or
(b) in the case of an article containing or embodying matter to be looked at or a record, shows, plays or projects it, or, where the matter is data stored electronically, transmits that data.

Thus the transfer of obscene material either manually by use of computer disks or other storage media, or electronically from one computer to another via a network or the Internet, clearly falls under section 1 (3). Thus obscene material sent by e-mail, or posted to UseNet newsgroups is going to be caught by the legislation. The Obscene Publications Act 1964, section 1 (2), makes it an offence to have an obscene article in ownership, possession or control with a view to publishing it for gain.

Thus, obscene material placed on a webserver will be caught even when an individual simply makes the data available to be transferred or downloaded electronically by others so that they can access the materials and copy them. This was demonstrated in the case of *R. v. Arnolds, R. v. Fellows*.[20] On appeal against their initial conviction the defendants argued that the act of placing material on an Internet site could not be regarded as a form of distribution or publication. The Court of Appeal, however, held that while the legislation required some activity on the part of the 'publisher', this seemed to be amply provided by the fact that one of the appellants had taken 'whatever steps were necessary not merely to store the data on his computer but also to make it available world wide to other computers via the Internet. He corresponded by e-mail with those who sought to have access to it and he imposed certain conditions before they were permitted to do so.'

The two main defences to obscenity charges contained in the Obscene Publications Act 1959 are innocent publication and publication in the public good. Innocent publication means that the person who published the material in question did not know that it was obscene and had no reasonable cause to believe that its publication would result in liability under the Act (s. 2 (5)). In the Internet context, it can be seen that while providers of facilities or ISPs are unaware that obscene material is being put onto the Internet via their system they cannot be liable. However, if they are put on notice that this is occurring, they will have to take action to bring the activity to a halt. Failure to take such action would leave them at significant risk of prosecution. An example of this has been the activities of the police in putting Internet service providers on notice of UseNet news-groups that contain potentially obscene material.[21] This provides great impetus to the ISPs to drop such newsgroups, as the notice would make it virtually impossible to run a successful defence of innocent publication. In contrast to providers who host webpages or newsgroups, those providers who simply provide a connection to the Internet are unlikely to be able, even if they wanted to, to be in a position to accurately assess the nature of even a fraction of the data that their systems carry. They are thus unlikely to incur liability, even if their systems are used as a conduit to access or distribute pornography, as there can be no actual knowledge of the material carried.

The defence of public good is found in section 4 of the Obscene Publications Act 1959, which states that 'publication of the article in question is justified as being for the public good on the ground that it is in the interests of science, literature, art or learning, or of other objects of general concern'. The defence does not mean that the article is not obscene, but rather that the obscene elements are outweighed by one of the interests listed. As may be gleaned from the discussion of the definition of pornography above, much may be read into the context in which the purportedly 'obscene' material is to be found. Indeed, the first case to arise under the legislation, in 1961, concerned D. H. Lawrence's book *Lady Chatterley's lover.* Undoubtedly, some of the passages of the book were rather explicit for the period, but taken as a whole, the book's clear literary merits, which were defended by a number of experts, helped ensure its acquittal. It has been argued that, in some cases, the concept of literary merit has been rather liberally construed, for example, the book *Inside Linda Lovelace*, about the porn actress who starred in *Deep throat,* was cleared on similar grounds in 1976.

A key problem with the Obscene Publications Acts is that the only certain way to test whether or not material is obscene, or if obscene serves the public good, is via the courts. The *Mapplethorpe* example cited above is a clear example of a work that in the eyes of a significant element in society (the police) is clearly obscene, and in the eyes of others (the University of Central England) is a work of artistic merit. The uncertainty that this generates tends to have a 'chilling' effect on the nature and scope of material that is created, published, and distributed, in the UK, as publishers and other distributors are less willing to publish controversial material.

The Protection of Children Act 1978; the Criminal Justice Act 1988; the Criminal Justice and Public Order Act 1994

The relevant parts of the amended Protection of Children Act 1978 deal with photographic representations of children under 16 (or persons who appear to be under 16). The Act makes it an offence to take, make, permit to be taken, distribute, show, possess intending to distribute or show, or publish indecent photographs or pseudo-photographs of children. The Act defines 'distribution' very broadly. It is not necessary for actual possession of the material to pass from one person to another; the material merely has to be exposed or offered for acquisition. The 1978 Act also criminalizes advertisements that suggest that the advertiser distributes or shows indecent photographs of children, or intends to do so. The legislative amendments made by the Criminal Justice Act 1988 further criminalize the mere possession of such photographs or pseudo-photographs.

Section 84 (4) of the Criminal Justice and Public Order Act 1994 inserted a subsection (b) to section 7 (4) of the 1978 Act stating that 'photograph' shall include 'data stored on a computer disc or by other electronic means which is capable of conversion into a photograph'.

While this definition of photograph covers digital representations of physical photographs (thus graphic files, such as GIF and JPEG images, downloaded from ftp sites, embedded in webpages, or compiled from UseNet messages, will be treated as photographs), it was not considered sufficiently broad. Section 84 of the Criminal Justice and Public Order Act 1994 added the concept of the pseudo-photograph: ' "Pseudo-photograph" means an image, whether made by computer-graphics or otherwise howsoever, which appears to be a photograph.' Thus a pseudo-photograph means any image that is capable of being resolved into an image that appears to be a photograph and, if the image appears to show a child, then the image is to be treated as if that of a child. This means that there is no need for a child to have been used in the creation of the image, indeed the Act covers an indecent image that may not be based on any living subject. The pseudo-photograph amendments deal with situations where, for instance, morphing software is used to create, from images of adults, images that look as if they are of children. Given the increasing difficulty of detecting faked photographs, and the tendency of defendants to argue that individuals in seized images were not in fact children, this change seems logical. Some have argued that the purpose of the Protection of Children Act 1978 was to prevent harm coming to actual children, and if no children are used in the making of pseudo-photographs, such photographs whether indecent or not should remain outside the law. Others counter that paedophiles have been known to use indecent photographs to persuade children that unlawful sexual activity is acceptable behaviour, and thus children may be harmed by the existence of such material.

Unlike obscenity, the term 'indecency' is not defined in either the Protection of Children Act 1978, or any other statute in which it occurs. When one examines statutes that refer to indecency, such as those that prohibit the import of indecent materials (see Customs Consolidation Act 1876; the Customs and Excise Management Act 1979), sending such materials through the post (the Post Office Act 1953) or their public display (the Indecent Display (Control) Act 1981), it appears that 'indecency' relates to material that is considered 'shocking and disgusting', but less 'shocking and disgusting' than material that is considered obscene. In practice, the test for indecency remains just as subjective, and thus just as difficult to pin down, as that for obscenity. In essence, the test would seem to be whether the item in question offends current standards of propriety, or to put it in the American phraseology, whether it offends contemporary community standards.[22] Given that community standards of adult behaviour tend to be rather higher where children are involved, an image involving an naked adult that might be perfectly acceptable could well be treated as indecent if a child or pseudo-child image were to be portrayed in a similar manner.

The provisions discussed above have clear relevance to activities on the Internet. It would seem to follow from the *Arnold* case mentioned above that placing of indecent pictures of children on a webserver will almost inevitably mean that they will be distributed; when such pictures are held on a computer they can be plausibly said to be in someone's possession; a link to a website may be considered an advertisement; and a e-mail offering such pictures in digital or paper form certainly would.

A person or company charged under the 1978 Act with distributing, showing, or possessing intending to show or distribute, has two potential defences, the first being that the person or company charged did not see the image and had no knowledge or suspicion that the image was indecent, and the second that there was a legitimate reason for possessing or distributing the image, for example, for academic research.

It is also an offence to possess an indecent image of a child or indecent child-like image. The defences available are to be found in the amended version of section 160 of the 1988 Act. These are similar to those contained in the 1978 Act, but include what might be termed an 'unsolicited indecent material' defence:

(1) It is an offence for a person to have any indecent photograph or pseudo-photograph of a child in his possession.
(2) Where a person is charged with an offence under subs. (1) above, it shall be a defence for him to prove
   (a) that he had a legitimate reason for having the photograph or pseudo-photograph in his possession, or
   (b) that he had not himself seen the photograph or pseudo-photograph and did not know, nor had any cause to suspect, it to be indecent, or
   (c) that the photograph or pseudo-photograph was sent to him without any prior request made by him or on his behalf and that he did not keep it for an unreasonable time.

The Telecommunications Act 1984

Section 43 of the 1984 Act makes it an offence to send 'by means of a public telecommunications system, a message or other matter that is grossly offensive or of an indecent, obscene or menacing character'. While the Act deals in principle with indecent, obscene or offensive telephone calls, it is also capable of covering the transmission of obscene materials via public telecommunications systems in the form of electronic data. The meaning of a 'public telecommunication system' is 'any telecommunications system designated by the Secretary of State', and thus any of the British telecommunications companies so designated will be covered. Unlike the Computer Misuse Act 1990, which allows an element of extra-territorial jurisdiction, the Telecommunications Act 1984 does not give British courts jurisdiction in circumstances where a non-UK telecommunication system is used to send obscene materials into the UK. It will also not apply in circumstances where the obscene material is transmitted via a local area network unless at some point in its passage via the local area network the material is routed through a public telecommunications system. It seems that the use of leased lines will fall outside the scope of the Act.[23]

Unsolicited Goods and Services Act 1971

While the main focus of this Act was to put an end to the practice of sending people unsolicited goods, with a message that if the goods were not returned within a certain time the recipients would have to pay for them (which is in any case legally unenforceable), section 4 of the Act deals with unsolicited explicit sexual material. It is an offence under the Act to send an unsolicited book, magazine, or leaflet that describes or depicts human sexual techniques. It is also an offence to send unsolicited advertising material for such a publication. The advertising material does not have to describe or depict human sexual techniques. The definitions used in the Act seem to relate more obviously to books or magazines, and it has been claimed that this renders it inapplicable to material transmitted electronically.[24] Certainly, as of 1998, there have been no cases where the Act has been used against online materials. However, as junk e-mail, much of which advertises pornographic material, both digital and paper-based, becomes more of a problem, it may well be that either the courts will be asked to consider applying the Act to the online environment, or Parliament will be asked to consider extending the definitions.

Racial hatred

Key UK legislation

- The Public Order Act 1986, ss. 17–19, 23

It has been suggested that certain sections of the Public Order Act 1986 (see s. 42 for those sections of the Act applicable to Scotland) may also be relevant to any discussion of criminal liability on the Internet. Sections of the Act that are concerned with racial hatred state that an individual who publishes or distributes written material that is abusive, threatening or insulting to the public, or to a section of the public, or who has such material intending it to be displayed, published or distributed, will be guilty of an offence if that person intends to stir up racial hatred, or if in the circumstances racial hatred is likely to be stirred up (s. 17).

This may take the form of:

- the display of written material (s. 18);
- the publication or distribution of written material (s. 19)
- the distribution, showing, or playing of a recording of visual images (s. 21)

where these are threatening, abusive or insulting, and are intended to, or are likely to, stir up racial hatred.

It is a defence for an accused who is not shown to have intended to stir up racial hatred to prove that he was not aware of the content of the material and did not suspect, and had no reason to suspect, that it was threatening, abusive or insulting.

The provisions appear to be applicable to webpages that are overtly racist. It is also possible that a webpage that is not expressly racist, but has links to other webpages that are, may be covered by the Act. In that case, as with libel, the important issue would be proving whether the owner of the linking webpage knew that the material linked to was 'threatening, abusive or insulting'. However, the issue remains theoretical, as at present relatively little use appears to have been made of this law in electronic, or indeed any other, forums. It is worth noting that some other countries – for example, Germany – have extremely stringent laws in this regard, such that online service providers, such as CompuServe, have fallen foul of laws relating to the prevention of pornography, Neo-Nazi propaganda, and Holocaust denial.

Contempt of court

Key UK legislation

• Contempt of Court Act 1981

In England, but not in Scotland, a distinction is drawn between 'civil' and 'criminal' contempts. Civil contempt relates to circumstances where parties breach an order of court made in civil proceedings, for example injunctions or undertakings, and as such are not relevant here. Criminal contempt deals with various types of conduct that if allowed to go unchecked would have the effect of interfering with the administration of justice, and is designed to have a punitive and deterrent effect.[25-6]

Criminal contempts essentially fall into five categories:

• publications prejudicial to a fair criminal trial
• publications prejudicial to fair civil proceedings
• publications interfering with the course of justice as a continuing process
• contempt in the face of the court
• acts that interfere with the course of justice.

While the law of the contempt of court was developed by the judiciary through the common law, it has been modified to some extent by the Contempt of Court Act 1981 (however the Act does not codify or replace entirely the common law; it does, however, apply to Scotland (s. 15)).

The CCA 1981 makes it an offence of strict liability to publish a '. . . publication [that] includes any speech, writing, broadcast, cable programme or other communication in whatever form, which is addressed to the public at large, or any section of the public' (s. 2 (1)) where such a publication '. . . creates a substantial risk that the course of justice in the proceedings in question will be seriously impeded or prejudiced' (s. 2 (2)).

The fact that it is a 'strict liability' offence means that an offence occurs even where the person making the publication did not intend to interfere with the course of justice. The broad definition of 'publication' would cover UseNet messages, e-mail messages sent to mailing lists, and webpages. The publication of material relating to a case will be an offence only where it occurs when the case is still *sub judice*. The statutory 'strict liability' rule is only applied during the period that the case is 'active', and the definition of 'active' is laid down in the Act. However, where an individual knows or has good reason to believe that proceedings are imminent, and publishes material that is likely or calculated to impede or prejudice the course of justice before the point laid down in the Act as the time when the case is 'active', this may be a common law contempt.

Actions that would commonly draw charges of contempt include:

- publication of material that prejudges the case, especially where it makes the express or tacit assumption that the accused in a criminal trial is guilty[27]
- publication of material that is emotive or disparaging, especially where there is an insinuation of complicity or guilt by association
- publication of material that is likely to be inadmissible at trial, such as previous convictions, or mention of evidence likely to be excluded as having been improperly [28]
- publication of material, such as a photograph of the defendant, where the issue of identification forms part of the trial proceedings
- publication of material hostile or abusive towards potential witnesses with the intention of coercing them into not testifying, or disclosure of witnesses' names following a court order that their names should not be disclosed if there was a danger that lack of anonymity would prevent them from coming forward[29]
- publication of jury deliberations
- publication of material breaching reporting restrictions in cases such as those where in open court there is identification of children involved in the proceedings, or identification of rape victims[30]
- publication of material relating to court proceedings closed to the public, including where there is an issue of national security.

There are several defences to the 'strict liability' offence:

- a person is not guilty of contempt of court under the strict liability rule as the publisher of any matter to which that rule applies if at the time of publication (having taken all reasonable care) he does not know and has no reason to suspect that the relevant proceedings are active (s. 3 (1))
- a person is not guilty of contempt of court under the strict liability rule as the distributor of a publication containing any such matter if at the time of publication (having taken all reasonable care) he does not know that it contains such matter and has no reason to suspect that it is likely to do so (s. 3 (2))

- a person is not guilty of contempt of court under the strict liability rule in respect of a fair and accurate report of legal proceedings held in public, published contemporaneously and in good faith (s. 4 (1)).

The enforcement of the law of contempt has been rendered more difficult in modern times by the ability of individuals to publish material in countries outside the court's jurisdiction, in both traditional and digital media. Consider, for instance, the *Spycatcher* saga, where the book in question was freely available outside the UK, but could not be published or excerpted in the UK. A Canadian example concerns the trials in Ontario of Karla Homolka and Paul Bernado. During Homolka's trial for the murders of two teenaged girls, Kristen French and Leslie Muhaffy, the court ordered a publication ban on reports of the trial in Ontario, in order to ensure a fair trial for Homolka's husband, Paul Bernado (a.k.a. Paul Teale), who was also charged with the murders.[31] Despite the ban, information was widely available, due to coverage by US newspapers, cable and TV stations, and at least one Website based at a US university. A UseNet newsgroup **alt.fan.karla-homolka** set up to disseminate and discuss information about the trial was censored by many Canadian universities.

The Internet has in many ways exacerbated problems associated with jurisdiction. It has been suggested, with regard to the Internet, that where the court cannot bring contempt proceedings against the original publisher, it may seek to do so against the Internet service provider that distributed the material within the court's jurisdiction. Such an approach would, however, potentially create similar problems to those found in libel cases, where ISPs have argued that the sheer volume of e-mail traffic, or the vast number of webpages on their systems, makes it impossible for them all to be checked for possible libellous statements. As with libel, the courts are likely to treat rather more favourably (with regard to punitive measures) those ISPs and website owners who, once notified that material likely to constitute the basis for a contempt offence, is held on their systems, do everything in their power to remove it as rapidly as possible.

Criminal provisions under intellectual property legislation

Key UK legislation

- Copyright, Designs and Patents Act 1988

Sections 107 and 110 of the CDPA 1988 contain the criminal offences for breach of copyright. Section 16 of the CDPA 1988 describes those rights exclusively afforded by law to a copyright owner, and thus outlines the civil protection element.

When a legal copy of a computer program is acquired, the user acquires the rights to use that program within the terms of the licence provided with it. If the user performs an act that falls outside the terms of the licence, he or she is in breach of the licence, and this breach is actionable in the courts. Creating copies of software beyond the number allowed by the licence, or in the absence of a valid licence, would mean the creation of infringing copies, and this is actionable in the courts.

It is not necessary to sell infringing copies to be subject to criminal prosecution. Possession of infringing copies for use within a business is a criminal offence. A company will be held liable for the action of its employees when they produce, or use, infringing copies in the course of their employment. A company is legally expected to take reasonable steps to avoid breaches of relevant law, such as regular software audits. However, all auditing procedures are only as effective as the institutional commitment to good software management. Employees could be personally liable for infringement of copyright that is directly attributable to their actions.

Section 110 provides that where an offence under s. 107 has been committed by a corporate body, and it can be proved that this offence took place with the consent or connivance of a director, manager, secretary or other similar officer of the body, then that person is also guilty of an offence and may be prosecuted.[34] Thus, both the corporate body and its senior officers may be held liable for the same offence.

Consent or connivance

For a section 110 offence to be proven there must be 'consent or connivance on the part of a director, manager, secretary or other similar officer of the body'. The term 'consent' would appear to cover the situation where the individual in question was actively aware of, and involved in instructing or permitting, the breach of copyright that was to take place. The term 'connivance' would appear to cover those circumstances where the individual concerned did not play an active role in the breach of copyright, but was either aware of an on-going breach and did not act to stop it, or provided a corporate environment in which breaches of copyright were either tolerated or ignored.

Other criminal provisions

Blasphemy

Blasphemy is considered to be denial of the truth of Christian doctrine or the Bible, using words that are 'scurrilous, abusive or offensive to vilify the Christian religion'. The offence is a common law one, and has been since 1676. However, in the twentieth century the law of blasphemy fell into disuse, with no prosecutions for blasphemy for over 50 years between 1922 and 1978. Despite the then widely felt view that the offence had become an unusable historical anachronism, it resurfaced in 1979, when a successful action for blasphemous libel was brought against the publishers of *Gay news* for publishing a poem linking homosexual practices with the life and crucifixion of Christ.[35-6] More recently, in 1995, a UK website with a link to the banned poem was the subject of an investigation by the police after complaints from the public. The CPS eventually decided not to bring a prosecution.[37] It should be noted that the common law offence can only be invoked in the case of blasphemy against Christianity and the established church. This was demonstrated in 1991, when a group of Muslims unsuccessfully sought to invoke the offence against Salman Rushdie and the publishers of his book *The satanic verses*.[38]

Gambling

Internet gambling is by all accounts a boom industry, with some estimates suggesting it will become a $25-billion-a-year industry by 2000. In the UK, betting, gaming and lotteries are covered by an array of regulatory laws, including the Betting Gaming and Lotteries Act 1963, the Gaming Act 1968, the Lotteries and Amusements Act 1976 and the Betting and Gaming Duties Act 1981. While there do not appear to have been any prosecutions in the UK relating to online gambling, the rules surrounding the area are complicated enough that those wishing to host a site for the purpose of gambling would be well advised to seek legal advice. [39]

Regulation of trans-border flows of electronic information – international liability?

The growth of the Internet, and in particular the expansion of the World Wide Web has led many countries to examine whether their existing law is able to cope with the potential problems that may arise. In the main, however, countries have refrained from rushing to create Internet-specific laws. This is due in part to the volatility of the current situation, whereby it is impossible to predict either the speed of development or the direction of this medium. Many countries, even traditionally conservative states such as Singapore, are unwilling to pass legislation that might have the effect of damaging their ability to take advantage of the commercial opportunities that may arise from such advances in technology.

The US has been a significant exception to this, most notably with the passage of the Communications Decency Act 1996 (hereafter the CDA).[40] This Act sought to criminalize the activities of anyone who:

(B) by means of a telecommunications device knowingly –
(i) makes, creates, or solicits, and
(ii) initiates the transmission of, any comment, request, suggestion, proposal, image, or other communication which is obscene or indecent knowing that the recipient of the communication is under 18 years of age regardless of whether the maker of such communication placed the call or initiated the communication

or

(A) uses an interactive computer service to send to a specific person or persons under 18 years of age, or
(B) uses any interactive computer service to display in a manner available to a person under 18 years of age,
(1) any comment, request, suggestion, proposal, image, or other communication that, in context, depicts or describes, in terms patently offensive as measured by contemporary community standards, sexual or excretory activities or organs, regardless of whether the user of such service placed the call or initiated the communication; or
(2) knowingly permits any telecommunications facility under such person's control to be used for an activity prohibited by paragraph (1) with the intent that it be used for such activity.

One of the main problems with the CDA was the use of the terms 'indecent' and 'patently offensive', which appeared to fall foul of the First Amendment to the US Constitution in that they were too broad in scope and unduly restricted freedom of speech. According to E. F. Fector,

The constitutional challenge to the Communications Decency Act has been grounded in four basic arguments – that the law is unconstitutionally overbroad (criminalizing protected speech), that it is unconstitutionally vague (making it difficult for individuals and organizations to comply), that it fails what the judiciary calls the 'least restrictive means' test for speech regulation, and that there is no basic constitutional authority under the First Amendment to engage in this type of content regulation in any nonbroadcast medium.[41]

The Act attracted a great deal of controversy during its passage through the US legislature, and an action to have it declared unconstitutional was filed by the American Civil Liberties Union shortly after it was signed into law by the US President. In June 1996, Philadelphia's federal court found the CDA to be unconstitutional on the grounds that it breached the US constitutional guarantees of freedom of speech and of the press.

> Amendment 1: Congress shall make no law respecting an establishment of religion, or prohibiting the free exercise thereof; or abridging the freedom of speech, or of the press; or the right of the people peaceably to assemble, and to petition the government for a redress of grievances.

A government appeal of that judgment was subsequently rejected by the US Supreme Court, which affirmed the judgment of the lower court. However, despite the failure of the Communications Decency Act, the issue of Internet regulation in the US has not gone away, and further attempts to curtail what is seen by many as the anarchy on the Internet have followed.

Thus far, only the Child Online Protection Act 1998 (COPA),[42] which amends section 223 of the US Communications Act of 1934 has successfully negotiated the US political system. COPA requires persons who, via the World Wide Web, sell or transfer material that 'the average person, applying contemporary community standards', would find 'prurient' or 'patently offensive' for children to see, and which is without serious artistic, political or scientific value, to restrict access to such material by minors. (The fact that a significant proportion of the objectionable material available on the Internet never passes via the Web being sent via UseNet newsgroups or e-mail, seems to have been overlooked by those drafting the COPA.) More narrowly tailored than its predecessor, COPA allows websites to distribute pornography, but requires websites that distribute material deemed 'harmful to children' to verify adult status through the use of credit cards, adult access codes, adult PINs (personal identification numbers), or other future technologies.

The day after COPA was signed into law, the American Civil Liberties Union and other media industry groups filed a lawsuit alleging that the Act violates the First Amendment. They were successful in obtaining a temporary restraining order, preventing the US Justice Department from enforcing the law, in mid-November 1998. The judge granting the order held that 'the plaintiffs have shown (1) a likelihood of success on the merits of at least some of their claims, (2) that they will suffer irreparable harm if a temporary restraining order is not issued, and (3) that the balance of harms and the public interest weigh in favor of granting the temporary restraining order'.[43] It seems likely that, when the full case comes to trial, COPA will go the way of the CDA, as the US Justice

Department itself does not seem to think that the Act will survive judicial scrutiny. However, it is equally likely that the proponents of such legislation will continue to test the boundaries of the First Amendment until they find a formulation that is judicially acceptable.

From a UK legal position, a rather more important set of developments have arisen in the EU where the Green Paper on the protection of minors and human dignity (COM (96) 483 final) was published in 1996. This opened a debate on the protection of minors and human dignity in audiovisual and information services, including Internet services. An extensive consultation process led to the adoption of the Council Recommendation on the protection of minors and human dignity in audiovisual and information services.[44] Amongst its other provisions online Internet service providers are asked to develop codes of good conduct so as to better apply and clarify current legislation.

The Recommendation offers guidelines for the development of national self-regulation regarding the protection of minors and human dignity. Self-regulation is based on three key elements:

- the involvement of all the interested parties (government, industry, service and access providers, user associations) in the production of codes of conduct
- the implementation of codes of conduct by the industry
- the evaluation of measures taken.

The Recommendation is closely linked to the Action Plan on Promoting Safe Use on the Internet,[45] which in turn refers directly to the Communication on Illegal and Harmful Content on the Internet.[46]

It would appear that, to some extent at least, there is a degree of consensus between the EU member states that some regulation of Internet content is both desirable and achievable, and that some changes in the laws of the Member States may well yet be necessary. How practicable this will turn out to be is, of course, debatable, but it will add a further element to those issues that content providers should consider before placing material on the Internet.

Thus, despite the attention paid in this chapter to the provisions of UK law, it is important never to forget the international nature of the Web. A webpage is usually accessible worldwide, and, when putting either institutional or personal webpages on the Web, it is worth considering who may view them. While there are jurisdictions more liberal than the UK with regard to freedom of speech, such as the US, where pornography may, under certain circumstances, attract First Amendment protection, there are many that are not. At present, owing to a lack of international agreement over Internet jurisdictional issues, it seems unlikely that an educational institution in the UK could be successfully prosecuted (in terms of the actual application of a penal sanction) for one of its machines holding a webpage containing material considered offensive or obscene by nationals of another country, whether the criminal prosecution was brought there, or in the UK. However, such a webpage might prove costly with regard to other activities of the educational institution, such as overseas student recruitment and research ventures, because of the negative publicity.

Looking to the future, as national law enforcement agencies worldwide develop new cooperative agreements in combating criminal activity, such as child pornography, it seems likely that organized multi-jurisdictional investigations and jurisdiction-hopping to find the most favourable national venue for a successful prosecution may yet become more prevalent. In such a cooperative climate, webpage owners may have to be prepared to deal sympathetically with the laws and values of countries other than their own, as the traditional print publishers have had to do, or consider restricting the accessibility of their material to specific Internet domains.

References

1   O'Hanlon, D. and Blair, J., 'Mediation on the Net: a unique jurisdiction with unique possibilities',
    http://www.wvjolt.wvu.edu/wvjolt/current/issue1/articles/ohanlon/jolt.htm.
2   Gesetz zur Regelung der Rahmenbedingungen für Informations- und Kommunikationsdienste (Informations- und Kommunikationsdienste-Gesetz IuKDG):
    http://www.iid.de/rahmen/iukdgbt.html [German – visited 20/07/98] and http://www.kuner.com/data/reg/multimd3.htm [English translation – visited 20/07/98].
3   http://pedowatch.org/arresti5.htm [visited 20/07/98].
4   European Commission Legal Advisory Board, 'Issues raised by Internet', http://www2.echo.lu/legal/en/internet/internet.html [gives details of the latest developments; visited 20/07/98].
5   Charlesworth, A., 'Legislating against computer misuse: the trials and tribulations of the Computer Misuse Act 1990', *Journal of law and information science*, **80** (2), 1993.
6   Charlesworth, A., 'Between flesh and sand: rethinking the Computer Misuse Act 1990', *International yearbook of law, computers and technology*, **31** (9), 1995.
7   Johnson, D. R. and Post, D. G., 'Law and borders—the rise of law in cyberspacee', http://www.cli.org/X0025_LBFIN.html [visited 20/07/98].
8   Rimm, M., 'Marketing pornography on the information superhighway', *Georgetown law journal*, **83** (June), 1995, 1849–1934; archived at http://TRFN.pgh.pa.us/guest/mrstudy.html [visited 20/07/98].

9   See, for more details,
     http://www2000.ogsm.vanderbilt.edu/cyberporn.debate.html [visited 20/07/98].

10   http://www.yahoo.com/Business_and_Economy/Companies/Sex/Directories/
     [visited 20/07/98].

11   'Industry focuses on cleaning up its act', Guardian, 27 September 1994, 8.

12   'Computer going down', *Guardian*, 24 August 1994

13   For example: http://www.playboy.com and http://www.penthouse.com [visited
     08/09/98].

14   For example: **alt.binaries.pictures.erotica** and **alt.binaries.pictures.blondes**.

15   Quoted in Heins, M., *Indecency: the ongoing american debate over sex, children, free
     speech, and dirty words*, Andy Warhol Foundation for the Visual Arts Paper Series
     on the Arts, Culture and Society Paper No. 7;
     http://www.warholfoundation.org/article7.htm [visited 08/09/98].

16   See, for example, Cloonan, M., 'Free speech or aural pornography? 'Niggers with
     attitude' (NWA) and 'Obscenity legislation',
     http://www.lmu.ac.uk/lss/ls/infosvce/lib/max/cstu21a.htm [visited 08/09/98].

17   *Calder* v. *Powell* [1965] 1 QB 509; *R.* v. *Skirving* [1985] QB 819.

18   *DPP* v. *A & B Chewing Gum* [1968] 1 QB 119.

19   S. 168 and schedule 9, para. 3.

20   *The Times*, 27 September 1996.

21   *Independent*, 20 December 1995.

22   See *United States* v. *Thomas* 74 F.3d 701 (6th Cir. 1996).

23   Gibbons, T., 'Computer generated pornography', *International yearbook of law,
     computers and technology*, **9**, 1995, 83–95.

24   Lloyd, I. J., 'Shopping in cyberspace',
     http://law-www-server.law.strath.ac.uk/diglib/pub/mall.html.

25   Bailey, S. H., Harris, D. J. and Jones, B. L., 'Freedom of expression: contempt of
     court', *Civil liberties: cases and materials*, 3rd edn, London: Butterworth, 1991,
     Chapter 6.

26   Smith, G. (ed.), 'Internet law and regulation', *FT law and tax*, 1996.

27   *A-G* v. *TVS Television* (1989), The Times 7 July (DC).

28   *S-G* v. *Henry* [1990] COD 307.

29   *R* v. *Socialist Worker Printers and Publishers Ltd, Ex parte A-G* [1975] QB 637 (DC).

30   *Pickering* v. *Liverpool Daily Post and Echo Newspapers plc* [1991] 1 All ER 622
     (HL).

31   See Action No. 125/93, [R. v. Bernardo], [1993] OJ No. 2047,
     http://www2.magmacom.com/~djakob/censor/mediaban.txt [visited 08/09/98].

32   http://www.cs.indiana.edu/canada/karla.html.

33   http://www.cs.indiana.edu/canada/BannedInCanada.txt [visited 08/09/98].

34   See *Thames & Hudson Ltd* v. *Design and Artists Copyright Society Ltd and others*
     [1995] FSR 153.

35 R. v. *Lemon* [1979] AC 617.
36 See Cumper, P., 'Religious human rights in the United Kingdom', http://www.law.emory.edu/EILR/volumes/spring96/cumper.html [visited 08/09/98].
37 See http://www.queer.org.au/QRD/news/world/1997/hunt-688.html [visited 08/09/98].
38 R. v. *Chief Metropolitan Stipendiary Magistrate ex parte Choudhury* [1991] 1 All ER 306.
39 Smith, G. (ed.), op. cit., 125.
40 CDA text at http://www.cpsr.org/cpsr/nii/cyber-rights/web/cda/cda.final.html [visited 08/09/98].
41 Fector, E. F., 'A publication of the electronic frontier foundation', *Online*, 9 (8), 12 June 1996.
42 COPA text at http://www.epic.org/free_speech/house_cda2.html
43 *ACLU et al.* v. *Reno* 98-5591 (E.D. Pa. 1998).
44 See Council Recommendation 98/560/EC on the development of the competitiveness of the European audio-visual and information services industry by promoting national frameworks aimed at achieving a comparable and effective level of protection of minors and human dignity (24 September 1998 OJ L270 1998, 48).
45 See the Common Position on Decision No /98/EC of the European Parliament and of the Council adopting a Multiannual Community Action Plan on promoting safer use of the Internet by combating illegal and harmful content on global networks, http://www2.echo.lu/iap/position/en.html
46 See Communication to the European Parliament, the Council, the Economic and Social Committee, and the Committee of the Regions on Illegal and harmful content on the Internet, http://www2.echo.lu/legal/en/internet/communic.html

8

Self-regulation and other issues

Heather Rowe and Mark Taylor

Introduction

Some of the great attractions of the Internet are its flexibility and international reach and, some might say, its anarchic nature. However, to say that it is not regulated is simply not true.

This chapter focuses primarily on the self-regulation of the multimedia and the Internet, particularly in the area of advertising. A number of specific examples are given relating to the financial services field. These are included because they give some excellent examples of how existing regulation is applied in the context of the Internet – and highlight some of the problems. In addition, this chapter touches on the areas of liability for content, discrimination and computer misuse, and considers some of the knotty jurisdictional issues that can arise when advertising on the Internet.

This chapter is prepared from the perspective of English law and regulation. However, it mentions one or two initiatives emanating from the European Commission that may be relevant in this area in the future and affect the activities of EU member states doing business and advertising on the Internet. It also considers some relevant voluntary codes of practice from bodies such as the International Chamber of Commerce.

New issues arising from use of the Internet

The Internet is simply a medium of communication and, as such, is subject to many areas of law of general application. For example a libel, an act of harassment, a breach of copyright or a fraudulent activity is just as actionable when perpetrated through the Internet as when perpetrated through a more conventional medium.

The Internet also raises the issue of where a transaction takes place. This is relevant because it determines the regulatory and legal system(s) to which a party or transaction is subject. Problems in determining the location of a cross-border transaction and its governing law are by no means new but, given the global nature of the Internet, these issues are going to come up time and time again with no absolute solutions. It has long been unclear, for example, *exactly* when an overseas firm is deemed to carry on business in the UK. Could it ever be said that, if you have a website hosted on a UK server and can deal with people in the UK from that website, you could (even without a physical presence in the country) nevertheless be carrying on business in the UK?

There are complex rules of contract law that relate to international contracts with a connection with more than one jurisdiction, for example, where the contracting party controlling the website is in country A, the server where the website is physically located is in country B, and the proposed customer is in country C (the variables can be even more complex than this). Even if a website includes a statement containing an express clause stating the governing law, the laws of the proposed customer's country may have public policy rules, for example, that might refuse to recognize an express choice of law.

Even assuming a valid contract and a valid governing law clause, the country of the other contracting party may have consumer protection laws that it would apply to the transaction to protect its national consumers. Again, that country might do so as a matter of public policy. If nothing else, this could prevent action being taken against customers in their own country for breaching the contract, even if it is a valid contract.

The primary new regulatory problems are:

(i)   the ease with which the Internet can be used for cross-border transactions involving customers having access to UK or overseas product providers

(ii)   the ease with which overseas product providers can set up a website and access prospective customers worldwide, advertising products aimed beyond their local market

(iii) the ease with which UK consumers can access websites of overseas providers of goods and services

(iv)   the increased use of 'electronic' documents to carry out investment transactions brings a particular new feature – the use of search engines and intelligent agents to help navigate through the vast volumes of information available and to sift through that information to find what is most relevant. Taken together with hypertext links, search engines are capable of bypassing existing regulatory structures or safeguards (such as consumer protection health warnings), particularly when the search engine summarizes a website in its own words

(v)   use of electronic payment systems (which raises issues relating to security of payments and other transactions over the Internet)

(vi)   the concerns regarding security of unencrypted messages sent over the Internet, and

(vii) the extent to which 'health warnings' required or recommended by relevant laws, regulations and codes can be circumvented.

The whole question of 'intelligent agents' is an interesting one. An intelligent agent is a small program that can be assigned to each customer to collate information about him and offer financial advice. The agent performs these tasks while sitting on the technology-based distributor channel (be it an ATM, bank kiosk, mobile phone, PC or television) used by the customer. The agent appears on channel when the customer logs on. By switching on his PC, for example, the customer sends a signal for the agent to attend. When not at work, the agent sits on an agent server. The key feature is that you cannot *see* an agent and the customer may be unaware of its presence.

An intelligent agent can have a dual function – advice and information getting. In handling customer inquiries and requests, the agent asks customers personalized questions about, say, the customer's life style – thereby 'getting to know' the customer.

The economics of Internet use appear to be overwhelming. It is relatively cheap and an effective means of advertising to set up a website. It would be relatively inexpensive for investment firms to sell their products by means of intelligent agents. Employees and premises are expensive. Software, on the other hand, whilst it may be relatively expensive to develop, is subsequently very cheap to replicate. Soon, software will be able to interrogate an individual, find out that individual's requirements from a financial product, his assets and his inclination to take risk. That software can then sift through the 1000s of products that will be advertised on the Internet and come up with some sort of recommendation – thus potentially making independent financial advisers or appointed representatives redundant.

Professional investment advisers have to manifest their skills to the public – they take examinations. How will regulators judge a software package? When will the day come when an action is brought by a disgruntled investor on the basis that a software agent has made a recommendation which has caused loss? Who will take responsibility?

In fact, this is *not* just idle speculation. In recent months, there has been a case on exactly this point – that software can give advice. Judgement was delivered on 14 July 1998 in 'Re Market Wizard Systems (UK) Limited'.

The Defendant, Market Wizard Systems (UK) Ltd, marketed and sold a computer software package known as the Market Wizard Equity Options Trading System. Mr Justice Carnworth held, in a reserved judgement in the Chancery Division, pursuant to a petition of the Secretary of State for Trade and Industry, that the computer package provided signals to users indicating the current positions to be held by selected traded stocks on that particular day and which also provided guidance as to the course of action the user should take in relation to the buying or selling of the investment.

The brochure which accompanied the package described the product as providing 'critical guidance when you need to make intelligent, disciplined trading decisions . . . '. Mr Justice Carnworth held that the software package provided investment advice within the meaning of paragraph 15 in Part 11 of Schedule 1 to the Financial Services Act 1986. As such, the Defendant was required to obtain authorization under the Act. Since no authorization had been obtained, the Defendant's business was illegal.

In his judgement, His Lordship thought it necessary to identify when the advice was actually given. If it had been the Defendant operating the program, in response to specific requests from customers, there would be no doubt that it was providing investment advice. The fact, however, that the customer, not the Defendant, actually operated the program, did not change the nature of the advice or its source. The software program therefore fell within the scope of the Financial Services Act.

General regulation of advertising in the UK

It is now clear that the rules that apply to advertising generally will apply equally to advertising on the Internet, including advertising paid for by other people on a site. What is less clear is the extent to which any commercial website might be treated as advertising. For instance, a website established in the name of a retail store might not of itself be considered to be advertising. However, such sites sometimes include journalistic style material in an effort to flesh out the retailer's marketing. That could be advertising. Once the site starts describing products, it probably would be regarded as advertising those products.

Another example of uncertainty is the electronic version of a product such as a newspaper: is the electronic version a product itself, or simply an advertisement for the 'real' product? In essence, commercial websites are blurring the sharp line in other forms of advertising between the advertisers and a journal's editors. Thus, in practice, if a site is clearly there to sell something, rather than simply consisting of access to the site itself (and perhaps some basic factual information), then it will probably be seen as advertising and the following regulations should be kept in mind.

Overview of UK advertising regulation

Advertising in the UK is regulated through a system of self regulation. The Committee of Advertising Practice (CAP) writes and enforces the British codes of advertising and sales promotion. It is through CAP that all parts of the advertising industry agree to support both the codes and the Advertising Standards Authority (ASA), which supervises the codes and the system of self-regulation. The idea behind this system is that unless consumers can trust the advertisements they see, advertising in any medium would not be regarded as credible. The system relies on consensus and persuasion, backed up by a series of sanctions, which have successfully kept the various forms of advertising in check (without legislation) for over 30 years.

In 1995 CAP expressly included within its scope non-broadcast electronic media, including advertisements on CD-ROM and the Internet, and this brings the self-regulation of such media into line with that for press, poster and screen advertising.

The ASA have already expressed the view that they take jurisdiction over UK websites and that they will apply the same rules to the content of advertisements on a UK website as they do to other types of 'traditional' advertising. This means that the British Code of Advertising Practice and the British Code of Sales Promotion administered by the ASA apply to UK websites and multimedia products.

The ASA acts independently of the Government and aims to operate in the public interest. If an advertisement or promotion breaks the codes, advertisers are asked to amend or withdraw it. If they do not do so, there are a number of sanctions available:

1 Adverse publicity
Every month the ASA publishes a report containing details of complaint adjudications, including the advertiser's name, agency and the medium involved. These reports are circulated to the media, government agencies, the advertising industry, consumer bodies and the public. They can often result in wide (and probably unwelcome) media coverage.
2 Refusal of advertising space
Newspapers, for example, can be asked to enforce their standard terms of business which require compliance with the codes. They may decide to refuse further space to advertisers who have breached the codes and chosen not to comply with the ASA's request for a withdrawal.
3 Legal proceedings
As a last resort, the ASA can refer repeatedly misleading advertisements to the Office of Fair Trading (OFT). The director general of the OFT can make an application to court under the Control of Misleading Advertisements Regulations 1988 and obtain an injunction in the courts to prevent advertisers using the same or similar claims in future advertisements.

The British Code of Advertising Practice[1]

The ninth edition of the advertising code and also the sixth edition of the sales promotion code, are published by the Committee of Advertising Practice. They came into force on 1 February 1995. The codes apply to advertisements in newspapers, magazines, cinema and video commercials, mailing lists (except business-to-business), sales promotions and advertisement promotions. However, fly-posting, classified private advertisements, private correspondence and communications, health-related claims in advertisements and television commercials are not covered by the codes.

The advertising code sets out a number of principles that must be complied with by all advertisers, such as the general requirements that advertisements must:

(a) be legal, decent, honest and truthful
(b) be prepared with a sense of responsibility to consumers and society
(c) respect the principles of fair competition, and
(d) not bring advertising into disrepute.

The code states that the advertisers have primary responsibility for ensuring that their advertisements are legal (clause 4) and must hold documentary evidence to prove all claims (clause 3). Advertisers must not exploit the 'credulity, lack of knowledge or inexperience of consumers' and should not mislead consumers through inaccuracy and ambiguity, exaggeration, omission or otherwise (clause 7). The code is to be 'applied in the spirit as well as in the letter'.

The code also covers issues such as violence and anti-social behaviour, political advertising, fear and distress, matters of opinion, protection of privacy, the advertising of prices, comparisons and denigration.

Although the code does not have the force of law, failure to comply may lead to the ASA applying the appropriate sanctions listed above. Consequently those choosing the Internet for their advertising medium cannot afford to ignore the code.

The British Code of Sales Promotion [2]

This contains similar principles to the advertising code in that sales promotions should be legal, decent, honest and truthful. Similarly, it is not legally binding, but can result in certain sanctions.

It also provides (as does the advertising code) specific rules for, for example, financial services and products, medicines and advertising for children.

Both the advertising code and the sales promotion code have additional provisions relating to distance selling, which is described as offering goods or services to consumers without the buyer and seller meeting at any time face-to-face. This clearly includes Internet and multimedia based advertising and promotions. It is worth noting that advertisers, promoters and all others involved in handling responses must observe the codes. The provisions state, *inter alia,* that:

(a) advertisements should state the full name and address of the advertisers outside the coupon or other response mechanism so that it can be retained by consumers. Advertisements should include, unless obvious from the context: the main characteristics of the products or service; the amount and number of any transport charges; any VAT payable, unless the advertisement is addressed exclusively to a trade; a statement that goods can be returned; any limitation on the offer and any conditions that affect its validity, the estimated delivery time, etc.

(b) advertisers should not take longer than 30 days to fulfil an order except in certain circumstances

(c) advertisers should provide customers with written information on payment arrangements, credit, instalments, rights to withdraw, cancellation, other terms and conditions, as well as the most appropriate address for contact

(d) advertisers must refund money promptly in the following circumstances: if consumers have not received their goods or services; if goods are returned because they are damaged; if unwanted goods are returned undamaged within seven working days; if an unconditional money-back guarantee is given and the goods are returned within a reasonable period, as well as where the consumer can produce proof of posting for goods that have been returned but are not received

(e) advertisers do not have to provide a full refund on perishable, personalized or hand-made goods, high-value products or goods that can be copied

(f) if advertisers intend to call on respondents personally this should be made clear in the advertisement or in a follow-up mailing. To allow consumers an adequate opportunity to refuse a personal visit, advertisers should provide a reply-paid postcard or free-phone telephone contact instructions.

Clearly not all of the above (reply-paid cards, for example) work in relation to the Internet but compliance with the above provisions must be ensured, insofar as it is relevant.

International Chamber of Commerce International Code of Advertising Practice[3]

This code aims to promote high standards of ethics in marketing via self-regula-tory codes that are intended to complement existing frameworks of national and international law. A new edition of the code was released in 1997. The code also ties in with the ICC International Code of Practice on Direct Marketing (see below). There is no sanction to enforce the code: rather it is expected to be fol-lowed as a matter of good practice, both in the spirit as well as in the letter.

The code aims to cover advertisements in their broadest sense, regardless of the medium used, and thus covers webpages and the like, which in essence aim to promote the webpage owner. The term 'consumer' refers to any person to whom an advertisement is addressed or who can reasonably be expected to be reached by it, while 'product' refers to any goods or services offered.

The code sets out the basic principle that all advertising should be legal, decent, honest and truthful, prepared with a due sense of social responsibility and conform to the principles of fair competition. There are specific articles in the code on all these topics, as well as on truthful presentation, comparisons, testi-monials, exploitation of goodwill and imitation.

Article 11, on Imitation, is interesting in that it suggests that where advertisers have established distinctive advertising campaigns in one or more countries, other advertisers should not unduly imitate them in the other countries where the former may operate, so as to prevent the initial advertisers from extending their campaigns within a reasonable period of time to such countries. Due to the acces-sibility of one Internet page from around the world, care should be taken that the look, feel and layout of a webpage does not imitate any other known webpage wherever it may be based and whatever country it may be aimed at primarily.

In summary, the ICC code is very similar to the British code on advertising, and thus although the ICC code has no sanctions to enforce it, a breach of it is likely to be a breach of the British code, which has the sanctions already outlined above.

International Chamber of Commerce Code of Practice on Direct Marketing[4]

This code of practice was first published by the ICC in 1992 and was revised in 1998. The code is intended to provide individuals and organizations involved in direct marketing with a basic set of rules that are generally acceptable nationally and internationally. The purpose of the code is to enhance the general confidence in direct marketing and to foster a sense of responsibility towards the consumer and the general public. In line with other codes of practice, the ICC code outlines a number of basic principles dealing with, *inter alia*, truthful presentation, integrity and honesty, clarity, decency, comparison and fair competition, guarantees, etc. There are also specific principles relating to telemarketing, for example.

It should not be assumed that the current code applies to the Internet but in some ways use of unsolicited e-mail is in many ways similar to use of the telephone. The code is designed as an international instrument of self-regulation and the prime responsibility for observance is placed on the seller. The code is mainly concerned with active marketing organizations (i.e. those making contact with customers). The code is currently being revised, specifically to address the Internet, although there is no clear indication of when it will be finished.

Draft International Chamber of Commerce Guidelines on Interactive Marketing Communications[5]

The draft guidelines aim to lay down principles for responsible commercial communication over the Internet, World Wide Web and other online services. This goes wider than advertising. Their objectives are to enhance the confidence of the public at large in marketing provided over these new interactive systems, to safeguard an optimum of freedom of expression for advertisers, and to minimize the incentive for governmental and/or intergovernmental regulations. The transformation of the guidelines into an ICC code is currently being considered.

Guideline 2 states that users should be given the opportunity to decide not to receive unsolicited commercial messages, and such messages should not be directed to users who ask not to be so approached.

To give examples of its provisions, Guideline 4 deals with respect for public groups. Commercial content-providers should respect the role of particular electronic newsgroups, forums or bulletin boards as public meeting places that may have rules as to what is acceptable commercial behaviour. The posting of commercial messages to such sites should be very carefully considered in the light of whether a site has a commercial nature or activity, or has implicitly or explicitly indicated consent to the receipt of commercial messages. Off-topic commercial messages to non-commercial sites are only appropriate when the site operator has specifically allowed such messages. In particular, the practice of sending multiple postings to non-pertinent public sites in disregard of the sites' express rules should be shunned by responsible advertisers.

Guideline 5 regards respect for data privacy issues. It states that providers should be sensitive to data privacy issues, particularly with regard to the storage, reuse and/or sale of consumer data. Marketers wishing to share customer data with other commercial entities may commit themselves in advance to informing customers of this, and allowing them to block such sharing if they wish. Marketers should inform customers upon their request as to the information they have kept on record for them. Customers should also be given the opportunity to correct such information, to request that it be removed or to request that the marketer no longer solicits them.

Guideline 6 makes an important point about the potential sensitivities of a global audience. Given the global reach of a website and the Internet, and the variety and diversity of possible recipients of messages through it, special sensitivity should be taken as regards the possibility that a particular message will be perceived as pornographic, violent, racist or sexist, if not in the marketer's own country then in other countries where the message may be accessed.

As with the ICC code, these Guidelines are not legally binding (and are not quite finalized). However, they are a good measure of what is considered appropriate practice for an organization interested in complying with suggested codes of self-regulation. If the self regulatory approach does not work, there is always the possibility that governments will step in to legislate instead – surely not the option to be preferred.

Direct Marketing Association Code of Practice [6]

The first edition of the code of practice was published by the Direct Marketing Association back in 1993. The second edition was published in 1997. The revised Code sets standards of ethical conduct and best practice that members must adhere to, including data users and other agents involved in direct marketing using personal information.

The general rules (section 4) of the code cover the use of personal information for direct marketing purposes and apply to data owners, data users, list brokers, list managers and data processors, whether or not any payment is made in relation to the information. The rules will certainly apply to marketing by telephone.

As with the ICC code on direct marketing, it should be assumed this code applies to the Internet as much as to the telephone. In addition, institutions intending to be involved in the area of direct marketing might wish, for all sorts of publicity reasons, to use a marketing entity to carry out direct marketing that observes the code of conduct.

The Control of Misleading Advertisements Regulations 1988 (SI 1988 No. 915)

These regulations cover any form of representation (including ones made via multimedia and the Internet) that is made in connection with a trade, business, craft or profession in order to promote the supply or transfer of goods or services, but do not apply to 'investment advertisements' and any advertisement for 'investment business'.

The regulations impose a duty upon the Director General of Fair Trading, the Independent Television Commission and the Cable Authority to consider complaints about misleading advertisements, unless the complaint appears to be frivolous or vexatious. If the Director General considers an advertisement to be misleading, he or she may bring proceedings for an injunction against any person concerned with the publication of the advertisement, and has powers to obtain information from any person to enable the above functions to be carried out.

The court may grant an injunction on such terms as it thinks fit, but only providing that it is satisfied that the advertisement to which the application relates is misleading. In granting an injunction the court has regard to all the interests involved, and in particular the public interest. The court can require any person who appears to be responsible for the publication of the advertisement to furnish the court with evidence of the accuracy of any factual claim made in it. The court will not refuse to grant an injunction for lack of evidence that the publication of the advertisement has given rise to loss or damage to any person, or the person responsible for the advertisement intended it to be misleading or failed to exercise care to prevent its being misleading.

The Distance Selling Directive (97/7/EC)

The European Union Directive on the Protection of Consumers in respect of Distance Contracts (OJ R144/19) was published in June 1997. In essence, it is a directive on distance selling, and it has taken some time for the various European Union bodies to agree upon the provisions. The directive must be brought into force in each member state by 4 June 2000. There are practical matters that need to be addressed in relation to compliance, which could affect design and content of a website.

The directive aims to standardize the laws of the various member states concerning distance contracts between consumers and suppliers. The aim of this is to promote, in line with the EU's 'principle aim', free movement of goods and services throughout member states, so that consumers can have access to the goods and services of another member state on the same terms as the population of that state. The aim of the directive is to set a minimum community level of law required in this area (recital 4). Member states may introduce more stringent provision to ensure a higher level of consumer protection, provided they are compatible with the European Union treaties (such as the Treaty of Rome).

Scope

The directive applies to 'any contract concerning goods or services concluded between a supplier and a consumer under an organized distance sales or service scheme run by the supplier, who, for the purpose of the contract, makes exclusive use of one or more means of Distance Communication up to and including the moment at which the contract is concluded'.

'Means of Distance Communication' are any means that, without the simultaneous physical presence of the supplier and the consumer, may be used for the conclusion of a contract between those parties. An annex to the directive lists some of these, and specifically mentions electronic mail and 'videotex' (personal computer and television screen with keyboard or touch screen). Thus, the directive covers the sale of goods or services concluded over the Internet or by a mixture of distance communication methods. For example, an advert on a CD-ROM that gives a telephone number to ring to conclude a contract could fall under the terms of the directive, as all methods of communication are 'distance' ones. A similar argument could apply to advertisements on websites that invite orders to be placed by telephone or by electronic mail. The scope of the directive is thus potentially quite wide.

Exemptions

The directive does not apply to contracts relating to financial services, including investment services and banking services.

The following contracts are exempted from the directive's requirements on prior information (Article 4), written confirmation of information (Article 5), right of withdrawal (Article 6) and time to perform (Article 7(1)):

(i) contracts for the supply of foodstuffs, beverages or other goods intended for everyday consumption, supplied to the consumer's home, his residence or workplace by regular roundsmen; and

(ii) contracts for the provision of accommodation, transport, catering or leisure services where the supplier undertakes to provide the services on a specific date or within a specific period.

Prior information

Article 4 requires the provision of several pieces of information to the consumer prior to the conclusion of any distance contract, including: the identity of the supplier; the supplier's address (where advance payment is required); the main characteristics of the goods or services; the price; delivery costs; arrangements for payment and delivery; the existence of a right of withdrawal under Article 6; the cost of using the means of distance communication, where it is calculated other than at the basic rate; and the period for which the offer or the price remains valid. The requirement is to provide the information in a clear manner appropriate to the means of distance communication used, and it appears that the European Commission's view is that the Internet is an acceptable means of providing such information. Due regard must be made to the usual principles governing the protection of those who are unable to give their consent, such as minors.

Written confirmation

Article 5 requires the consumer to receive confirmation in another durable medium of most of the information referred to in Article 4 in good time during the performance of the contract, and at least by the time of delivery, unless the information has already been given to the consumer in an appropriate medium. In addition, the following must be provided: written information on how to exercise the right of withdrawal; the address of the place of business of the supplier; information on after sale service and any guarantees; and the conclusion for cancelling the contract.

There has been some debate as to whether e-mail is an acceptable form of confirmation due to the directive's conclusion that 'information disseminated by certain electronic technologies is often ephemeral in nature insofar as it is not a permanent medium'.

Right of withdrawal

Article 6 creates a right of withdrawal for the consumer. The consumer will have a period of at least seven working days in which to withdraw from any distance contract without penalty and without giving any reason. The only charge that may be made because of the consumer's exercise of this right is the direct cost of returning the goods. In the case of goods, the seven-day period runs from the day of receipt. If the supplier fails to provide the information required by Article 5, then the period shall be three months instead, unless the information is supplied within the three months, in which case the seven-day period starts from that moment.

However, the right of withdrawal is not exercisable in respect of contracts for: the provision of services if performance has begun; the supply of goods or services where the price is dependent on market fluctuations uncontrollable by the supplier; the supply of goods made to the consumer's specification, or which are liable to deteriorate or expire rapidly; the supply of audiovideo recordings or computer software that the consumer has unsealed; the supply of newspapers, periodicals and magazines; and gaming and lottery services. If the price of goods or services is covered to some extent by credit from the supplier, the latter should also be cancelable without penalty if the right to withdrawal is exercised.

Other provisions

Article 7 requires, subject to any agreement to the contrary, the supplier to execute the order within 30 days. Where he or she fails to do this, the consumer must be informed and be able to obtain a refund as soon as possible. The provision of goods or services of equivalent quality and price may be permitted if this was provided for in or prior to the contract.

It is worth noting that, under Article 12, the consumer may not waive the rights conferred on him by the implementation of the directive into member states law. Also, this article provides that a consumer does not lose the protection granted by the directive by virtue of the choice of law of a non-member country as the law applicable to the contract if the contract has close connection with the territory of one or more member states. In other words, this means that a supplier cannot seek to circumvent the directive by stating in an advertisement or contract that the law of a non-member state is the applicable law to the contract. Quite how effective this would be may depend also on the choice of jurisdiction clause (i.e. where any litigation about the agreement would occur) and the law claimed to apply to the contract. For instance, the claimed applicable law of a non-member state might provide that the new law is not to take precedence over it.

In summary, the impact of the directive on some commercial organizations' use of the Internet could be significant. There is now a draft directive specifically for distance selling in the financial services sector which is proving very controversial.

Other legislation

In addition a mass of other UK legislation is potentially applicable to electronic adverts, including the Trade Descriptions Act 1968, the Consumer Credit Act 1974, The Prices Act 1974, the Unsolicited Goods and Services Act 1971, the Consumer Protection Act 1987, and the Trade Marks Act 1994 (to name but a few!)

Examples of some specific regulation – the financial services industry

The Banking Act 1987 (Advertisements) Regulations 1988

These regulations came into force on 29 April 1988 and apply (with certain exceptions) to advertisements containing an invitation to make a deposit. They set out general requirements for advertisements with which any person or company making deposit advertisements must comply.

Code of Conduct for the Advertising of Interest Bearing Accounts [7]

This applies to the advertising of all interest bearing accounts maintained within the United Kingdom and is published by the British Bankers' Association. Advertisers must take special care to ensure that members of the general public are fully aware of the nature of any commitment into which they may enter as a result of responding to an advertisement and the registered or business name of the deposit-taking institution must be clearly stated in the advertisement.

'Good Banking' – the Banking Code of Practice [8]

The 'Good Banking' code of practice was drawn up by the British Bankers' Association, the Building Societies Association and the Association for Payment Clearing Services to be observed by banks, building societies and card issuers in their relations with personal customers. The code is reviewed every three years, and the third edition was published in 1997, took general effect from 1 July 1997 and was revised in 1998. The code is voluntary, although most banks active in the UK (over 100) and building societies comply to a greater or lesser extent with its provisions. The code applies to the relationship between banks and their *personal* customers only.

Clauses 2.13 to 2.18 deal with the marketing of services. Clause 2.18 states that 'We will ensure that all advertising and promotional material is clear, fair, reasonable and not misleading'. In addition, clause 5.12 states that signatories to the code will comply with the law and follow relevant codes of practice or similar documents as members of the British Bankers' Association, the Building Societies Association and the Association for Payment Clearing Services. The main codes of practice are listed above, and include the British Code of Advertising Practice and the British Code of Sales Promotion Practice (see above).

In addition to the Banking Code of Practice, there is a Code of Mortgage Lending Practice. This is a voluntary code followed by lenders in their relations with personal customers in the UK. It sets out almost identical provisions on advertising and compliance with codes of practice as the Banking code.

The new Banking code is already in existence and came into force on 31 March 1999. It does not expressly mention the Internet but is clearly looking at new 'electronic' products as it mentions 'electronic purses' (such as Mondex cards where value is stored on the card).

The Financial Services Act 1986 (FSA)

The FSA applies to the activities of investment professionals (fund managers, stockbrokers, market makers and other intermediaries) when they carry out 'investment activities' that will occur when they, amongst other things: deal in investments (i.e. shares, stocks, options, futures etc.) as principal or agent, manage assets belonging to another person that may include investments and/or give advice.

Section 57 of the FSA regulates advertising and makes it an offence to issue or cause to be issued an investment advertisement unless it is issued by an authorized person and the contents are approved by an authorized person or an exemption (listed in section 58) applies. An investment advertisement may include any form of advertising (specifically film, broadcast or video) that invites persons to enter into any agreement, the entering or performance of which by either party constitutes investment activity. There are a large number of exemptions to this provision.

The criteria governing the approval of investment advertisements are contained in the rules of the various recognized Self-regulating organizations (SROs). The applicable rules will be those of the SRO of which the authorized person is a member (for example, the Securities and Futures Authority, and the Personal Investment Authority).

Broadly speaking, where authorized persons issue or approve an investment advertisement, they must apply appropriate expertise and be able to show that they believe on reasonable grounds that the advertisement is fair and not misleading. The rule books of the SROs set out the standards that members should consider in judging whether any advertisement is fair and not misleading. In addition, the rule books contain requirements for the contents of investment advertisements, some of which are mandatory and some of which are optional. Where investment products are to be marketed to private customers, the rule books of the SROs require the authorized person to take reasonable steps to ensure that the advertisement contains adequate and fair information about the investment product being offered, the terms of the offer and the risks involved. Indeed, certain direct advertisements must contain written contractual terms.

Material circulated on the Internet or in multimedia form could fall within the definition of 'an investment advertisement' in section 57 (2) of the FSA if it contains an invitation or information likely to lead directly or indirectly to persons entering into or offering to enter into investment agreements (such as agreements for the purchase or sale of investments or the provision of investment services).

Section 56 of the FSA regulates unsolicited calls, which are defined as a personal visit or other oral communication made without express invitation. An investment agreement entered into as a result of an unsolicited call may be unenforceable against the recipient of the call. Such diverse activities as changing the subject with a colleague at the golf club or a presentation about a company organized by its brokers could be classified as 'unsolicited calls'. The section will not apply where the call is permitted by the Common Unsolicited Calls Regulations. These permit amongst other things solicitation in relation to:

(a) transactions with anyone who is not a private investor
(b) certain existing customers of the caller or the persons proposing to enter the transaction or of certain associates of either
(c) employee share schemes, and
(d) corporate acquisitions and disposals.

There are also provisions under section 47 of the FSA concerning misleading statements and practices. Under section 47 any person who makes a statement, promise or forecast that he or she knows to be misleading, false or deceptive is guilty of a criminal offence if the statement is made for the purpose of inducing or is reckless as to whether it may induce another person to enter (or to refrain from entering or offering to enter into) an investment agreement.

The restrictions in section 57 (1) of the FSA apply where an investment advertisement is issued in the UK. It is the general view of the Financial Services Authority (the former Securities and Investment Board) that, for the purposes of the FSA, where an advertisement held anywhere on the Internet is made available to or can be obtained by someone in the UK (e.g. it can be pulled up on a computer screen in the UK), that advertisement may be viewed as having been issued in the UK (at the point it is made available to or is pulled up on a computer screen by a person in the UK).

Section 57 is qualified by section 207 (3), which sets out the circumstances when an investment advertisement issued outside the UK is treated as issued in the UK. This is particularly relevant to the operation of the Internet or multimedia products that are produced abroad and used in the UK. The implication of section 207 (3) is that an advertisement issued overseas will be considered to have been issued in the UK if either it is directed at people in the UK or made available to them other than by way of a periodical published overseas and circulating principally overseas (or sound or television broadcast transmitted principally for reception outside the UK).

Whether or not any material made available to Internet users in the UK will be an investment advertisement, and, if so, whether or not its issue in the UK would constitute a breach of section 57 (1) will depend on the precise facts in each case.

Contravention of Section 57 is a criminal offence punishable on conviction by imprisonment or a fine, or both, and can also form the basis of civil proceedings by the authority. The authority decides whether to take enforcement action, looking at each particular case and any other relevant factors, which may include the following (not an exhaustive list):

(a) whether any risks to investors are such that authority action is needed to protect their interests
(b) whether there are any other potential infringements of the FSA in addition to a potential section 57 breach
(c) whether as a matter of fact any offer was directed at potential UK investors, and
(d) the degree to which, given the nature of the Internet, someone had taken positive steps to avoid the material's being made available to or receivable by persons in the UK.

The positive steps mentioned above might include requiring pre-registration (before access to any potentially offending material) to ensure that only those at whom the material was aimed had access.

This is a prime example of regulation applying in circumstances where it may not entirely have been intended.

The Data Protection Act 1984 (DPA)

The DPA 'regulates the use of automatically processed information relating to individuals and the provision of services in respect of such information', and applies throughout the United Kingdom. As such, the DPA can apply to a host of situations relating to electronic media. The 1984 and 1998 Data Protection Acts are discussed in Chapter 6. The new 1998 Act should come into force in April–June 1999. It does create some important new provisions which could affect use of websites.

The ISDN Directive

The directive concerns the processing of personal data and the protection of privacy in the telecommunications sector, in particular, in the integrated services digital network (ISDN) and in the public digital mobile networks.

The directive *sounds* as if it is only relevant in limited areas related to telecommunications, but it has much wider ramifications as it is specifically aimed at digital technologies, new telecommunications services and the successful cross-border development of such services.

Although much of the directive clearly affects public telecommunications operators specifically, some provisions have implications for others. For example, Article 5 requires member states to legislate to protect confidentiality of communications over the public network. This includes future changes to the current English law on recording or monitoring calls. More interestingly, Article 12 relates to unsolicited calls. It is primarily aimed at automatic calling machines (without human intervention) or use of faxes to send unsolicited messages that cannot be used without prior consent of the subscriber. However, member states are supposed to legislate so that consent is also required for any other sorts of calls being made for direct marketing. This could include e-mail.

The ISDN directive was supposed to be brought into English law by 24 October 1998, save for Article 5, which will affect the current English law in relation to the recording and monitoring of telephone calls but which does not have to come into force until October 2000. It will come into force some time in the first half of 1999 and will be implemented by statutory instruments rather than by laws.

Jurisdictional problems

Jurisdiction is by far the most problematic and vexed legal issue relating to the Internet. It is far from clear to what extent the mere fact of having a website will subject the site owner to the laws of a given country. This is an area of law that is likely to develop substantially and one that will affect the utility of the Internet as a business tool or forum. The key issue will be whether or not the contents of a particular webpage will, unwittingly, mean that the site owner is subject to foreign laws or, in particular instances where the site owner has offshore business units with a website accessible from the UK, subject to English law and regulation. At present each case must be considered on its own facts, and in many instances the answer will depend on the laws in force in the country in which the question is being raised. Potentially, the laws regulating advertising in each country from which the webpage can be accessed may apply which, in essence, is every country in the world. Clearly it is impractical to seek advice to ensure compliance in each jurisdiction.

English criminal law is, broadly, based on physical presence within the territory. Thus English courts would not have jurisdiction to try matters that relate to activities overseas. For example, a person in Germany or France who dealt in infringing copies of software could probably not be tried in an English court for his sales in Germany. However, if he or she set up a website in Germany, the position is less clear, especially if the site is targeted towards English customers.

An example of the jurisdictional issues that can arise in the area of financial services is on p.166.

Forming a contract – general points

Whilst there is some debate as to how best to achieve the formation of a contract over the Internet, under English law electronic media should not prove to be an obstacle to a valid contract being formed. After all, contracts are formed all the time over the telephone and by fax. The international dimension may, however, complicate matters and it is possible that courts other than the English courts may have jurisdiction in the event of a dispute (for example where the other contracting party resides overseas and the services or goods are to be provided to him or her there) and they may hold that the local legal requirements to form a valid contract have not been complied with.

Under English law, there are four essential elements to a contract:

(i)   an offer
(ii) acceptance of the offer
(iii) an intention to create legal relations, and
(iv) consideration.

In many common situations, the four elements are obvious: you see a mobile phone in a show room; you make an offer which is accepted; you tender the purchase price (the consideration) and the relevant rental papers are handed over by the seller and a binding contract has been formed. However, if the potential purchaser saw the phone advertised in the newspaper and tendered the asking price, a valid contract would not be formed unless the dealer accepted the offer: advertisements are generally only 'invitations to treat', that is, invitations to the world at large to make an offer *to buy*. In other examples, it is less clear which party is the offeror and which the acceptor. The distinction between being an *offeror* or an *acceptor* is a subtle but important one, as it affects the parties' respective abilities to withdraw or reject an offer.

Websites and advertisements

In the majority of cases where a company is likely to enter into contracts over the Internet, it will do so by way of an advertisement which, if worded correctly, would amount to an 'invitation to treat'. Thus, where a potential customer is applying for some service or the like, the website owner would be entitled to turn down the application. Each case will turn on its own facts and the intended objectives of the owner should dictate how the advertisement is worded.

In addition, it is important that the terms and conditions underpinning the transaction must be referred to and available for the user to read. These are not the same as the terms and conditions governing access to the site (see 'health warnings' in the following section). Where services or goods are to be ordered over the Internet, the user should be made clearly aware of the terms and conditions that are to apply. Views differ even within the UK on the best way of achieving this. Ideally, the users should be obliged to scroll through the terms and conditions and confirm that they have read them and accepted them. It would be very difficult, under English law, for users to deny they were aware of the relevant terms if such a procedure *has* to be followed before any purchase or order takes place. From a marketing and presentational perspective, this is not attractive. However, if this is not done, a court may hold that the terms and conditions would not apply, especially if they contained unusual or onerous provisions (which should be highlighted and brought to the user's attention in any event).

The terms and conditions should at least be referred to (prominently) on the first webpage relating to the services or goods, with a hypertext link to the actual terms and conditions. In addition they should be available from the webpage from which the order is placed or application made. The objective is to bring the terms and conditions to the attention of the users and to give them every opportunity to read and accept them. Immediately prior to the users' finalizing a transaction they should be asked to confirm that they have read the relevant terms and conditions and that they accept them. In the event that they do not do so, the users should be offered the opportunity to cancel the transaction or review the terms and conditions. The transaction should not be completed without confirmation that the terms and conditions have been accepted. All this should be borne in mind when designing a webpage.

Timing and place of formation

Another question that may need to be considered is at what *time* a contract will be deemed to be formed and *where*. Whilst there is no specific legislation on this and there is no judicial guidance on how the courts are likely to address the issues in the context of the Internet, it is instructive to consider how the law has developed over the years and how it has been applied in the past.

As a general rule in English law, a contract will not be formed until *acceptance* of the offer has been communicated to the offeror. However, as an exception to the general rule, the courts have developed a rule that where an offeror has explicitly or implicitly agreed to the offer being accepted by post, once the letter accepting the offer has been posted, the contract is deemed to have been formed even if the offeror does not receive the letter accepting the offer. This rule, known as the *postal rule*, is well established and was developed in the early nineteenth century as representing the fairest method of allocating the risk and consequence of letters going astray in the post. By analogy, one could argue that where the offeror has expressly (or impliedly) agreed to acceptance by e-mail, once the acceptance has been sent by the acceptor into the ether, the contract is formed even though the e-mail message is never received by the offeror. Until the courts have ruled on the point, there must be uncertainty as to whether or not a contract has been formed where the e-mail accepting the offer is not (or where it is alleged that it was not) received. To avoid this situation in circumstances where the contract is to be formed without any further approval by the website owner, it should be made clear in the relevant terms and conditions or by a statement that will be seen by the user *before* sending an e-mail that the contract will not be formed until the website owner has received the e-mail accepting its offer.

Further rules have developed to take into account the use of the telex in international commerce. The English courts have held that where a contract is formed by exchanges of telex, the contract is concluded *in the country where the telex accepting the offer is received*. By analogy, it could be argued that a contract is concluded where the e-mail accepting an offer is received. The significance of this is that English law might recognize that courts overseas may be able to assume jurisdiction merely because the message is received in their jurisdiction.

The offeror could pre-empt matters by specifying in the terms of trading from a website the law which is to apply to the contract (e.g. English law) and which courts are to have jurisdiction in the event of a dispute. However, the effectiveness of these measures could perhaps fall to be determined by the foreign court and, in any event, the measures would not bind third parties (such as a person who had been defamed on an electronic bulletin board run by a website owner), nor would they be effective to avoid regulatory regimes or criminal sanctions.

Health warnings and disclaimers – efficacy in an Internet environment?

Many existing statutes, regulations and rules of regulatory bodies (or simple prudence) require 'health warnings' to appear on written materials – for example, the standard caveats seen on investment and unit trust advertisements.

Organizations may also wish to include other provisions on their website or CD-ROM to protect themselves, though they are not driven to do so by any relevant statute; for example, a clause restricting those downloading content from their website replicating it for gain, or clauses excluding liability for content (especially if that content has been obtained from third parties).

Some industry sectors may wish to impose terms and conditions on people accessing their websites to: reduce the risk of their being subject to foreign legislation and supervision, prevent third parties from making unauthorized use of the site and restrict the use to which the copyrighted materials on a site may be put. Those familiar with the Internet will appreciate that many different methods are employed to try and impose terms and conditions on web users.

However, unless terms and conditions are brought to the attention of the user in question, the chances of their being enforceable must be remote. Terms and conditions hidden at the bottom of the homepage in small print are less likely to be enforceable than those that a user must scroll through (with unusual and onerous provisions highlighted or in bold), and having done so click on an 'accept' icon, although the latter may be unpalatable from a presentation point of view. In the end, a balance must be struck based on a sensible risk assessment that takes into account the nature of the website and the target audience.

One recommendation must surely be to discuss the whole area of 'best practice' on use of the Internet with all industry regulators relevant to a webpage's content in the hope that consistent strategies (which make regulators feel at least relatively comfortable) can emerge.

Intellectual property rights

While intellectual property rights (IPR) are dealt with in detail in Chapter 4, their demand for a degree of self-regulation suggests that some mention is necessary here.

Copyright

When preparing a webpage or transmitting material over a network, a number of legal issues relating to intellectual property rights (i.e. copyright, trade and service marks, etc.) must be addressed. Merely because materials (whether they are documents, images, sound recordings or video clips) have been digitized and are available over a network, does not mean they can be copied at will or that any intellectual property rights that attach to them have been waived. Whilst some rights holders are happy to make their works freely available to the world at large, most are not. The common perception of material being placed in the 'public domain', (that is to say it is not protected by copyright because it was not regis- tered, for example) is not generally recognized under English law – there is no requirement under English law to register a work for copyright protection. (There used to be some form of requirement under US law but this is no longer the case, although the US Library of Congress still maintains a copyright regis- ter.) In certain circumstances works that fall into categories that would ordinarily be protected by copyright may not be protected for a variety of reasons, such as that the author was not a *qualifying individual or person* for the purposes of the relevant legislation; however, this is quite rare. In addition, copyright in a partic- ular work may have expired. The most that one may say, where a rights holder claims to put his material into the *public domain*, is that third parties have been granted a licence, possibly implied, with regard to the material in question.

It should also be remembered that often the person who has placed digitized material on a network will not have been entitled to do so. In short, material downloaded from the Internet by an individual for his or her use should not be copied and used by that person unless the normal clearance procedures have been followed and the appropriate licence to use has been obtained.

A second point to remember arises where somebody proposes to put materials created by third parties on a network such as the Internet. Even if that person has used that material before, for example in an advertisement campaign in the national press, this does not mean that he or she is entitled to use the same mate- rial in other circumstances. The right to use a photograph in a newspaper may not grant the right to digitize it and use it on a website.

Another issue that needs to be considered when preparing a webpage or site is the impact that it could have on the owner's intellectual property rights. Once material is placed on the Internet, the owner effectively loses control in so far as it can be copied and redistributed without the website owner's consent. All of the owner's websites and pages should, of course, contain a copyright notice in the usual way, and an explicit licence setting out the extent to which the material may be copied or circulated. The licence wording need not be lengthy but should restrict use to personal use only, with no right to reproduce in any other materi- als. However, one should assume that at least some of those accessing the website might ignore the restrictions. It is therefore important to consider the conse- quences of this *before* it occurs and the true 'value' of what is put onto a website. Do you want to make it easy for your competitors to download and exploit your research reports, for example? If the research is intended for *clients* or a limited circulation only, you should instigate some form of password procedure to enable you to check and enforce this.

Trade marks

There may be countries where a website owner has not registered its trade marks. There could be a possibility, perhaps remote, that someone locally may have registered a mark that could lead to a local infringement or other claim against the website owner in another country.

Use of a competitor's name or logo could also cause potential problems. While the law on comparative advertising has changed recently, use of a potential competitor's trade mark, for example, could amount to trade mark infringement if the comparison is not presented fairly in all the circumstances.

A less obvious, but more significant, issue relates to the owner's trade and service marks and corporate identity generally. Many companies invest time and money in protecting their trade and service marks and ensuring that they are distinctive of the website owner. Deviations from the way the marks are presented and alterations to the marks themselves could dilute their distinctiveness and affect their validity. Many companies now seek to provide how their 'brand' is to be reflected in *all* their websites, in order to strengthen its recognition.

Software licences and Internet/intranet connections

Software licensing issues may arise in two ways. These are:

1 A company may wish to use existing software licences to exploit an Internet/intranet setup. One needs to consider whether or not the existing licences permit this new use or whether they are fairly specific as to a particular machine/website/purpose.
2 In addition, it may well be that a network designer/builder will write some bespoke software for the project. One would hope that title will pass to the commissioning entity, but if it is based on an existing product of the designer, he or she may not be willing to give up title. In such a case, the commissioner of the work will have to make sure that an appropriate licence for the software is in place, with an escrow agreement to protect the commissioner against the software house's insolvency.

Sex discrimination

The principles of sex discrimination and its associated legislation apply to electronic media such as the Internet and CD-ROMs as much as to any other situation. Thus, care must be taken to ensure that the material on such media is not in any way discriminatory between the sexes or indeed racially. This will require the same objective thought as is the case with any external publication or information issued by a company.

In addition, there is the issue of 'sexual harassment', which is defined in the European Recommendations and Code of Practice on the Dignity of Men and Women as 'unwanted conduct of a sexual nature or other conduct based on sex which affects the dignity of a man or woman'. While this clearly includes any unwelcome physical or verbal conduct, it should cover unwelcome non-verbal conduct by computer. Although such conduct usually brings to mind examples of repeated e-mail requests for a date, or other sexual advances or innuendoes, this is not the only conduct covered. Arguably, information, comments or digital pictures included in electronic media, for instance 'page 3-style' pictures, fall within this conduct as much as e-mails.

It is also worth noting that if such harassment takes place 'in the course of employment' the offence is treated as being carried out by the employer as well as by the employee, unless the employer can show that 'all reasonable steps' were taken to prevent the harassment. This is the case even where the electronic harassment occurred without the employer's knowledge or approval. Thus, liability for employees' actions can be quite wide-ranging and managers and employers in order to avoid liability for this type of misconduct should generally ensure that their employees are not abusing electronic media. Specific reference to the prohibition of this type of conduct in their terms of employment and a harassment policy should be sufficient, provided that they are communicated to, and understood by, all employees. In the context of production of information on electronic media, close supervision of the content would also be well advised.

Illegal material on the Internet

There is a measure of self-regulation in relation to illegal material on the Internet (in particular with reference to child pornography). In September 1996, the Internet Watch Foundation (IWF) was launched to address the problem of illegal material. It is an independent organization that implements proposals jointly agreed by the Government, the police and two major UK service provider trade associations (Internet Service Providers' Association (ISPA) and London Internet Exchange (LINX)). The organization encourages all users of the Internet to report potentially illegal material via a hotline, be it by phone, fax or e-mail. Users are encouraged to send reports if they see something that they believe to be illegal, even if not absolutely certain as to that fact. The information required in a report is a brief description of what has been seen and details of where it is located. However, reports of something that a user personally finds offensive as a matter of personal taste or morality rather than as a matter of law cannot be acted upon. When it receives a report, the IWF assesses the material, traces its origin, and if necessary then contacts the police and the service provider to remove the material. The appropriate reporter is advised of the progress of his or her report. The IWF stresses that there is little it can do about material that is not liable to prosecution under UK law, however offensive individuals may find it. The IWF procedure is something that webpage providers need to be aware of, as the potential is there for any user or visitor to their page to report them. Although the IWF cannot itself remove or block access to a webpage, it will forward what it considers to be illegal material to the police for transmission to the relevant law enforcement agency, and request the service provider involved to contact the webpage owner to have the webpage removed.

As always with the Internet, webpage owners should be aware that other jurisdictions may have their own laws on harassment and on illegal material that may affect webpages accessible in that jurisdiction.

The dangers of e-mail communications

Liability for defamatory communications

Liability is dealt with in detail elsewhere, but, as with IPR, the demand for a degree of self-regulation makes some mention necessary here.

In principle, a company's liability for defamatory e-mail messages sent by its staff does not differ from its liability in respect of any other communication written by its employees. Although the legal status of an e-mail message has not been determined (either by the courts or by Parliament), the generally accepted view is that it is actionable as a libel, that is to say, as a publication made in permanent form. This is because e-mail messages (although seemingly transient) are invariably stored on and retrieved from a computer's hard drive. E-mail messages will accordingly be treated in law as equivalent to letters, faxes and paper written documents. In order to bring a claim for libel based on the publication of such a document, it is not necessary to show that any loss or damage has been suffered; the law presumes that some damage will flow from publication.

A company will have a potential liability on two levels. It may be held vicariously liable if its employees themselves publish e-mail messages through the company's communications system. In addition, as the owner and controller of the communications system through which e-mail messages written by its staff are sent, the company may be directly liable itself for publishing those messages.

A company will be vicariously liable for defamatory e-mail messages sent by a member of its staff provided that the employee, when sending the e-mail, was 'acting within the scope of his employment'. Any e-mail that is sent by a member of staff as part of, or directly incidental to, the carrying out of his or her job will be deemed to have been sent while that person was so acting. This will be the case even if the member of staff was expressly forbidden from publishing defamatory material. A company will only escape the risk of vicarious liability if the sending of the e-mail message was completely unconnected with the employee's job and could properly be regarded as a wholly private communication.

The fact that an e-mail message is confined to the company's internal communications system will not prevent the company's being held vicariously liable. The courts have held that a communication between two individuals, even where they are both employed by the same company, is capable of amounting to a 'publication' for which the company can be vicariously liable. This arose in the case of *Western Provident Association Limited* v. *Norwich Union Healthcare Limited and The Norwich Union Life Insurance Company Limited* (formerly The Norwich Union Life Insurance Society), reported in the *Financial Times* on 18 July 1997. This case did not result in a judgment as it was settled.

Norwich Union paid £450,000 in settlement to Western Provident and issued an apology to Western Provident admitting that its staff libelled the private healthcare group by internal electronic mail. This is believed to be the first libel action brought involving messages sent by e-mail. Norwich Union staff spread rumours that Western Provident was being investigated by the Department of Trade and Industry that the group was close to insolvency. In a statement in open court Norwich Union admitted that rumours were false and deeply regretted and sincerely apologized to Western Provident for the dissemination of the rumours. Norwich Union stated that it had made every effort to ensure that such unacceptable practices did not occur again. It also undertook not to repeat the allegations. Although, of course, the potential for serious financial or other damage to a third party is greatly increased when e-mails are sent externally to outside bodies, such as clients or potential clients, a company should not ignore the fact that considerable damage can be caused by a defamatory allegation or rumour circulating internally. What is more, where it can be shown that an employee either intended or should reasonably have anticipated that the contents of the e-mail would be passed on to others either within or outside the organization in which he or she worked, the company will be vicariously liable for those further communications.

The extent of a company's direct liability in respect of staff e-mail communications is more uncertain. There is some authority that suggests that there cannot be direct liability for communications internally between staff members because a company cannot publish to itself. Even in respect of external communications, there is an unresolved question whether the mere act of providing staff with computers and a link to the Internet can constitute a sufficient act of publication. Assuming that it does amount to publication, the Defamation Act 1996 provides a possible defence to a company whose only involvement in the publication has been the operation or provision of the system or service by means of which the message was retrieved, copied, distributed or made available in electronic form.

In such circumstances, the company would have a defence if it could show that it had taken reasonable care in relation to the particular publication and did not know, and had no reason to believe, that what it did caused or contributed to the publication (*see* Defamation Act 1996, section 1). It is not clear what steps, if any, a company would need to demonstrate it had taken in order to bring itself within the terms of this recently enacted provision, which had not so far been tested in the courts by November 1998. Certainly, it would be prudent for the company to implement and enforce a strict office policy as to the use that staff make of the company's e-mail facility. It is not, however, recommended that a company takes more active steps, such as, for example, monitoring the contents of e-mail messages passing through its systems. Such action might take the company outside the statutory defence on the basis that it had ceased to be involved 'only' in the operation or provision of the communications system or service. It also risks a claim for infringement of privacy by the employee whose message is intercepted.

Any company which is sued (as either directly liable or vicariously liable or both) over the contents of an e-mail will be able potentially to rely on any of the normal libel defences, for example that the statement is true or is fair comment based on true facts. In addition, any e-mail communication that is legitimately sent to a person who has a genuine interest in its contents may be protected by the defence of qualified privilege, provided that the sender was not acting maliciously, and reasonably believed that the contents of the e-mail were true. The defence would commonly apply where, for example, job references or credit ratings are communicated between persons by e-mail for proper business purposes. Where, however, an employee publishes material for an ulterior purpose or without believing that it is true, the defence of qualified privilege will not be available.

The position becomes more complex where an e-mail is sent to a recipient outside the jurisdiction of England and Wales. This is likely to occur frequently, particularly in the case of a multi-national organization that has offices or branches worldwide. The question whether such a communication will be actionable in the sender's country will probably depend not only on the position under the law of this jurisdiction but also on the position under the law of the country in which the e-mail is received. In some circumstances, limitations imposed by the foreign law on the liability may be given effect in England and Wales.

For these reasons, a company would be well advised to ensure that its staff are properly versed in the potential liability attaching both to itself and its employees in respect of defamatory e-mail communications. The problem is accentuated by the fact that people have tended to treat e-mail as a relaxed and informal mode of communication. A written corporate policy should be implemented, including the following:

- staff should be required to confine their communications by e-mail to those that are properly required for business purposes
- staff should be expressly prohibited from publishing any material that is potentially libelous
- care should be taken to ensure that statements are true, could not be miscon-strued and are sent only to those with a legitimate interest in the subject matter
- staff should be told to take steps to validate incoming e-mails, as it is possible to mimic the sender's address and change contents en route
- staff should be instructed that, if they receive a defamatory e-mail, they should report it to their manager
- on no account should staff repeat the libel, which could include forwarding it to others.

It is to be hoped that such guidelines will help to instil a sense of responsibility amongst staff and minimize risks.

Precautions in respect of potential liability for other wrongs

It is recommended also that there be similar restraints on the sending of material that is obscene, discriminatory or that might be regarded as amounting to harassment.

Harassment

It is unlikely that harassment issues should arise except where there is use of, for example, bulletin boards or live chat. However, it is perhaps more likely to arise within a corporate's own intranet used by its employees. There are already cases pending in the United States (in which the damages being claimed are astronomical) where, for example, employees of companies are claiming that they are being harassed by sexually or racially discriminatory e-mail.

Probably the most publicized of these actions is *Owens* v. *Morgan Stanley & Co.*, which has been before the New York Courts.

A law suit was filed by two African/American employees of the investment banking firm who claimed they were subjected to a hostile work environment.

The original complaint which alleged violations of various statutes, including the New York Human Rights Law, sought $5 million in compensatory damages and $25 million in punitive damages per plaintiff. It is clear that sums involved are vast.

The basis of the suit was a racist e-mail message which became the subject of office jokes and of ridicule of the plaintiffs, as well as other African/American employees at Morgan Stanley. The plaintiffs even suggested that they were denied promotions despite demonstrating ability although, perhaps, this issue is not linked to the e-mail campaign. The plaintiffs have argued that it *is* directly related to the e-mail campaign. It is particularly so because, in the allegations, the alleged author of the e-mail message was named in the law suit, as well as other Morgan Stanley employees who were accused of further distributing the offending e-mail in question.

Since the terms of the settlement of this case are confidential, it is difficult to know how significant this case really is, although the figures initially bandied about were certainly fairly spectacular.

Looking at English law, it is important for an employer to avoid harassment by e-mail – if there is anything done by a person in the course of employment it is treated as done by the employer as well as by them, whether or not done with the employer's knowledge or approval – as in section 41 of the Discrimination Act 1975. What exactly is 'in the course of employment' in the context of this Act is not entirely clear, but the employer could be liable in certain circumstances.

The 1976 Race Relations Act contains similar provisions in relation to racial discrimination.

It is prudent to have warnings in both situations to assist the employer in attempting to avoid vicarious liability.

Companies Act 1985

Section 349 of this Act provides that:
  (1) Every company shall have its *name* mentioned *in legible characters*:
    (a) in all business letters of the company,
    (b) *in all its notices and other official publications,*
    (c) in all bills of exchange, promissory notes, endorsements, cheques and orders for money or goods purporting to be signed by or on behalf of the company, and
    (d) in all its bills of parcels, invoices, receipts and letters of credit.
  (2) If a company fails to comply with subsection (1) it is liable to a fine.
  (3) If an officer of a company or a person on its behalf:

(a) issues or authorizes the issue of any business letter of the company, or any notice or other official publication of the company, in which the company's name is not mentioned as required by subsection (1), or

(b) issues or authorizes the issue of any bill of parcels, invoice, receipt or letter of credit of the company in which its name is not so mentioned, he is liable to a fine.

E-mail could be used as a notice or receipt, for example. The company's name should therefore appear in all 'official' e-mail.

Confidentiality

Communications sent by e-mail are more easily intercepted, copied and read by strangers than more traditional forms of communication. In the circumstances, the best practice is for staff to avoid altogether sending confidential information by e-mail. However, if confidential information has to be communicated in this way, the company should provide a macro insert to its staff that they are required to use when sending e-mails, particularly externally. The macro should contain a confidentiality warning, in similar form to the wording that typically appears on faxes. The macro for external use should also contain the information that is required by the Business Names Act 1977 to be included on business letters.

The implications of discovery obligations

At an early stage in litigation, at least after the writ is issued and possibly before, a party comes under an obligation not to destroy documents that might be relevant to the action. If the company has in place a system for the deletion of e-mail files after the expiry of a fixed period of time, it may find itself inadvertently in breach of this obligation. Procedures should be put in place to avoid this possibility. The obligation to preserve documents and to disclose them arises in any litigation, not just libel claims. Staff should, accordingly, be required to act with caution when sending e-mails, not simply to minimize the company's exposure to a claim for libel or other action over the e-mail content, but also to avoid prejudicing the company's position generally with regard to litigation.

Conclusion

The above chapter provides an overview of the main areas of self-regulation and the legal issues that could be relevant to the Internet and multimedia products. It is not exhaustive and should act as a reminder to treat the Internet no less carefully as a medium than you would hard copy media.

References

1   British Code of Advertising Practice, February 1995 (9th edn), **http://www. asa.org.uk**

2   British Code of Sales Promotion, February 1995 (6th edn), **http://www.asa.org.uk**

3   International Chamber of Commerce International Code of Advertising Practice, 1997, **http://www.iccwbo.org**

4   International Chamber of Commerce Code of Practice on Direct Marketing, 1998, **http://www.iccwbo.org**

5   International Chamber of Commerce Revised Guidelines on Interactive Marketing Communications, 1998, **http://www.iccwbo.org**

6   Direct Marketing Association Code of Practice, 1997 (2nd edn).

7   Code of Conduct for the Advertising of Interest Bearing Accounts, January 1999.

8   Banking Code of Practice, 1998 (revised edn).

9

Agreements, user licences and codes of practice

Richard McCracken

The history and development of copyright are inextricably linked with the history and development of copying technology. As each new technological development makes it easier to reproduce master copies or to distribute works, or to copy and distribute works in new ways, so copyright legislation and practice have evolved to offer rights owners new forms of protection. And enforceable protection is the means of exploitation. From the early printing presses to the invention of film, from broadcast television and radio to the new and emerging digital communication and storage technologies, copyright law has expanded to offer rights owners increasingly sophisticated licensing options.

The question is this: why should any of this matter to someone dealing with an electronic archive or library? The answer, of course, is because digital or electronic networks and archives increasingly bring libraries into the sophisticated and complex areas of copyright management and licensing that have traditionally been the territory of the publishing and broadcasting industries. When digital systems remove the physical object (the book) from the archive, then all that is left is a form of rights licensing. This is intellectual property in its purest form. If books as physical objects have helped to define the library in the past, then the negotiation of licences will define the library of the future. That is why the business of licensing electronic rights is so difficult. If the licence itself defines the product, then what we are doing by negotiating and licensing electronic rights is trying to define an answer to the question 'what is a library?'. While this chapter cannot answer the question, it will attempt to help you develop a practical approach to defining and negotiating a licence to accommodate both present need and future plans.

Licensing rights is different from buying a physical object in a very important and fundamental way. Buy a hammer and the shopkeeper has no interest in whether you are using it to build a house or an ark or simply to hang a painting. License copyright, on the other hand, and the licensor will take a very close interest in how you intend making use of the material and will charge accordingly. Buy a copy of a book or subscribe to a magazine or learned journal and you will be able to retain your old copies as part of your archive even after your subscription lapses. If you subscribe to an electronic journal, your access to archive editions of the journal may evaporate along with your lapsed subscription. This places a responsibility on licensees to analyse their needs before entering into any negotiation regarding a licence.

The model I want to develop is that of networked city transport. We are familiar with the travel routes of major city centres being divided into travel zones, often shaped rather like the concentric circles of a bullseye target. There is an inner core and then successive outlying areas that are reached by crossing arbitrary fare boundaries that do not always correspond to physical geographical or administrative boundaries. Travellers on the network have choices that they exercise (often subliminally) in travelling within and between zones. Is it cheaper or more convenient to travel by taxi, bus, tram or rail or to walk? Is it cheaper or more convenient to combine several forms of transport? Is it possible to step off, pass through the barriers, walk, shop and then re-enter the system, all on the one ticket? In each case, the sensible traveller will balance criteria such as affordability, speed, distance, convenience and the need (or not) to combine two or more means of transport and the need (or desire) to travel. Prices, too, reflect a balancing of similar criteria with the need to set fares at a level and in a combination that will attract customers. Someone planning to travel solely in the central zone would be unlikely to buy a full price area pass as they would be buying a right to travel beyond the central zone that they are unlikely to exercise. However, a lower priced full area pass might be attractive for customers who, even though they know the bulk of their travel will be confined to the central area, anticipate also that in some circumstances they might travel further.

The travel zone model applies equally well to decisions that have to be made in the effective licensing of intellectual property. Budgetary constraints, the preferred or essential means of distribution, convenience and breadth of access must be taken into account in defining the core purpose of the licence, just as one might define 'destination and purpose of travel' when booking a travel ticket.

This means that there is essential preliminary work to be done before licensing negotiations start. While that analysis of need (balancing real need against the temptations of wish fulfilment) is often more difficult than reaching agreement in the negotiations themselves, it is essential if the resulting licence is to meet your needs. Defining need defines the licence, saves money, achieves a satisfactory licence and guides the negotiation.

The importance of clearly defining the core target audience or user group before entering negotiation is reinforced by the use of standard contracts. Such contracts agreed either between a single library and a rights owner or owners, or recommended nationally as a result of consensus reached between libraries and rights owners, bring many benefits, some disadvantages and a number of responsibilities if they are to work effectively.

Standard licences are an extremely effective way of handling the repetitive licensing of a large number of small and broadly similar transactions. They introduce clarity, consistency and speed into the licensing process. They make it possible to handle large numbers of individual licences without having to explain or negotiate terms and conditions. They allow licensees and licensor alike to be confident that they understand the level of rights granted across a range of material and encourage the growth of sustainable relationships between the parties.

Recognizing the importance of both groups' reaching agreement on a common set of licensing objectives, publishing and library associations in many countries have put in place working groups with a brief to develop a consensus approach towards generating a standard, recommended licence for electronic libraries, Tilburg Library, Denmark has developed electronic licensing principles for use by librarians in negotiating with publishers and other rights owners. The European Copyright Users Platform (ECUP) and European Bureau of Library, Information and Documentation Associations (EBLIDA) have provided pan-European forums as representative interest groups acting on behalf of libraries and other copyright user groups. In the US, similar representative bodies and user coalitions have worked to lobby on behalf of users, to provide a focus for debate, offer advice and draft model licences. In the UK, the Joint Information Systems Committee (JISC) and the Publishers Association (PA) set up a joint working group to discuss areas of agreement and conflict between their two constituencies. An original model licence was produced and has been followed up by further meetings of the working group, resulting in a toolkit designed for use by libraries and publishers engaged in licensing electronic product. The toolkit has three elements. The first, a standardized licensing framework, may be used to structure agreements. The second is a range of exemplar licences covering common situations, such as licensing access to a CD-ROM or the right to access a publisher's server or to digitize a text original. The third is an agreed set of definitions that can be referred to in licences as a reference standard. The working group has now developed a refined version of the original standard licence that takes account of feedback supplied by both users and rights owners.

Similarly, the Copyright Licensing Agency (CLA) in the UK, a collecting society representing the interests of both publishers and authors, is currently (January 1999) seeking a mandate from its members with a view to offering digital rights licences to educational institutions and libraries. As well as representing its members' interests, the CLA has engaged in extensive talks with representatives from user groups with an intention to develop consensus.

These moves, in the UK, across Europe and in the US, as well as in other countries, fit closely with the expressed intentions of many governments. Their common view seems to be that consensus between owners and users is a more workable way forward than one much-lobbied alternative – legislative change incorporating a widening of users' rights in the digital media.

Both the UK government and the EU draft directives on the harmonization of copyright seem to place similar emphasis on licensing solutions. The strength of collective licensing in managing huge numbers of multiple, small rights transactions seems, for the moment at least, to be the rights management system of choice for the digital environment.

While there has been much progress towards reaching a shared view of what may be achieved by standard licensing, achieving a single standard licence is still some long way off and may never be achieved. This is because, firstly, it is difficult to imagine a single licence whose terms are wide enough to encompass every possibility while at the same time being concise enough to be manageable. It seems more likely that a range of standard licences may evolve, each designed to meet a particular range of common circumstances. Secondly, as a view of what might constitute a digital library begins to emerge on the library side of negotiations, and as publishers begin to find new and better ways of defining (and widening?) the rights they are able to offer, so licences will evolve. We are in a time of evolution.

It is not the intention here to provide a single model licence. National negotiations between library associations and publishers will in the first place provide you with standard licensing outcomes better suited to your wider needs, and in any event any licence set in print today will rapidly become outdated. My intention here is rather to set out a range of general principles that will enable licensees to take a realistic approach to negotiating a licence and to assess the real value of licences that may be on offer.

Standard licences also, however well fitted to the purpose, come with limitations. The first of these is the care with which they must be drafted. Small-scale multiple negotiations, while cumbersome in handling volume clearances, at least have the advantage of allowing licensees to learn and develop their new skills in the process of undertaking the work. Get something wrong in one licence and it is possible to pick up on the mistake and correct it in the next. Get it wrong under a standard or blanket licence and the consequences can be long lasting.

The second limitation is the need to define clearly a core activity for which the standard licence will secure the rights. Standardization, by definition, cannot cover every eventuality. It relies, therefore, on an accurate analysis of activity as follows:

- those essential core activities without which the project (the library) will fail

- those activities that are attractive but not absolutely essential to the core
- peripheral activities which, however attractive, are unlikely either to arise or to be used in any meaningful way.

In drafting and negotiating a licence, the analysis should be used to define both the licence and the negotiations. The core activity is essential. It must be obtainable within budget (if not, then the material should be dropped) and cannot be bargained away in the course of negotiation. The surrounding activity may be secured under option (secure now, pay later). The fringe activities may be used as bargaining or negotiating points in the course of arriving at an agreed licensing arrangement.

Before going on to examine the structure and meaning of a typical standard licence in detail, I want to spend a little time in analysing the structure of the relationship between licensor and licensee. Just what is the licence supposed to deliver? Why is there a need to use a licence at all? Well, because there must be a grant of rights from the licensor (the publisher) to the licensee (the library). This is turn has implications for the two parties. Firstly, publishers can only grant or licence the rights that they control. If electronic rights have been retained by the author, or imbedded third-party materials have not been cleared for use in electronic formats, or the publication dates from a time when electronic rights were not anticipated, then the publisher will simply not be able to license electronic use. In circumstances such as these, some publishers may license material for electronic use by licensing those parts of the work for which they do have electronic rights but excluding those parts for which they do not. This option, which is sometimes employed by picture archives, for example, should be avoided wherever possible. Such licences will place an additional responsibility upon licensees to clear all copyright content.

The licence

This section looks at the most common components of any licence with a commentary on the purpose of each, together with the implications that each section has for the coherence of the licence as a whole and for the user.

Copyright licensing is determined by the conjunction of three elements: copyright law, contract law and the capabilities of the relevant technology. Publishers licensing the use of their copyright use the acts restricted by copyright as tools in order to define the extent of any licence. You should become familiar with the restricted acts in order to help you analyse your intended use of materials (and, therefore, licensing requirements). In UK copyright law the restricted acts are, in lay terms:

copying
issuing copies to the public
performing, showing or playing to the public
broadcasting
adapting
storing in any electronic medium
rental and lending
importing infringing copies
dealing in infringing copies
providing means for making infringing copies
provision of premises or apparatus for making infringing copies
provision of premises or apparatus for infringing performances
authorizing infringement.

In assessing licensing requirements, one would analyse the delivery process from supplier to end user. Which of the restricted acts are committed along the way? In the case of digital libraries, securing the right to copy, store in an electronic medium, issue copies to the public, perform, show or play to the public, adapt, rent and lend are obvious and essential components of any licence, though circumstances may change from library to library.

There are other restricted acts, however, which are less obviously related to libraries but which libraries may commit inadvertently and which should be avoided. These are acts that derive from staff or guidelines giving instructions to users to commit restricted acts. Libraries should be careful both to avoid *authorizing* activity that could be construed as infringing and to give users sufficient guidance on their responsibilities under copyright law, so as to avoid any suggestion that library equipment or facilities are being used for the purposes of infringement.

Balancing the copyright owner's monopoly right in controlling the use and exploitation of the work are fair dealing provisions or defences covering the free use of material for the purposes of criticism or review, research and private study, and so on. To these must be added the fact that it is possible to use an insubstantial portion of a work without charge. (If infringement depends upon using a *substantial* part of a work, then use of an *insubstantial* part does not infringe.) Libraries will be familiar with those provisions that apply to them and they are outlined in Chapter 4. However, the continuing availability of fair dealing exceptions and defences is under threat.

The threat to fair dealing provisions comes from both the technical characteristics of digital media and the use of contractual (licensing) conditions to override the provisions of copyright legislation.

Let us first examine the impact that the technical constraints of the digital environment may impose on the licensing culture. In the early days of broadcast television, the absence of playback facilities meant that in order to repeat the screening of a play the entire cast had to reassemble and perform the work again. This led to the practice of performers being paid repeat fees. Even following the introduction of recording technology, the practice was retained because by then the additional payments had become a recognized part of the culture. So the limitations of the technology had a direct impact upon the licensing and payment for rights in performances. In a similar way, the impossibility of developing digital technology that will identify and recognize the intent behind access to a digitized work (because intention is what determines the degree to which the fair dealing provision may apply) is a driver behind the argument that fair dealing provision does not apply in a digital environment. The fact that this argument coincides with the commercial interests of rights owners adds to its potency. It should be resisted. It is important for libraries (and other users) to retain provisions for fair dealing.

It has been argued by some that contractual undertakings freely entered into in a licensing agreement override provisions made under copyright law. Others argue that licensees cannot be forced to waive their access to fair dealing provision. The position is, therefore, confused. For the sake of clarity and in the interests of preventing the erosion of their statutory rights, licensees are advised to insist upon the inclusion of a clause stating that nothing in the licence shall be deemed to affect any statutory rights that may be granted under copyright law. A simple clause such as the following may be used: 'Nothing in this licence shall in any way exclude, alter or affect any statutory provision relating to acts permitted in relation to copyright works under the applicable national copyright legislation.'

Licence structure

All licences follow the same basic structure: an introductory section setting out the aims of the agreement and describing or defining the parties; a central section setting out the terms of the agreement (licence) itself, and a final nuts-and-bolts section dealing with issues of termination, applicable law, etc. The rest of this chapter addresses the more typical contractual elements in sequence.

Introduction

The licence will often commence with a brief introduction (or *recitals*) giving an outline of what the contract is intended to achieve. While it is easy to see this introductory section as being somehow separate from the body of the contract, it gives the context in which the rest of the contract may be interpreted in case of dispute and so should be treated with the same degree of respect accorded to the rest of the contract.

In this contextual role, the introductory section forms a connection with two other sections that also serve to address the interpretation of the contract: the *definitions* and the choice of *applicable law*. Of these, the selection of applicable law (the jurisdiction to which the parties agree to submit in interpreting the contract) is perhaps the most straightforward, as the jurisdiction of choice should always be your own – primarily, though not exclusively, for reasons of cost.

The definitions are much more contentious and should be approached with care. We have discussed previously the way in which the digital library is defined by the licence rather than by its capacity to store and display physical objects. In determining the definitions that will operate the licence, the parties are, to a large extent, determining many of the licensing features.

The definitions are an agreed, short, clearly defined interpretation of the larger concepts underlying the licence. What, for instance, is meant by the phrase 'the library' in an agreement between a publisher and a library? Is it the physical library building or the user community? Definitions will specify the parties to the licence and the licensing terms. As a general rule, the licensor will attempt to define the rights granted under licence as narrowly as possible, while the licensee will attempt to negotiate definitions that broaden the grant of rights under licence. As a brief but useful example, consider how you might define the body of users who will have access to a digital library. A definition that specifies a body of users simply as students of a university excludes from its definition use by any other category of user (including staff of the university). You might feel that staff use is something that would not be overlooked but what about other, less obvious user groups such as walk-in users, students accessing other campus libraries during vacations, reciprocal use or access by other libraries, and so on.

The physical location of the library may also be subject to definition. In arriving at a site licence, how should one best define the 'site'? Is it enough to limit the licence to a physical location (library premises located at the campus of a particular university?) or should the site be defined in terms of the institution? Is remote access from halls of residence or departmental centres or other remote users intended or required?

The answers to these questions will vary enormously according to individual conditions appropriate to each licence. Approach the task of defining the licence carefully. While the rights granted under the licence will be subject to separate definition in the central section of the licence, the definitions of the key players and the wider concepts underlying the licence are crucial to the licensee's ability to exercise the rights granted under licence.

Some licences attempt to subdivide users into two (or more) categories in an attempt to mirror current or traditional library models. Of these, the two most common categories are 'authorized users' (members of the institution) and 'walk-in users' (casual or drop-in users). The two groups may be given different levels of access under licence and may be further subdivided by differentiating between *ad-hoc* users who are members of the public and those who are, for example, users from another licensed institution simply making temporary use of the library (for example, students using another university's library during vacations).

What is important is that whatever definition you agree it is sufficient to cover your own identifiable user group. The four most common categories are based on the following user groups:

- members of the institution of which the licensed library is a part – staff and students of a university, for example
- users who are not members of the institution but who have access rights under a registration or access agreement
- users who are not registered – casual, *ad-hoc* or drop-in members of the public
- users who are registered with the library under an access agreement but who access the materials remotely, not by using on-site work stations.

The site itself may also be defined in this section. Site definitions should not be limited to the physical site of the library itself but should extend to cover other possible access points, such as halls of residence, regional offices, lodgings and homes of members, etc.

Central section

The central section of the licence will be taken up by the Agreement itself. Although the licence is the sum of its parts and the central section cannot be interpreted in isolation, this is often seen as the core of the contract. It sets out the rights that are being bought or licensed. It differs from the recitals section in that whereas the recitals may deal in wishes, desires, intentions and objectives, the Agreement must be stated in terms that can be clearly defined and are grounded in the practicalities of buying or licensing services or goods. In the case of a licence covering access to or use of digitized works, this will take the form of defining the rights being licensed, the price being paid and the scheduling and calculation of payment. It is an inclusive listing of the rights you are acquiring. If it subsequently emerges that you have neglected to cover rights that you need to exercise, there are only two possible outcomes: you have to live with a licence that does not meet your requirements fully or you have to renegotiate an extended licence, probably at additional cost.

The central section, therefore, focuses on the grant of rights. This defines what the licensee and its users are able to do with the materials licensed under the agreement. The needs of users are key. Users cannot be encouraged or authorized to perform activities that are not covered by the acquisition of rights. Make sure that the analysis of institutional and user requirements carried out as a preliminary to the negotiation of the licence is reflected in listing the rights acquired. It is essential that this list is a comprehensive and realistic reflection of the analysis. Any activities not covered by the listing will limit your ability to meet the objectives identified in the analysis. Remember, too, that the listing must be realistic. The more you buy, the more you pay. The wider the range of rights sought under licence, the more you may encounter rights owners' inability or reluctance to licence. This is a game that you are engaged in, a game in which the desire of licensees to licence as widely as possible at the lowest cost plays against the licensor's desire to retain control over the material in question. By so doing, rights owners seek to derive maximum benefit from the digital market by using licences to slice the rights available more thinly at maximum revenue. A similar game will also be played between primary and secondary rights owners for control over the use of the material and the revenue accruing from it. For example, publishers may not be in a position to license their entire catalogue. Authors may control the electronic rights in some work(s) and not have licensed them to their publisher. Should this be so, the publisher may be unable to license the rights you require. (The outcome of this, of course, is that the publisher should warrant that they own or control the rights you are acquiring under licence. Unless they do so, you may discover that you are subject to subsequent claims from other rights owners – authors, for instance – claiming licensing payments in respect of their own work. You might even be forced to withdraw the work from use. The licensor's warranties would be detailed in the latter stages of the contract.)

While the rights you seek under licence will vary from library to library, some of the more common requirements are listed below:

- the right to access the rights owner's server/or to digitize hard-copy originals
- the right to store the licensed materials electronically
- the right to make the materials available on the library's system infrastructure and information services
- the right to index the materials
- the right to make the materials accessible to users (as set out in the definitions section of the licence) for the purposes of research, teaching and (private) study

- the right to permit users to print materials and/or to download materials for the purposes specified above
- the right to permit the reproduction and inclusion of hard or soft copies of the materials in course packs.

The rights listed are, typically, those that the majority of rights owners are comfortable in licensing. They will as a rule relate to the digitization and use of materials in a way that maintains the integrity of the original documents, that is the right to manipulate content will not generally be licensed. In some current licences this restriction may take the form of specifying the electronic format in which the digitized works are licensed. For example, use in portable document format (PDF) only may be specified. There are disadvantages associated with specifying use in terms of format as opposed to specifying a form of use or function. By specifying PDF as the licensed format, the licensor and licensee are attempting to ensure that the integrity of the materials will be respected by means of a format that does not allow manipulation. They run the risk that PDF may become outdated over time and the licence may date alongside it. It would be better to specify that the licensee warrants that the integrity of the work will be maintained by means of using only formats that prevent manipulation. In that way the user is not tied into using a single, specified format that may become outdated over time as the technologies of the new media develop.

The specification of format is associated with other restrictions that are placed upon licensees. These are stated alongside the rights granted in the licence. The most common restrictions are:

- use by means of any network that is not secure
- use by persons who are not registered and issued with a password or other, similarly secure means of identification
- systematic reproduction
- distribution, loan or sale outside the defined library user group
- sub-licensing to third parties
- interlibrary loan.

You may also find that this section is often where an attempt is made to impose restrictions on the licensee's ability to make use of national fair dealing provisions.

Other restrictions

Other restrictions on the limit of the licence may not be expressed in terms of rights limitations but will have an equal effect on your use of the material.

The licence will have a *term*: start and finish dates. The commencement of the licence and the termination of the licence should be agreed and specified. The question of what happens as the termination date approaches also needs to be addressed and agreed. What are your exit options? While the termination date will be fixed, earlier cancellation will be possible if there is a fundamental breach of the licence or if a partner becomes insolvent or if either party is capable of terminating the agreement by giving the other an agreed period of notice of cancellation.

You must avoid becoming tied to a contract that has no termination date or termination facility. A contract that does not specify an agreed means of termination may oblige the library to continue paying for rights and services that it no longer requires. You must also deal with the issue of continuing access or right to use the materials after termination. One fundamental difference between subscribing to a hard-copy journal and an electronic journal is that if your hard-copy subscription ends, you may continue to keep and make use of your archive copies. When a licence to use electronic material ends, there is a possibility that the right to access and use the materials ends with it. The right to continuing access and user rights is not automatically granted, and unless provision is made in the licence you may find that your ability to use the material is limited to the duration of the licence. Negotiate the right to continued access and use of materials. Licensors will insist on a reciprocal commitment from the licensees regarding limitations on use, manipulation and respect for the integrity of the material and continuing compliance with security conditions.

Delivery and payment

What is the licensor undertaking to provide the licensee? Before agreeing to a licence you must be sure that the licensor undertakes to supply you with the services that you are expecting and require. Will the licensor provide materials in the form of electronic files – if so, in what form and by what date? Will the materials not be supplied but rather be made available under a licensee's right to access the licensor's server – if so, how and by what date? Or are the materials to be digitized by the licensee from hard copies already owned by the licensee? A licence may well cover all three possibilities. We have examined above the necessity of having a warranty from the licensor, which sets out the breadth and the nature of the rights controlled and granted so as to avoid the possibility of licensees' being hit twice by claims or counterclaims from several rights owners claiming to hold rights in the same material.

It is important to understand also the requirements of the licensor. Licensees, too, have responsibilities under any licence. We have seen how limitations imposed on licensees centre on rights owners' legitimate concerns that the integrity of material is respected. As well as limiting the rights granted, these concerns will be reflected in a desire for licensees to warrant that they will respect the licence terms and will do so in respect of both the institution, its employees and licensed users. This often takes the form of the licensee's undertaking to cooperate with rights owners in informing them of actual or potential breaches of their rights and in undertaking to be responsible and liable for the actions of the licensee's own staff and licensed users. While licensees may be able to commit themselves to this warranty in respect of staff, they will be vulnerable to the actions of licensed users. Here it is reasonable for licensees to be responsible for the actions of users only insofar as the licensee has been negligent in failing to make users aware of licence restrictions and to set in place codes of practice, including disciplinary codes, to handle instances of rights infringement. Licensees must be diligent. Avoid authorizing users to perform infringing acts. Once a possible breach has been identified, licensees must be speedy in keeping licensors informed and in bringing the infringement to a close. They must not collude, either openly or by omission, in any continuing breach of the licence.

Payment, of course, is an undertaking performed by the licensee. But what form will the payment take? As well as the total cost (and you should make certain that the fee quoted really is the total – that there are no hidden extras) you will want to consider how the fee is calculated. Is it an annual licensing fee, for instance? If so, will it be based on user numbers or on sampled usage? Who will pay? Are any of the costs for individual transactions met by users or is the entire licence fee met centrally? In addition to specifying the licence fee, the licence will make provision for how the fee will be paid, by whom, when the fee is due (in full or by instalments?) and how it will be calculated.

Standard conditions

The final part of the licence will include standard licensing clauses specifying under which legislation the contract will operate, how disputes may be settled, a reference to what happens if the contract is damaged by uncontrollable or unavoidable circumstances (*force majeure*) and a commitment by the parties to meet their responsibilities. Choose your own national courts in preference to any other. Discuss the possibility of submitting to agreed arbitration, for example by representatives from the national library and publishers' associations. Avoid non-specific phraseology in describing how undertakings will be performed. Contracts should minimize dispute, not generate room for further argument: the use of broad, descriptive phrases – such as 'best endeavours' – that are difficult to assess objectively provoke additional discussion in the case of dispute. Courts in common law jurisdictions, such as the UK, are notoriously loath to rule on guesswork about terms such as 'quality', 'reasonable', 'best', and so on, while those governed by civil codes may derive interpretations from loose phrasing that were not strictly intended.

Achieving a clearly defined contract is only possible if the parties themselves are clear about their intentions. Difficult though it may be to define requirements dispassionately and clearly, if the exercise helps to bring about a clear understanding within and between the parties then it is even more worthwhile and should be embraced fully.

Further information

This chapter has been written to provide a commentary on standard licensing agreements and to help you approach the business of negotiating a licence with confidence. It is not intended to replace the need for proper legal advice in drafting the licence itself. There are many sources of advice readily available. Of these, the most useful may come from your national library associations and the standard licence formats that many national associations have agreed with publishers' representatives and with collective licensing bodies representing publishers, authors, music rights owners, and so on. The principles of the approach outlined in this chapter are not intended to replace the use of standard, agreed licences recommended by national or other representative bodies. For advice tailored to the needs of your own circumstances, speak to your national association. For further background advice and shared experience, the following list of web resources will be useful.

Model licensing clauses (all sites visited 01/02/1999)

Copyright Licensing Agency, information at
    http://www.cla.co.uk
Definitions of common words and phrases,
    http://www.library.yale.edu/~llicense/definiti.shtml
European Bureau of Library, Information and Documentation Associations (EBLIDA), information at
    http://www.kaapeli.fi/~eblida
European Copyright Users Platform (ECUP) heads of agreements,
    http://www.eblida.org/ecup/
JISC/PA Working Party, 'Proposed model licence between UK universities and publishers',
    http://www.ukoln.ac.uk
Journal Storage Project (JSTOR) library license agreement,
    http://www.jstor.org/about/license.html

UK National Electronic Site Licence Initiative (NESLI) site licence,
   http://www.nesli.ac.uk

Licensing principles

American Association of Law Libraries, American Library Association, Association of
   Academic Health Science Libraries, Association of Research Libraries, Medical
   Library Association, Special Libraries Association: principles for licensing elec-
   tronic resources,
   http://www.arl.org/scomm/licensing/principles.html
International Coalition of Library Consortia, information at
   http://www.library.yale.edu/consortia/statement.html
National Humanities Alliance, 'Basic principles for managing intellectual property in
   the digital environment',
   http://www-ninch.cni.org/ISSUES/COPYRIGHT/PRINCIPLES/NHA_
   Complete.html
Tilbury Library. Guidelines and checklist for libraries,
   http://cwis.kuk.nl/~dbi/english/license/lcpnnc.ntm
University of California Libraries, 'Principles for acquiring and licensing information in
   digital formats',
   http://sunsite.berkeley.edu/Info/principles.html
WPU/IWI Scientific and Professional Publishers of the Dutch Publishers Association
   covenant for electronic information,
   http://www.surfbureau.nl/iwicovenant.htm

Intellectual property

Australian Copyright Council, information at
   http://www.copyright.org.au
Open Information Interchange (OII) (European Commission Info 2000), 'Guide to
   intellectual property rights for electronic information exchange',
   http://www2.echo.lu/oii/en/iprguide.html

Discussion forums

Discussion on copyright collectives and libraries,
   http://www.mcgrawhill.ca/copyrightlaw/collect.html
EBLIDA,
   http://www.eblida.org/

Examples of commercial contracts

Academic Press Print and Electronic Access License (APPEAL),
    http://www.apnet.com/www/ap/genlay.htm
MCB University Press, information at
    http://www.mcb.co.uk

10

Information security management

Tony Hadland

The author is Information Manager for Barclays Property Holdings Limited, a subsidiary of Barclays Bank plc. The opinions, views and recommendations set out in this chapter are the author's and do not necessarily represent those of Barclays Property Holdings Limited or Barclays Bank plc.

Introduction

The spread of information security management

Information security management is clearly a growth area. Twenty years ago it was largely confined to governments, which have always been obsessive about such matters. In the early 1980s it spread to the financial services industry. The telecommunications companies and the oil industry then adopted it, and by the early 1990s the rest of industry was taking the subject seriously.

Now information security management is being adopted on a wider scale. Furthermore, many organizations already committed to it are revisiting the subject. This is because of factors such as:

- an ever greater dependence on IT
- an increasing use of networks to provide links between geographically separate sites, and with both suppliers and customers
- new business opportunities offered by electronic commerce
- changing patterns of employment that reduce the loyalty of employees
- the threat of sophisticated industrial and commercial espionage, heightened by easy availability of expertise previously deployed in the Cold War.

For many organizations information security management (referred to hereafter as InfoSec) is therefore becoming a necessity rather than an option.

Involvement of information professionals

Among information professionals, attitudes to InfoSec will differ. It may be perceived variously as:

- an unwelcome complication
- a necessary evil
- a welcome enhancement to the information infrastructure
- a necessity to ensure organizational survival
- an opportunity for career development.

Like it or not, InfoSec is now a fact of life. In many cases the information management infrastructure cannot survive without it. It will therefore increasingly impinge on information professionals, many of whom will accrue InfoSec responsibilities of some sort. In some cases these will include high-level responsibility for creating, implementing and managing InfoSec programmes.

Many information professionals will take the view that active involvement in InfoSec is preferable to passive acceptance. They will also welcome the fact that interest in InfoSec highlights the perceived value of the information they manage.

Scope of this chapter

This chapter provides an introduction to InfoSec. In so doing it gives an overview of:

- the purpose of InfoSec
- its basic aims
- policy areas to address
- the components of a security architecture
- key elements of an InfoSec awareness programme.

The principles set out are reasonably scalable and should prove a useful basis for the development of an InfoSec programme, regardless of the size of an organization. Small, uncomplicated organizations may be able to omit certain policy areas cited below. Highly specialized concerns, on the other hand, may need to address some matters not covered. But on the whole what follows should have wide application.

A generalist approach

As with the medical profession, there are many specialisms within InfoSec. For example, there are people who work full-time on matters such as encryption (see Appendix 3) or firewalls (Appendix 4). However, detailed knowledge of such subjects is not normally required by an information manager such as this author, whose role in InfoSec is likely to be more akin to that of a general practitioner. The GP deals with the day-to-day matters, the long-term relationship, the big picture, yet has sufficient awareness and knowledge of specialist areas to enable reference to the right specialist at the appropriate time. The same should normally apply to an information professional with responsibility for InfoSec.

BS 7799

British Standard BS 7799 is a 'Code of Practice for Information Security Management' and was formally adopted in February 1995. Unlike many traditional standards, it is not particularly prescriptive, as its foreword makes clear: 'As a Code of Practice, this British Standard takes the form of guidance and recommendations. It should not be quoted as if it were a specification, and in particular care should be taken to ensure that claims of compliance are not misleading.' Most of the standard describes a series of 109 controls, these being grouped into 10 sections. As with the ISO 9000 series of standards on quality management, whether or not an organization formally adopts BS 7799 will depend on factors such as:

- will clients or customers impose it?
- will the organization wish to impose it on others, such as suppliers and consultants?
- is there advantage in adopting it as an internal standard?

Regardless of whether they formally adopt the standard, reference to the code of practice may well prove useful to information professionals wishing to learn more about InfoSec. For contact details see Appendix 5.

Purpose of information security management

Why information security management? At the highest level, the purpose of InfoSec is to protect an organization's information assets from all threats. In so doing, business continuity must be assured and the impact of security incidents minimized.

A further aim is to protect the reputation of the organization.

Information assets

What are these information assets? Obviously many comprise computer-based information – network traffic and material held on servers, hard disk, diskette, tape and optical disk. But they also include information held on or transmitted via paper, microform, fax, telephone and the spoken word.

The key factor is the *importance* of the asset, rather than the sophistication of the medium on which it is stored, or through which it is accessed.

Threats

The threats to an organization's assets may be:

- internal
- external
- deliberate
- accidental.

In each of these cases the threat may be sudden or incremental. There is an analogy here with buildings, where undetected woodworm can, over time, do more damage than a small explosion.

The balance of risk

The aim should be to safeguard information assets *adequately*. As with all risk management, there is a balance to be struck between the cost of control and the cost of loss. It is not the role of InfoSec to stifle opportunity, but rather to *enable* it.

Basic aims

To achieve the purpose set out above, all InfoSec policies and procedures serve one or more of three basic aims. A widely adopted security-evocative mnemonic for these is *CIA*. This stands for:

- confidentiality
- integrity
- availability.

Confidentiality covers the protection of valuable or sensitive information from unauthorized disclosure or interception – for example, hacking, bugging, electronic or aural eavesdropping, and physical theft of paperwork or electronic media.

Integrity is the safeguarding of the completeness and accuracy of information, by protecting it against unauthorized modification, whether accidental or deliberate.

Availability means ensuring that the organization's information assets are available in a usable form whenever required. It implies such measures as backup regimes, uninterruptible power supplies, equipment duplication, support staff availability and the whole issue of business continuity planning.

Key policy areas

To achieve the aims of confidentiality, integrity and availability, a practical approach is to address seven key policy areas:

1 responsibility and accountability
2 release of intellectual property
3 risk assessment and management
4 legislation and regulation
5 access to systems and networks
6 integrity and audit
7 business continuity planning.

Responsibility and accountability

Responsibility and accountability for maintaining the required level of InfoSec must be assigned to, and accepted by, all information users within the scope of their job function. However, there are typically four categories of people with more specific responsibilities and accountabilities:

- chief executive officer and senior managers
- information security manager
- InfoSec policy owners
- system sponsors.

Chief executive officer and senior managers

It is vital to secure the support and 'buy in' of the CEO and senior managers within the organization. They must accept ultimate responsibility for ensuring:

- successful implementation of security mechanisms and procedures

- adequate security awareness of their staff
- provision of appropriate skills and expertise to enable security responsibilities to be met.

The head of each major department or business stream should also be responsible for appointing an information security manager (ISM) to provide specialist support. In smaller organizations, one ISM can serve several departments.

Information security manager

The ISM is the custodian of security standards and is responsible for:

- ensuring security controls and solutions meet policy and business requirements
- providing and supporting suitable standards, procedures and solutions to enable implementation of the required level of security
- ensuring security standards keep pace with new equipment and technology
- improving and monitoring general staff awareness of InfoSec requirements.

In a large organization there may be several ISMs. If so, close liaison between them should be encouraged and an informal InfoSec community created. Within this community the principle of 'constructive plagiarism' of InfoSec documentation can prevent unnecessary duplication and foster consistency of approach.

In some cases an ISM will recruit *local security coordinators* (LSCs) from among the staff of departments or business streams. In InfoSec terms LSCs are the equivalent of special constables or reservists. They have normal full-time jobs but can rapidly be deployed on key InfoSec matters when needed.

LSCs also help ensure that an appropriate risk balance is maintained. On the one hand, they act as the eyes and ears of the ISM in their area. On the other, they ensure that their area's organizational or business aims are given appropriate support by InfoSec and are not stifled by unnecessarily onerous controls.

Policy owners

The ownership, communication and implementation monitoring of InfoSec policies must be clearly assigned. Depending on the scale of the organization, this may be the role of:

- a small specialist central body
- the ISM community, or
- a solo ISM.

Policies should not be devised unilaterally. They must reflect the aims of the organization. It is therefore essential that they are signed-off by the CEO or a senior nominee. Without this it can be extremely difficult to 'sell' within the organization the need for the policy.

System sponsors

It is advisable to designate a system sponsor for each major IT service, such as operating systems, networks and major business applications. The system sponsor should be drawn from the line management of the relevant department or business unit.

System sponsors are responsible for:

- liasing with the ISM
- ensuring their systems comply with InfoSec policy requirements
- accepting the security risks inherent in their systems.

Audit

Ideally the functioning of InfoSec within the organization should be audited on a regular basis. Some large organizations may have internal audit functions with adequate skills and independence. Others might need to engage the services of an external specialist consultancy.

It is important that the audit function be independent of the ISM function.

Release of intellectual property

Most organizations have a fundamental need to protect their intellectual property. Therefore a policy is required to ensure that software, systems and other intellectual information compiled or developed by or for the organization are:

- the property of the organization
- suitably protected by copyright legislation
- not used, sold or copied externally, or provided to third parties, without formal authorization.

Special measures may be needed to determine ownership in joint venture situations.

Risk assessment and management

In some cases the level or stringency of InfoSec control measures may be predicated by policy. In most other cases these factors should be determined by formal risk assessment. A policy is therefore needed to cover this aspect.

Risk assessments are used to identify:

- specific risks
- their potential impact on the organization
- appropriate levels of control to counter any identified risks.

A number of formal risk assessment methodologies exist. Their complexity varies according to the organizational criticality of the risk. The methodologies employed by the author in his role are those published by the European Security Forum (ESF):

- SARA (Simple to Apply Risk Assessment), for business-critical systems
- SPRINT (Simplified Process for Risk Identification), a simplified derivative of SARA for less critical systems
- OSCAR (Optimized System for CArrying out Risk assessments), a PC-based risk assessment tool derived from SARA.

For ESF contact details see Appendix 5.

Legislation and regulation

Policy should reflect the need to comply with legislation applicable to the local environment. The organization may operate branches beyond its home jurisdiction, in territories with less stringent legal requirements. In such cases it may make a policy that the *spirit* of relevant home (e.g. UK) legislation should apply, provided it does not conflict with other local laws. Conversely, if local laws are more stringent then *they* should apply.

In policies on legislation and regulation it is common to highlight certain key topics, especially:

- software copyright
- computer misuse
- protection of personal data.

Software copyright

Policy should stress that:

* copying and use of software shall be in strict accordance with the terms and conditions of the software licence
* unauthorized use or copying of software by employees or agents is prohibited.

Computer misuse

The organization's IT resources shall be used only for authorized purposes. Specifically, they shall not be used to:

* copy, store, create or distribute illegal or offensive material
* copy or distribute material in contravention of copyright
* perform private business processing.

Personal data

Personal data must be maintained in strict accordance with:

* relevant local legislation
* the terms and conditions under which it is obtained, stored and used.

Access to systems and networks

This is a major topic, with policy requirements in the following five areas:

1   third-party access
2   PC security
3   physical protection of IT equipment
4   IT connectivity
5   dial-in security.

The underlying requirement is that all access or connection to the organization's IT resources shall be:

* formally authorized and authenticated (i.e. positively recognized)
* accountable to an individual.

Systems must be able to detect potentially unauthorized access and take appropriate evasive action. (For example, by barring access completely after three unsuccessful attempts to use a password.)

Third-party access

Access by third parties to the organization's IT resources or data shall be subject to a formal contract or service level agreement (SLA). This must address security and control issues, and define responsibility for them.

The organization must designate someone to:

* manage the contractual relationship
* monitor third-party compliance against the contract or SLA.

PC security

All PCs used to store or process the organization's information must have controls in place to:

* identify and authenticate all their users (e.g. via log-on IDs and passwords)
* prevent introduction of malicious code (e.g. viruses)
* trace all access to its originating source.

Specific controls may be necessary for portable PCs. For example, to minimize the risk of unauthorized access to information held on the PC, automatic encryption of the hard disk may be employed (see Appendix 3).

Physical security of equipment

To minimize risk of damage, tampering, unauthorized use or theft, the organization's IT equipment must be appropriately physically protected.

The level of protection must be commensurate with:

* the criticality or sensitivity of the data or function supported
* business requirements
* equipment value
* assessment of any associated risks.

IT connectivity

Care is needed when connecting the organization's computers and networks to those owned or managed by third parties, including public networks – *how much* will depend on the nature of the business transacted and the trustworthiness of the third parties.

Connections should not be permitted except where:

- formally authorized by the ISM, system sponsor and, where appropriate, the CEO
- all risks have been formally assessed
- the connection prevents, or at least detects, attempts by unauthorized users to access the system (e.g. a firewall is in place – see Appendix 4).

Dial-in security

Demand for dial-in access to networks and information systems is increasing, particularly as more people work from home. If not properly controlled, dial-in can make the organization's networks and systems easily accessible to unauthorized individuals via a public telephone network.

To counter this, dial-in access should be only through an authorized entry point, which uses a strong authentication mechanism, to ensure that person's trying to access the system or network are who they claim to be. Typically this might employ a *one-time password*, possibly combined with *dial-back*.

A *one-time password* is especially secure as it is generated for a specific person to use once only. The password is an apparently random string of characters. It is produced either by software on the PC or by a credit card size electronic token. The password generator is synchronized with the network/system access control, which can identify a valid one-time password.

Dial-back involves the network/system control terminating the incoming telephone call via which authentication has been achieved, and then dialling back the caller's pre-registered telephone number. This is to verify that the call has indeed come from that number.

The ISM should be made responsible for ensuring authorization and documenting of entry points.

Integrity and audit

The underlying requirements of this policy are twofold. System sponsors must:

- be assured that controls are in place, to give them confidence that a system has been correctly designed and developed to meet essential business functionality
- ensure that data and functions of the system are protected from unauthorized change, and that attempts to make such changes can be detected.

To achieve this, four main topics need to be addressed:

- use of third-party software
- system development security
- integrity of the live business environment
- audit and review.

Use of third-party software

When purchasing software, assurance must be obtained that the developer or supplier can provide adequate levels of support and maintenance. Where there is any doubt, and the software is employed as part of a critical system, consideration should be given to an escrow arrangement for the source code, in case the developer goes out of business.

System development security

The development and testing environment must be managed and controlled to ensure that the final products function correctly and as authorized.

Integrity of the live business environment

The system sponsor must ensure that the live system's software and data is protected against unauthorized modification, whether accidental or deliberate.

Audit and review

Where an auditing process is employed in respect of security and control of systems, the systems must be capable of producing supporting evidence. This evidence must enable transactions to be traced for their entire passage through the system. Critical or sensitive activity performed by individual users should also be traceable.

Business continuity planning

A business continuity plan (BCP) details the steps necessary for a business to continue functioning in the event of a crisis or disaster. Business continuity planning has much wider scope than InfoSec. However, the IT contingency plan forms a key part of the overall business continuity plan.

A typical BCP policy would require that:

- each location and department/business stream has a business continuity plan
- the detail and scope of the plan must be appropriate to the assessed risks
- each plan has a designated crisis manager with complete authority to manage a crisis or disaster
- departments/business streams must make adequate budget provision for BCP
- plans must be tested at least annually.

The IT contingency plan should form part of the overall BCP and require the following:

- all critical computer facilities and resources must have a formal contingency plan
- contingency facilities must be commensurate with assessed risks
- the IT contingency plan must be formally documented and cover:
  – survival – the period immediately following the incident
  – recovery – a planned and orderly return to normal operations
- adequate budgeting and testing procedures must be in place.

Establishing a security architecture

Having established policies in the seven key subject areas, how best should these policies be implemented?

In the long term it is ineffective to address security weaknesses in a piecemeal fashion, as and when problems arise. Generally this type of tactical approach leads to operational inefficiencies and high administration overheads.

It should therefore be a policy requirement that an IT security architecture be adopted and implemented. Just as a building's architecture brings together and integrates its disparate constructional, technical and functional elements, so an IT security architecture pulls together key elements of InfoSec.

The objective is to take a strategic (rather than tactical) approach, and thereby to:

- minimize administrative overheads

- simplify user interfaces
- facilitate interoperability.

A good approach is to take each brief InfoSec policy statement and develop subsidiary codes of practice. These codes set out how to implement the policy. They may be relatively high level and generic, dealing with performance criteria and general technical requirements. Alternatively (or additionally) they may fully specify technical solutions. Much will depend on the type of organization, the risks it faces, their volatility, and the InfoSec resources available.

Appendix 1 provides an example of a policy statement with an associated code of practice. A checklist of sample policy statements to consider for a security architecture is given in Appendix 2.

Baseline controls

Often, especially in larger organizations, it is cost effective to establish a set of baseline controls rather than to re-invent security solutions for each system. Effort can then be concentrated on providing any necessary additional controls over and above the baseline.

Hence a local area network and the PCs connected to it running ordinary desktop packages might be subject merely to baseline controls, whereas a financial management system and a wide area network accessed via the same LAN might require additional controls above the baseline.

Risk assessment techniques would be used to determine when additional controls are needed and which issues they need to address.

Dispensation procedure

Successful implementation of InfoSec necessitates making compliance with its policies mandatory. Exceptional circumstances, however, may make full compliance impossible in the short term. There should therefore be provision for the head of department or business stream to request a *temporary* dispensation.

A careful balance needs to be struck here: 'dispensation on demand' would seriously undermine InfoSec. Therefore temporary dispensations must be considered in terms of impact and duration, and only permitted if both are acceptable to the organization.

Dispensation requests should be routed through the ISM to the policy owners for adjudication. Depending on the impact and risks involved, referral to the CEO may be necessary.

Running an awareness programme

Although technology can considerably assist InfoSec, it is equally important to invest in raising the security awareness of all staff. This may be done by a variety of methods.

At the most basic level it is important to ensure that new recruits are made aware of key security policies. A brief 'Ten Commandments of IT Security' document may be handed to new recruits. In some cases it may be appropriate that they sign a copy. Indeed, it might form part of their contract of employment.

Commonly a warning message may be incorporated into the PC log-on process, perhaps directing users to a screen-based summary of security requirements. However, once the new recruit settles in it is easy to become blind to log-on messages, and to forget what was read on joining. Mechanisms are therefore needed to deepen security awareness and relate it to the IT user's own situation.

Seminars based on use of information security videos are a good approach, especially when supported by good quality booklets or leaflets that staff can retain for reference. Some large organizations commission their own videos. Sometimes they make them available to others for whom a bespoke production would be prohibitively expensive.

Information security awareness programmes commonly cover more than just IT security. Topics likely to be included are:

- *incident reporting* – e.g. theft of equipment, or suspected virus infection
- *passwords* – cautions against sharing passwords, writing them down or not changing them regularly
- *fax and e-mail security* – confidentiality considerations and the possible need to confirm destinations
- *unauthorized software* – copyright issues and virus protection
- *laptop security* – secure storage of unattended machines, encryption of sensitive files, cautions against working on confidential information in public places
- *conversational security* – cautions against discussing sensitive matters in public places or on mobile telephones, particularly analogue ones
- *remote access security* – Internet and dial-in security
- *physical security* – challenging unknown individuals in the workplace, not leaving visitors unattended, ensuring security doors are kept shut, etc.
- *secure office* – locking away confidential information, whether on magnetic, optical or paper media, and ensuring screens cannot be overlooked by unauthorized persons
- *secure waste* – secure disposal of sensitive paper and other media

- *workstation* – switching off PCs at the end of the working day, and invoking password-protected screen savers when leaving the PC unattended
- *back-up* – ensuring regular back-ups are made, and that they are stored both on and off site.

Summary

The aim of this chapter has been to provide an introduction to information security management. In so doing it has highlighted the spread of InfoSec, the increasing involvement of information professionals, and the merits of a generalist approach that does not require deep specialist technical knowledge. Reference has also been made to the relevant British Standard, BS 7799.

The purpose of InfoSec – to protect an organization's information assets and reputation – has been explained. The types of threats to information assets have been outlined. Importantly, attention has been drawn to the need to strike a balance between the cost of control and the cost of loss: InfoSec should enable opportunity rather than stifle it.

The three basic aims of InfoSec – confidentiality, integrity and availability – have been identified. To achieve these three aims, seven key policy areas have been suggested: responsibility and accountability, release of intellectual property, risk assessment and management, legislation and regulation, access to systems and networks, integrity and audit, and business continuity planning.

To put the key policies into effect, the adoption and implementation of an IT security Architecture has been advocated. A policy checklist has been provided for consideration when creating such an architecture.

Finally, the need has been stressed to invest in raising the security awareness of all staff. Outline guidance has been provided and suggestions have been offered as to the main topics to cover.

The author hopes that readers will find this information useful in taking their first steps into the world of InfoSec.

Appendix 1

SAMPLE POLICY STATEMENT AND CODE OF PRACTICE

A security architecture foundation document typically comprises a series of policy statements and associated codes of practice, supported by appropriate background information. Below is an example dealing with dial-in access.

Example: dial-in access

Background

The provision of dial-in access to our networks and computing resources requires the use of public telecommunications facilities, which fall outside our control. It must be assumed that such environments are 'hostile'. This is particularly so when the connectivity is provided by, or interfaces with, public domain networks such as the Internet.

To protect our organization from this external environment, a boundary must be defined, through which only positively identified and authorized callers are able to pass.

Policy statement

Any dial-in access must be authorized. It must be via an approved entry point using a strong authentication mechanism.

Code of practice

1 The network service provider or local network owner must approve authentication mechanisms. In addition, the mechanism must be approved by the director of information systems and logged by the information security manager.
2 Two-factor authentication should be used. This would include:

   • user ID and password
   • a further more stringent means, such as a PIN-protected token that can enter into a challenge/response dialogue with the gateway.

3 Dial-back facilities in modems should be considered as a method of reinforcing authentication.

4 The details recorded about each entry point must include:

- reason or justification for access
- authorization for the entry point
- who is authorized to use the entry point
- authentication mechanism(s) used
- identity of system sponsor
- who is responsible for administration (for example, issuing authentication tokens).

5 Gateway users and access permissions must be reviewed on a regular basis.
6 Each gateway should present the unauthorized access warning screen advising unauthorized users not to attempt to access the system.
7 The gateway must provide sufficient management audit trails to allow activity to be reviewed. The trails should include:

- all successful and unsuccessful connections
- all management activities
- the destination of outward connections.

8 Depending on the nature of the system being accessed, the use of encryption, digital signature or message authentication techniques may be recommended by the information security manager.
9 PC logical access controls should be considered to enhance the security of PCs in insecure locations.

Appendix 2

SECURITY ARCHITECTURE POLICY CHECKLIST

This appendix provides a reasonably comprehensive checklist of topics to be considered in constructing a security architecture. For each topic a brief sample policy statement has been provided. These statements can be adopted, rejected, simplified or developed in accordance with your own organization's needs.

Lest any potential information security manager finds the checklist daunting, it may be comforting to note that InfoSec responsibilities are spread right across the organization, from temporary staff to senior management. Whilst the ISM has the key role, this does not involve taking ultimate responsibility. That rightly rests with the chief executive officer.

Introduction and overview

The purpose of the security architecture is to avoid security weaknesses and operational inefficiencies, facilitate interoperability, simplify interfaces and minimize administrative overheads.

- *Creating the IT security architecture:* the information security manager (ISM) will create, implement and maintain the IT security architecture.
- *Propagating the IT security architecture:* the ISM will propagate the security architecture.
- *Security architecture in system development:* the security architecture will provide direction for system development.
- *Ensuring conformance to the security architecture:* all security policies are mandatory. Ultimate responsibility for ensuring implementation lies with the chief executive officer.

Security responsibilities of individuals

All employees and agents who use IT resources are responsible for maintaining the required level of IT security for their job function.

- *Management IT security responsibilities:* managers with responsibility for users of IT resources are responsible for ensuring implementation and correct use of IT security mechanisms and procedures. They must ensure that the necessary knowledge, skills, expertise and documentation are available for staff to fulfil their IT security responsibilities.

- *General employee responsibilities:* permanent, temporary and contract staff and agents must be made aware of their responsibilities for IT security.
- *Information security management responsibilities:* the ISM is responsible for:
  - ensuring IT security controls meet business requirements
  - providing appropriate policies, standards, procedures and support to implement the required level of security
  - ensuring appropriate security standards are available prior to implementation of new equipment or technology
  - liaison with senior managers on matters concerning IT security
  - monitoring and raising staff security awareness.
- *Local security coordinators:* each senior manager will nominate an LSC who will be the routine point of contact with the ISM.
- *Responsibility for managing third party access:* all access to IT resources or data by third parties (such as outsourced services, contractors or consultants) will be subject to a formal contract or service level agreement. This will address security issues and define responsibility for them. A designated 'owner' will be responsible for the contractual relationship.

Employing staff

Management must minimize the possibility of employing an individual who represents an unacceptable security risk.

- *New employees:* All new employees must be familiarized with their responsibilities towards IT security.
- *Agency staff:* Agency staff should be hired only from approved agencies.
- *Termination of employment:* Procedures for termination or transfer of employment must ensure the maintenance of security for the information and systems to which the employee has had access.

Risk assessment and management

When not mandated by policy, IT security will be determined via a risk assessment. This will identify security risks and their impact on the organization, allowing appropriate controls to be applied.

- *Acceptance of risk:* security risks may be accepted for overriding business reasons. In such a case the risks must be properly analysed and justified by the system sponsor. The potential impact must not go beyond the sponsor's control.

- *Methodologies:* the risk assessment methodologies adopted will be those published by the European Security Forum.

Legislation and regulation

The IT environment will operate within the locally applicable law. In territories where specific legislation is less stringent than in the United Kingdom, the spirit of the UK legislation should be followed.

- *Compliance with legal and external obligations:* when considering legal and external obligations, advice should be sought from our legal advisors.
- *Data protection:* personal data will be collected, stored, maintained and used in strict accordance with legislative requirements.
- *Prevention of computer misuse:* IT resources will be used only for official purposes. They will not be used for private business processing; copying or distributing material that would breach copyright; or storing, copying or distributing illegal or offensive material. Prior to access, unauthorized users will be made aware that access is prohibited.
- *Software copyright:* copying and use of software will be in strict accordance with the software licence.
- *Release of intellectual information and proprietary products:* management responsible for IT systems will ensure that all products, tools and intellectual property developed by or for us remain our property.
- *Restriction of technical information:* technical information about our systems could provide an unauthorized user with sufficient knowledge to breach security. Knowledge must therefore be restricted to authorized persons that have a need to know.
- *Imposing appropriate controls:* these controls must ensure that systems and products developed by us are not sold or copied without appropriate authorization.

Systems access and authorization policy

All access or connection to IT resources will be formally authorized and authenticated, and accountable to an individual. Systems must be able to detect potentially unauthorized access and take evasive action. The ability of staff to use functions or access data will be limited to that appropriate to their role.

- *Log-on:* authorized access must be via secure and approved log-on processes. Unauthorized users must be denied access and warned against further attempts to access the system.

- *Authorized activity access:* access to systems, services and data must be allowed only while users are undertaking authorized activity. Services will be suspended or withdrawn if unused or unattended.
- *Dual authorization:* where appropriate, the security infrastructure should support dual authorization for tasks split between users.
- *Authentication:* before being granted access to systems, services and data, users must authenticate themselves using an approved and appropriate method.
- *Data and functions access:* user access permissions must allow access only to the functions and data required by users to perform their normal duties.
- *Logical access administration:* logical access must be controlled.
- *Use of personal computers:* all PC-based systems used to process or store our information will have sufficient controls to identify and authenticate all their users.

Physical security

All computer hardware and associated IT equipment will be physically protected to minimize risk of unauthorized access and damage. The measures used will be commensurate with business requirements, equipment value, criticality/sensitivity of the functions or data supported and level of risk.

- *Physical protection of IT equipment:* any location housing IT equipment must have appropriate levels of physical and environmental protection.
- *Protection for specific locations:* access to servers, routers, gateways, hubs and other network equipment that holds, processes or routes sensitive or business-critical information must be limited to authorized persons.
- *Access to hardcopy devices:* printers and plotters must be adequately protected from unauthorized access.
- *Media storage:* areas used to store tapes, diskettes, optical discs, etc. must be secure. They must also meet the minimum environmental requirements recommended by the media supplier.
- *Media movement:* movement of media must be appropriately controlled, for example by using secure transport where necessary.
- *Disposal of media and equipment:* all media and equipment containing sensitive information must be disposed of in a manner commensurate with the sensitivity of information they hold.
- *Logging of hardware resources:* hardware must be properly logged for insurance and business recovery. Location of these assets must be accurately tracked.
- *PC systems:* these must have adequate physical controls.

- *Clear desk policy:* information must not be left where unauthorized persons may have access to it.

Network security

Connections between our networks and any others must be formally authorized. Our networks will be managed to prevent unauthorized connections.

- *Network integrity and connectivity:* the network security system will be capable of detecting and preventing unauthorized use of the network. Any data stored or transmitted must be capable of satisfying criteria of authenticity, uniqueness, accuracy, completeness and timeliness. Control of access and restriction of user privileges must be applied on an authorized need-to-know basis.
- *Network management:* network management systems must be capable of controlling and monitoring access.
- *Network confidentiality:* where data of varying sensitivity may be carried over the network, multi-level security should be considered. Selective encryption techniques or total transmission encryption should be considered at hardware or software level to include protection for both passwords and data.
- *Network availability:* sufficient resilience should be built into networks to ensure continuous availability. Availability should be measured routinely and trends acted upon to ensure optimum availability.
- *Dial-in security:* dial-in access to our networks will only be through an authorized entry point. This must have a strong authentication mechanism, such as one-time passwords. Records must be kept of all entry points.
- *Modems:* use of modems must be adequately controlled.
- *Internet access and usage:* access to the Internet must be authorized and will be permitted only via an approved secure gateway. Users must be aware of the security limitations relating to use of the Internet.

Application processing integrity

System owners will ensure that data and functions are protected from unauthorized change, and that such changes can be detected.

- *IT procurement:* all IT and related equipment must be procured in accordance with our technical strategy.
- *Project inception:* security requirements must be considered as part of project inception.

- *Security requirements definition and documentation:* system security requirements must be fully defined and documented. They must be kept up to date
  throughout the development process.
- *System design:* all system design work must accord with the security architecture.
- *User acceptance testing:* this must be adequate.
- *Integrity checks:* these must be performed regularly to confirm that no unauthorized alterations to system or business software have taken place.
- *File version control:* file version control techniques should be used to facilitate
  data integrity.
- *Changes to reference tables:* all changes to reference tables, standing data or
  look-up tables should be controlled appropriately.
- *Management (audit) trail recording:* all input, output, rejected and generated
  data should be recorded on a management trail, allowing identification of
  source.
- *Transferring and converting data:* there should be a structured mechanism for
  achieving initial data take-on and transferring or converting data from one
  system to another.
- *Cryptography:* this must only be used in conjunction with our approved algorithms and techniques.

System development environment security

The environment in which systems are developed, tested and enhanced will be
managed to ensure their final products function correctly.

- *Separation of development and live environments:* controls must be in place to
  maintain separation between development and live system environments.
- *Security profile:* a documented security profile for each system must be produced and maintained. This will map the system against the security architecture.
- *Program and system testing:* adequate testing must be undertaken.
- *Program coding and unit testing:* program coding and unit level testing must
  be appropriately controlled via a formal quality mechanism.
- *Prototyping, piloting and trialling:* prototyping, including piloting, must be
  appropriately controlled.
- *Change management:* appropriate procedures must be used to control the resolution and testing/retesting of errors and enhancements.
- *Procedural manuals:* these (whether hard copy or screen-based) should adequately detail the appropriate controls. These procedures should be verified
  before the system goes live.

- *Project sign-off:* on completion of the project it must be properly signed-off.
- *Software implementation plans:* controlled implementation of software must follow a plan.

Integrity of the live business environment

The system owner will ensure that the correctness of live business systems software and data can be maintained.

- *Unauthorized alterations:* these must not be made to either the hardware or the system configuration/set-up.
- *Change management:* formal change management procedures must be followed when applying fixes, alterations or upgrades to any software.
- *Data adjustments:* these must be controlled.
- *Distributed data processing integrity:* data file and program library integrity checking facilities should be available for distributed data processing sites.
- *Emergency support access:* such access to IT resources and software changes must be controlled.

Use of third-party software

Managers purchasing software must assure themselves that the supplier/developer is able to provide adequate levels of support and maintenance. Software that cannot meet the requirements of the IT security architecture will not be used.

- *Security and controls:* the acceptability of security and control facilities within the software will be determined before purchase.
- *Escrow:* an escrow agreement should cover third-party application source code.

Personal computer security policy

All PCs used to process or store our information will have sufficient controls to prevent introduction of malicious code.

Management trail facilities (audit and review)

All IT systems will provide a mechanism to record relevant, sensitive or critical activity performed by individual users. All business systems will enable adequate production of evidence of processing. Appropriate resources and facilities will be available for the timely review of management trail records and their protection from tampering.

- *Business application management trail facilities:* all applications must provide evidence of processing that enables transactions to be traced through the system from the initiating document or entry to the final destination or ultimate output, and vice versa.
- *Infrastructure activity management trail:* appropriate security-related events on systems infrastructure must be reported for subsequent review and analysis.

Business continuity

Each location or department must have a business continuity plan, appropriate to the risk identified. A crisis manager will be designated for each plan and will have complete authority in the event of a disaster. Senior managers will ensure adequate budget provision for their business continuity plan. The ISM will ensure coordination of the plans.

- *Business Continuity Plan testing:* each plan must be tested at least annually.
- *IT back-up and contingency:* adequate system back-up procedures and proven recovery mechanisms should be in place.
- *Minimizing single point of failure:* where necessary, there should be redundancy of storage media, processors and networks to obviate single points of failure.
- *Back-up management:* data retained for archival or other purposes must be managed appropriately for their classification and sensitivity.
- *PC back-ups:* it must be possible for information on PCs to be restored or recreated if lost or corrupted.

Appendix 3

ENCRYPTION

Private key cryptography

Cryptography of some sort or another has been used for centuries. Much 'secret writing' depends on a shared private key (i.e. a secret symmetric code), both to encipher and decipher the message. Traditional computer cryptography likewise uses a shared private key. It works well where the parties know and trust each other.

Private key cryptography still has a role today in InfoSec. For example, it can be very useful for encrypting the hard disks of portable computers to make it harder for thieves to access useful data. In normal use the data are automatically decrypted via software activated by a reinforced log-on ID and password procedure. The user does not need to know the key.

Public key cryptography

Increasing use of relatively insecure means of distributing data, such as the Internet, has raised interest in *public* key cryptography. This employs two different (i.e. asymmetric) keys. Either can be used to encrypt the message, then only the other can decrypt it. The one key cannot be deduced from the other.

Public key cryptography is so named because each user has two keys, one of which is 'public' (just as most telephone numbers are public). So, if person A uses her *private* key to 'sign' a message to person B, B can then use A's *public* key to verify that the message is really from A and has not been tampered with. Alternatively, A can encrypt a message to B using B's *public* key. B (and nobody else) can then use his *private* key to decrypt the message.

Public key cryptography is of particular interest in the context of open electronic commerce (e-commerce) and government-to-citizen transactions (taxes, licences, social security payments, etc.). It depends largely on trusted third parties (TTPs) or certifying authorities (CAs) to deal with matters such as maintaining public key directories and member registers, certificating keys and generating pairs of keys that are mathematically independent.

There are well-publicized problems due to the official controls placed on cryptography by some governments, notably that of the USA. The issues revolve around restricting the use of strong algorithms and enabling government access to keys. The government aims are to protect national security and fight organized crime. If criminal or anti-government elements encrypt their traffic in very strong encryption, this limits the availability of 'eavesdropping' as a security or police option. Hence, at the time of writing, the strongest encryption originated in the USA is rarely licensed for use outside that country.

Digital signatures

These offer proof of integrity and authenticity of information. They rely heavily on cryptographic techniques, and may therefore be subject to the same regulatory, legal and deployment considerations.

Appendix 4

FIREWALLS

Firewalls are the most important and effective means of protecting an Internet protocol (IP) network from an external threat. A firewall is a combination of hardware and software controlling access between networks. Hence a firewall may form the gateway between your 'trusted' corporate network and the 'untrusted' Internet, or between your corporate network and that of a third party to whom network monitoring has been outsourced.

A firewall may do one or more of the following:

- keep out specific types of traffic whilst letting other traffic through
- provide an audit trail of network traffic passing through
- prevent or authenticate specific types of outgoing traffic.

For example, firewalls are sometimes used to strip the Java and Active-X Code out of incoming Internet traffic. This is to prevent malicious code entering a network via a standard web browser.

Some organizations also use firewalls to bar access to 'inappropriate' Internet sites. Certain URLs (uniform resource locators) and TCP/IP addresses are filtered, and audit trails produced identifying individuals who deliberately try to access them.

For a firewall to make a significant contribution to network security, the organization must have a policy setting out what traffic it wants to control. Knowledgeable staff must also manage the firewall. It will be of little use if merely taken 'out of the box' and interposed between networks.

A key point is that the firewall must be the only connection point to another network. It can easily be circumvented by uncontrolled connection of the protected network to another via a modem – for example, if a member of staff connects a networked PC to the Internet via a telephone socket. Hence the importance of network access policy.

Appendix 5

SOURCES OF ADDITIONAL INFORMATION

This appendix provides contact information for:

- a selection of InfoSec-orientated websites
- free guidance on InfoSec from the UK government
- information about BS 7799 and related certification
- documentation on risk assessment methodologies and Internet security guidance from the European Security Forum
- a leading provider of InfoSec training
- a major InfoSec journal.

InfoSec websites

- Security Server: **http://www.securityserver.com/index.html**
  Security Server provides many links to different security topics, companies and relevant literature.
- National Computing Centre Limited: **http://www.ncc.co.uk/**
  National Computing Centre provides impartial advice and consultancy on all aspects of IT, including security. Their factsheet '30 essential actions for IT security' can be accessed from this site.
- International Computer Security Association (ICSA): **http://www.icsa.com** *or* **http://www.monopoly.org/**
  International Computer Security Association is a US-based independent corporation promoting improvement of commercial digital security.

Guidance from the UK government

The Department of Trade and Industry (DTI) publishes several useful InfoSec-related documents. These are listed below together with their respective telephone numbers for ordering.

- Mail: Information Security Policy Group, CII Directorate, Department of Trade and Industry, 151 Buckingham Palace Road, London SW1W 9SS; tel.: 0171 215 1962; fax: 0171 931 7194.

Documents and telephone numbers for ordering:

- *The business manager's guide to information security*: 0171 215 1202 (also on the World Wide Web at **http://dtiinfo1.dti.gov.uk/security/**)
- *Draft information security policy document*: 0171 215 1206
- *Computer assurance guidelines for the commercial sector*: 0171 215 1206
- *Information society initiative information security booklet*: 0345 15 2000.

BS 7799 code of practice for information security

For further information on BS 7799 contact the British Standards Institution:

- Mail: British Standards House, 389 Chiswick High Road, London W4 4AL; tel.: 0181 996 9000; fax: 0181 996 7400; webpage: **http://www. bsi.org.uk/bsi/disc/hot_topics/bs7799.html**; e-mail: **disc@bsi.org.uk**

BS 7799 certification

SGS Yarsley International Certification Services Limited is a leading independent certification body. Its many quality assurance services include BS 7799 certification.

- Mail: SGS House, Portland Road, East Grinstead, West Sussex RH19 4ET; tel.: 01342 410088; fax: 01342 305305; homepage: **http://www.sgs.co.uk/ Home.htm**; e-mail: **gary.baker@sgsgroup.com**

Risk assessment methodologies and Internet security guidance

The European Security Forum is an independent, non-profit-making association of leading organizations. It is dedicated to clarifying and resolving key issues in information security and developing security solutions that meet the business needs of members. Publications include: *SARA, OSCAR* and *SPRINT* risk assessment guides, manuals and related documentation; the ESF *standard of good practice for information security*; *The Internet and security* implementation overview and implementation guide.

- Mail: Room PCG8, Plumtree Court, London EC4A 4HT; tel.: 0171 213 1745; fax: 0171 213 4813.

Journal

Information management and computer security (ISSN 0968-5227) is a leading international and interdisciplinary journal on InfoSec. It is available in print, on CD-ROM or via the World Wide Web. The publisher is MCB University Press.

* Mail: 60/62 Tooler Lane, Bradford, West Yorkshire BD8 9BY; tel.: 01274 777700; homepage: **http://www.mcb.co.uk/cgi-bin/journal1/imcs**; e-mail: **akaminska@mcb.co.uk**

Training

Among the best known and most reputable training companies is Zergo Limited. The company provides a comprehensive range of information security courses, workshops, seminars and technical updates. Zergo is also a leading security consultancy and solution provider.

* Mail: The Square, Basing View, Basingstoke, Hampshire RG21 4EG; tel.: 01256 818 800; fax: 01256 812 901; homepage: **http://www.zergo.co.uk** or **http://www.zergo.com**

Appendix 6

INTERNET GUIDELINES

This appendix suggests basic InfoSec guidelines for Internet users.

General user guidelines

*   If using a networked PC, access the Internet only via an approved gateway/firewall.
*   Don't send confidential information over the Internet unless special measures have been taken to ensure protection.
*   Respect copyright in software, images, logos, etc.
*   Don't download, create, copy, store or distribute offensive or illegal material.

Electronic mail

*   Take care when receiving file attachments via e-mail. Macros could contain viruses.
*   Ensure virus protection is available to scan any document or executable file downloaded from the Internet prior to use.
*   Remember that under some legislative regimes, e-mail can be used as evidence of contract.
*   Bear in mind that e-mail is easily forged.
*   Don't send confidential or sensitive information by e-mail unless special security measures have been taken.

World Wide Web

*   Don't modify web browser security, as this may leave the PC and local network open to attack.
*   Don't download 'plug-ins' without obtaining authority.
*   Don't use 'beta' releases of browser software.
*   Don't use downloaded software without checking it for viruses.

11

Database production: a commercial view of the law

Michelle Green

Introduction

This chapter contains some limited advice to anyone venturing into electronic publishing. When I agreed to write this chapter, The Library Association sent me a contract to sign along with some instructions. Amongst the instructions was a paper entitled *Copyright permissions: a guide for authors*. The important concepts it covers are as relevant to electronic publishing as they are to paper publishing. That is true of most of the legal issues involved in electronic publishing. Copyright, intellectual property, authors' royalties, liability, and libel – all these issues apply equally to any publishing project regardless of media. Electronic publishing then adds a few twists and turns of its own.

This paper does not cover all the advantages and benefits open to electronic publishers. As in most spheres, the law usually comes into electronic publishing when something has the potential to go, or has already gone, wrong. Even with full knowledge of the risks and assuming some level of misuse, electronic publishers can and do derive concrete benefits from their publications. Do not believe the hype, though: electronic publishing of any weight or size is neither cheap nor easy.

Not every legal issue that affects electronic publishing is dealt with in-depth by this paper. Nor should the information given here be misconstrued as legal advice. The author is not a lawyer. If you are intending to publish anything, no matter how little and to what size an audience, you should make yourself aware of some of the basic concepts touched on here. If you plan on entering into a serious commercial publishing venture, you should get competent specialist legal advice, educate yourself thoroughly in this area or – preferably – do both.

Some of the UK and EU legislation discussed in the paper is very new and is largely untested by litigation. Application and interpretation of the new database rights and changes to copyright in the year following publication of this book may alter some of the views expressed in this paper, which in any case are largely my opinions only.

Throughout the paper scenarios are used to illustrate more vividly some of the dry legal concepts being discussed. Some of the scenarios are absolutely true; others are wholly fictional but should be plausible.

Finally, these are the personal views of the author and do not necessarily represent those of her company.

A summary and a list of some recommended reading and useful websites round off the paper.

Am I a publisher?

It doesn't take much to be a publisher these days. If you have put up your own website – Congratulations! – you are a publisher. It could easily be argued that putting up information on an intranet is also publishing. Most people accept that producing a CD-ROM or diskette database for dissemination is an act of publishing, but the Internet equivalent is not always recognized as such.

The Internet offers a new publishing medium that is being embraced by many different types of organizations and individuals. Many of these are entirely new to publishing. The Internet is not the only medium used for electronic publishing, though. CD-ROM, traditional online services and diskettes have been and will continue to be very widely used. It is true, though, that most non-publishers considering entering the electronic publishing arena will be focusing on the Internet and more specifically the Web rather than other possibilities.

Rights, risks and responsibilities

There are two categories of risks, rights and responsibilities facing an electronic publisher. The first category is made up of those issues that could damage the publication and therefore the publisher. The second category includes those issues that could damage any user of a publication or even third parties.

Users of publications do have rights and responsibilities of their own and may take on some risk by using your publication or by relying on the information contained in it. Inevitably though it is the publisher's ultimate responsibility to consider both categories. What damages an end user may, in turn, damage the publisher.

It should also be remembered that many electronic publications contain at least two elements – software and data. Both carry their own separate rights, risks and responsibilities.

The following is just a short list of the types of things that can go wrong with an electronic publication:

- end users can make illicit copies of databases or extracts of data
- a publisher who fails to reach agreement with authors or other copyright owners prior to publication can suffer compensation demands or other legal action
- end users can break the terms of licence agreements by any number of means
- piracy both on a small scale and on larger more organized level can damage revenue potential and confuse the market
- legal action can be taken against the publisher for publication of libellous, obscene or otherwise unlawful material
- lawsuits or compensation demands can be brought claiming liability for damage to end users or third parties due to alleged faulty software or data
- actual damage can be caused to publishers' own computer systems by malicious attacks from hackers
- compensation demands or legal action taken for breaks in an online information service to paying customers.

The wild, wild Web

One of the characteristics of the Internet is that the original community of users tended to have quite different and strongly held views about information and its exploitation. The culture is and to some extent continues to be one where cooperation and sharing are the dominant traits. Anyone intending to publish on the Internet should be very familiar with this culture and its own set of unwritten rules, called netiquette.

The open nature of the Internet subculture can be a boon and is certainly refreshing, but it also raises some potential risks for publishers. Publishers should be aware of the following risks to themselves:

- Software piracy is one of those crimes that unfortunately still hold some level of social acceptability, although this is changing. Electronic information suffers a similar fate due to its inevitable association in people's minds with software.
- There is a widely held belief that electronic publishing is cheap and easy. A small minority of the people who believe that have no compunction against knowingly abusing publishers' legitimate rights.
- The Internet community is an international one. Some nations do not have, nor do their citizens honour, legal concepts such as copyright. Even where copyright and other legislation protect a publisher's rights, the protections and the vigour with which they are enforced are not identical in all jurisdictions.

- Some users feel that all information should be public domain and therefore free of charge. A very small minority of those people is perfectly prepared to flout the law in this matter.
- A tiny minority of people enjoy breaking into electronic systems either to prove that they can or in order to do serious damage.

Some of the wilder elements on the Internet have formed such groups and publications as the following:

Information Liberation Front: Their website holds information for hackers, some deliberate copyright rip-offs of US government and other publications, viruses, etc.
Worldwide Piracy Initiative: Their mission statement is 'The Worldwide Piracy Initiative indexes resources regarding freedom of information and expression, and forbidden knowledge. Security through obscurity has no place in a modern technocratic society. Prohibition of knowledge and of ideas must be stopped whenever possible, even when that knowledge may be dangerous or unpleasant.'[1]

Publishers will have to decide for themselves how much of a threat if any such people pose to them.

Damage to publishers

Intellectual property and unauthorized use

The Web, e-mail and push technology (broadcast information published in the absence of the normal Web client browser request for information) all facilitate both commercial and non-commercial publishing. These same technologies also leave publishers much more vulnerable to abuse or misuse of their copyright and intellectual property and damage to their revenue potential. CD-ROM and traditional online publications can also be misused to a greater extent than their paper equivalents. While other legal pitfalls such as libel are more remote possibilities, abuse of intellectual property is relatively common.

Electronic publications suffer the following types of damage to intellectual property on a fairly regular basis:

- illicit copying of extracts or of the entire publication
- illicit republication of extracts or of the entire publication
- network installations giving access to more users than the licence allows

- network installations giving access to users not authorized by the licence. (In this instance networks include any kind of interconnected computers, including local area networks, wide area networks, intranets, Internet, etc.)

The amount of damage caused and the frequency with which such abuse occurs are exacerbated by the fact that electronic information is so easy to copy, republication can be global on the Internet, and because of the mindset of people who have the technological capability to cause such damage. Some misuse is carried out by people who are simply ignorant or careless about the rights of publishers. Some abuse is carried out by people who know perfectly well that they are damaging the publisher. For the most part illicit republication of, or unauthorized access to, electronic information can be done on a much wider scale at much lower cost to the misuser than with paper-based information.

Networking

Networking is the one, admittedly broad, area of technology that effects electronic publishing the most. CD-ROMs exemplify the problem. When they started to emerge as a serious publishing medium, most publishers and end-users assumed that each CD-ROM would be used on a single stand-alone PC. Software and prices were designed with this in mind.

Just a couple of years later the potential for putting CD-ROMs on local area networks (LANs) began to be exploited. This immediately put pressures on publishers to upgrade their software and the cost of supporting end users shot up. At the same time there was some surprise expressed from a minority of end users when they were asked to pay for the additional value they were getting out of the networked version of the product.

There was a period of a few years in the UK when mechanisms for networking surcharges were very disparate. There still exists a wide variation in the charges electronic publishers make for networking their products, but most pricing policies for local area networking are now more logical and economically understandable. They have to be or markets will not tolerate them.

Unfortunately the situation is now even cloudier. After LANs came wide area networks (WANs), intranets, extranets, the Internet, remote access by telephone lines, ISDN, etc. Even in 1995 it was technologically possible to give global access to a CD-ROM database supplied for use on a single stand-alone licence.

Publishers have legitimate rights to determine how their databases are going to be used. On the other hand some end users are willing to ignore those clearly expressed intentions and are happy to exploit the available technology to its fullest limit, disregarding publishers' legal and moral rights.

Scenario 1

A publisher is launching a new product – Database X. It had been decided to price the product very low and make it available for standalone use only at launch. An American university buys a copy of Database X from a distributor as soon as it is launched. There is a shrink-wrap licence, in the inevitable small print, indicating that the product should not be networked. In addition, that condition is reiterated on the packaging in a 10-point type size along with other information about installing the product.

Six months later the publisher gets an e-mail from a librarian in a UK university. The e-mail gives a web address and instructions on how to log into the US university's campus network and gain full access to Database X. The instructions have been making the rounds of various e-mail lists and websites.

The publisher immediately contacts the US university, which apologizes on behalf of the associate professor responsible for publicizing the availability of Database X. The product is withdrawn from the network.

Security systems

Publishers should evaluate the likelihood of exploitation occurring, the extent of the actual damage that could be caused by illicit exploitation and how much they intend to spend to make the exploitation more difficult. There are no guarantees and no 100% secure systems in publishing.

Scenario 2

The publisher in Scenario 1 decides to take steps to avoid future exploitation of Database X. By now the market has moved on and it must publish both standalone and network versions of the product. It invests considerable amounts of money in developing sophisticated security software that will ensure that the product will only work after a particular password is entered. That password is checked against amount paid and determines whether the product can be used on a network or not and if so how many simultaneous users are allowed.

The administration of issuing passwords adds overheads to the publisher's costs. With an international market it must run a 24-hour helpline to issue the passwords. Furthermore the security software is incompatible with a number of network installations, so the publisher must make further investments in software development. The administration and technical support costs escalate, and the publisher takes the decision to remove the security software entirely.

The greatest loss from intellectual property violations is the loss of potential revenue. This is extremely difficult to quantify. One must strive, however, to be realistic in arriving at such estimates. Publishers must also decide if they are going to stand on principle or pragmatism. Are they prepared to use every possible mechanism and spare no expense to minimize the potential for illicit use?

Pragmatic publishers will spend some time balancing their security risks and the needs of their end users against the costs of implementing security measures. They may then decide to implement minimal or even no specific security measures, knowing full well that some exploitation may occur. Or they may choose to invest in very secure technological solutions. Regardless of the decision taken they may also wish to become involved in one of the organizations such as BSA or FAST described later in this chapter.

There are many means to increase the security of electronic databases. One can use a password system, or diskette keys, or dongles (mechanical devices often connected to a computer's parallel port that meters or otherwise controls the use of software and electronic databases). The Internet and traditional online systems primarily work with user ID and password systems.

There are many systems available commercially, and publishers can develop their own if none of these is suitable. There are no security systems that are entirely without cost. The greatest on-going cost is caused by the increased technical support and administration that are required.

Publishers should also consider the effect of security measures on their end users. Are they going to make life more difficult for normal users? Are users suffering undue inconvenience because of a few rogues? In its evaluation of database security, the publisher must also include the number of cancellations or non-sales made because of the security device itself.

Intellectual property and non-commercial publishers

It is not only publishers hoping to gain revenue out of their publications that are concerned about intellectual property issues. Publishers are not wholly altruistic. They are publishing for some reason that they hope will bring benefit to them. They have also most probably put some effort, resource or money into producing their work. The last thing they want to see is all their hard work being exploited by someone else for their own benefit and to the detriment of the original publisher.

Scenario 3

The university admissions department is asking each department to upgrade its contribution to the university website to attract student applications. The library department decides to demonstrate its modernity and at the same time promote the use of electronic sources to the library users.

Members of the department write extensive instruction sheets for various CD-ROM and online databases, as well as guidance notes on which databases to use for which types of searches. They also review many free Internet sites and make recommendations for the best ones for certain subjects.

Their new webpages draw much more traffic from both existing and prospective students as well as other librarians. The library department gains some kudos for the excellent work.

Five months later it is discovered that another university has essentially copied the pages and just reformatted them, removing instructions for databases to which it does not subscribe and adding a few new ones. The Web review is reproduced verbatim and a copyright statement attributing it to the original university is displayed.

Not only is this a violation of copyright, but it is extremely galling for the people who have invested their own time and effort. In all likelihood the librarians would probably have given permission to have some of the material reused anyway if they had been asked.

For the university admissions department the situation is more fundamental. An investment the university made in an attempt to set itself apart has been undermined by being copied.

Putting a copyright notice correctly attributing authorship is not sufficient. You must also have the author's permission to use copyright material.

Damage done by publishers

Liability

The question of who precisely is liable for any damage caused by published material or who is breaking the law by publishing illegal material is confused considerably by the new technological possibilities. The European Commission in its latest proposal for another copyright directive says: 'It is clear that . . . liability is a horizontal issue affecting a number of areas other than copyright and related rights (from trade marks or misleading advertising to defamation or obscene content). There is a need to clarify the situation for the various parties concerned (notably access providers, service providers, others).' [2]

In addition to the problem areas noted above, other potential pitfalls for electronic publishers include actual or consequential damage to end users' computer systems caused by the publishers' faulty software, consequential damage to end users' business caused by poor quality or incorrect information, and damage and inconvenience caused by viruses supplied inadvertently with electronic databases. Consumer rights and related legislation will give end users some statutory rights in most jurisdictions. However, a carefully drafted end-user licence agreement is the electronic publisher's strongest protection in this area.

Damage to end-users' computer systems is particularly tricky because of the complexity of today's computer systems. If something goes wrong with a computer or a network, it is not always possible to determine precisely what caused the error. Many end users are quite sure that any problem that arises must have been caused by the last application they were using or the last application they installed. While clearly such applications have to be suspects in determining the cause of the problem, they are often wholly innocent.

For example, if a computer hard disk is itself physically faulty, it may appear to work perfectly well for quite a period of time, until at some point it will fail and will almost certainly cause some data on the hard disk to be lost irretrievably. The publisher or any software supplier may end up in a situation similar to the one below. One ought to at least consider what action one would take.

Scenario 4

An end user does not run Scandisk on his PC and therefore has no idea that in fact his hard disk is building up large areas of bad sectors indicating a physical fault on the hard disk. While downloading some documents from Database X, a system error message is displayed on his screen. His PC hangs and he reboots it. Later that day, to his dismay, he discovers that certain applications no longer run at all and that others crash. Documents that he knows should be there are missing. Remembering that Database X had 'crashed' earlier in the day, he immediately assumes that all of the damage has been caused at that time. He contacts the publisher of Database X demanding their assistance in recovering his lost data or, failing that, compensation for the losses and inconvenience.

Database X's publisher now needs to determine if indeed it is possible that it could have caused the problem. This could be extremely difficult to prove either way. The publisher also has to consider issues of good customer relations and possible bad publicity. A publisher with an adequately robust licence agreement should at least have the comfort of knowing the full limitation of its

In the scenario above, if the damage is clearly not the fault of the publisher it may still be the commercially sensible, if somewhat galling, thing to do to offer some limited assistance or compensation to the end user without admitting any liability. Such offers should be in writing and must be extremely carefully worded according to the legal advice given for the jurisdiction.

If the publisher is absolutely certain that it has not caused the damage and is large and callous enough not to worry about customer relations, bad publicity or possible legal action, it can choose to simply stand on its absolutely correct and legal grounds. It can deny all responsibility and refuse any assistance or compensation whatsoever. If the claim from the end user is blatantly opportunistic, this is probably also the correct tactic.

Year 2000 compliance

By now everyone should be aware of the problems that could potentially be caused by software or hardware that does not use four digits to represent years. One can read about the horror stories and actual problems being caused by this short-sightedness elsewhere. Publishers should consider two things. If they are supplying software to end users, software by now should be Year 2000 compliant. Peter Bullock, partner in Masons' I&T Group warns of the dangers:

> There can be little doubt that any wholly new program supplied in the future which is not 2000-compliant (the nature of the problem having become now so well known) would be regarded as unfit for the purpose for which it was supplied . . . The recipient would accordingly be entitled to the usual panoply of contractual remedies for breach, including a claim for damages and the right to reject the program.[3]

Republication and authors' rights

The issues raised by reusing material originally produced for printed publications in electronic databases are contentious and no clear solution is evident. Authors generate material for a specific, often printed, publication. After initial publication that material is reused either in electronic versions of the printed publication or in entirely different electronic publications.

Authors can feel that their intellectual property is being exploited in a way that they did not envisage and for which they have not been compensated. In a recent article in *Information world review,* Northern Light was reported as being the latest organization to run up against this problem: 'Northern Light has been accused of flouting copyright by the US National Writers Union (NWU), but the company says it is following the same licensing practices as traditional online vendors such as LEXIS-NEXIS and Dialog.'[4] At the beginning of 1999 there is a case pending in the US courts on the same issue mentioned in the report: 'The NWU is in the process of appealing against a case it lost last year [1998] in which a judge ruled that LEXIS-NEXIS, UMI, *Time*, the *New York Times* and *Newsday* were not infringing the rights of freelance writers by selling articles electronically' (see Chapter 4, p.69).

Any electronic publisher reusing data originally published for paper publications should be very aware of the issues involved and should either already have sought legal counsel or be in a position to get access to good legal advice relatively quickly. This issue is a fluid one. Treaties are in the process of being signed; legislation is being drafted. Both large publishers and organizations representing authors should already be involved in lobbying the EU and national governments on these issues.

The European Commission published a proposal in December 1997 entitled *Proposal for a European Parliament and Council Directive on the harmonization of certain aspects of copyright and related rights in the information society*.[5] In this proposal, the Commission acknowledges that the recent directives, the Computer Programs Directive[6] and the Database Directive,[7] have harmonized the reproduction rights for those two categories of work. The Rental Right Directive has also provided some harmonization of reproduction rights for performers, film and music producers, and broadcasters, but in a less precise way. The Commission concludes that further legislation is required for a number of reasons: to define all acts of reproduction including digital reproduction for all copyright material throughout the Union and to harmonize exceptions 'to comply with obligations arising from the two new WIPO treaties',[8] and to cover the newly emerging technologically possibilities for transmitting copyright material to the public.

In Section B (7) of proposal, the Commission finds that: 'On the whole, it can be stated that the existing situation in Member States with respect to the communication to the public of works and other subject matter is characterized by significant legal uncertainty and legal differences between Member States in the nature and characteristics of protection.' [9]

As required, there is an impact assessment form published with the proposal. This clearly states that electronic publishers along with a range of other types of businesses will be affected should the proposal be adopted. Section 3 of the impact assessment deals with what businesses will have to do to comply with the proposal:

> Harmonization is proposed on four elements: the reproduction right, the right of communication to the public, including making available 'on-demand' over the net, the right of distribution of physical copies and the protection of technological measures and rights-management information. . . . The proposed directive will not force

business to make major adjustments, since it mainly implies a fine-tuning of the Member States' laws within their existing concepts and traditions.[10]

Similar legislation is pending in the United States, as shown in this Business Software Alliance news release made on 26 February 1998:

BSA President Robert Holleyman Hails House Subcommittee Support for Digital Age International Copyright Laws

The Business Software Alliance applauds the members of the House Judiciary Subcommittee on Courts and Intellectual Property for their vote today for legislation which would protect the rights of authors who sell software, books, music and other valuable works over the Internet.

H.R. 2281, The WIPO Copyright Treaties Implementation Act, favorably reported by the House Subcommittee today, would establish an international standard for online copyright laws and assure software developers and other authors that their works and creativity will be protected on the Internet.[11]

With any new publications, both publishers and authors should be aware of the multimedia publication possibilities of the material they are commissioning and/or creating. Good, clear contracts addressing the issues of copyright, republication rights and permitted as well as prohibited use will benefit the author greatly, and at least leave the publisher in a clearer position for the future.

Other legal issues

Copyright and database rights

Copyright law varies from country to country. Some countries do not even recognize the concept of copyright. In the UK virtually everything you could possibly want to publish is subject to copyright – text, images, programs, audio files, etc. The main issues of copyright are covered by the Copyright, Designs and Patents Act 1988 and are dealt with in Chapter 4. The 1988 law makes no reference to databases but instead confers some protection to compilations. Copyright law, especially that dealing with databases, has recently changed in the European Union and many member states.

EU legislation in the form of Council Directive No. 96/9/EC was adopted to harmonize the laws of EU member states in this area. The Directive has been implemented in the UK by the Copyright and Rights in Databases Regulations 1997 (SI 1997 No. 3032), which came into force on 1 January 1998.

The Regulation gives definitions for a database in Part II: Amendment of the Copyright, Designs and Patents Act 1988, Section 6. It says:

Meaning of 'database'
6. After section 3 insert –
'Databases 3A. – (1) In this Part "database" means a collection of independent works, data or other materials which –
    (a) are arranged in a systematic or methodical way, and
    (b) are individually accessible by electronic or other means.
(2) For the purposes of this Part a literary work consisting of a database is original if, and only if, by reason of the selection or arrangement of the contents of the database the database constitutes the author's own intellectual creation.

The Directive introduced a new right – the database right. The right is applicable whether or not copyright exists with the database publisher. The database maker is entitled to these rights where there has been a substantial investment in the obtaining, verification or presentation of the contents of the database. Database rights prevent extraction and reuse of the whole or a substantial part of the data from a database.

Copyright protection is only accorded to a database that by virtue of the selection or arrangement of the contents constitutes the author's own intellectual creation. Part III: Database Right, Section 13 of the Regulation says:

Database right
13. – (1) A property right ('database right') subsists, in accordance with this Part, in a database if there has been a substantial investment in obtaining, verifying or presenting the contents of the database.
(2) For the purposes of paragraph (1) it is immaterial whether or not the database or any of its contents is a copyright work, within the meaning of Part I of the 1988 Act.

Database rights expire after 15 years. But crucially the clock on that 15-year limit is reset each time 'substantial change' is made to the database. Part III: Database right, Section 17 says:

Term of protection
17. – (1) Database right in a database expires at the end of the period of fifteen years from the end of the calendar year in which the making of the database was completed.
(2) Where a database is made available to the public before the end of the period referred to in paragraph (1), database right in the database shall expire fifteen years from the end of the calendar year in which the database was first made available to the public.

(3) Any substantial change to the contents of a database, including a substantial change resulting from the accumulation of successive additions, deletions or alterations, which would result in the database being considered to be a substantial new investment shall qualify the database resulting from that investment for its own term of protection.

Fair dealing

Fair dealing is a legal provision that allows readers to use extracts or quotations from a copyright work without violating the copyright owner's rights or having to pay a fee. The rules on how much can be used and for what purposes are somewhat vague. In any case those legal definitions that do exist vary quite substantially even within member states of the European Union. For serious commercial electronic publishers, fair dealing is unlikely to apply to anything they might wish to republish themselves.

On the other hand, end users of electronic titles will want to take extracts from those titles. They will want to have at least the same general principles of fair dealing applied to the electronic title as they would expect from a printed publication. Often, however, they wish to make extracts from electronic titles that far outstrips what would be considered fair dealing in the printed realm. They will often ask if they can download extracts or whole documents or even the whole database to their own intranet and mix it in with their own data. They will ask if they can send copies of a document downloaded from a database and then e-mail it to 200 employees in their organization. They will ask if they can take 10 documents from a publication and load them on their homepage on the Internet. They *will* ask. What are you, the publisher, going to say? What is electronic fair dealing?

The UK Copyright and Rights in Databases Regulations 1997 deals with a few aspects of electronic fair dealing. It removes researching a database for a commercial purpose from the definition of fair dealing. That means that to do so without permission of the copyright owner is not fair dealing and is a violation of copyright. On the other hand it does give users some leeway to extract data from databases without violating copyright. Section 19 of the Regulation says:

19. – (1) A lawful user of a database which has been made available to the public in any manner shall be entitled to extract or re-utilise insubstantial parts of the contents of the database for any purpose.

Section 20 of the Regulation deals with some other allowed activities under the concept of fair dealing.

Exceptions to database right

20. – (1) Database right in a database which has been made available to the public in any manner is not infringed by fair dealing with a substantial part of its contents if –

(a) that part is extracted from the database by a person who is apart from this paragraph a lawful user of the database,

(b) it is extracted for the purpose of illustration for teaching or research and not for any commercial purpose, and

(c) the source is indicated.

(2) The provisions of Schedule 1 specify other acts which may be done in relation to a database notwithstanding the existence of database right.

Schedule 1 of the Regulation deals with exceptions exclusively for the purpose of public administration.

Insurance

If your organization is not established already in the publishing field, the general liability clauses of your organization's insurance cover may not be valid for your new publishing activities. Some American insurance companies have put together policies specifically for website owners. Policies cover business interruption, liability for libel and slander as well as 'errors and omissions' cover.

Licence agreements

If you intend to publish a database, then you should seriously consider how you intend to license it. Licences are important regardless of whether the data are being used commercially or not. Apart from those permissions granted in law, all forms of copying, adaptation and distribution need the licence of the copyright owner. In addition your liability as the publisher does not depend on whether end-users pay to access your database. A report commissioned by the then CD-ROM Standards and Practices Action Group states

> The grant to the customer of the licence entitles the customer to do acts which would otherwise be prohibited. Distinguish this from the use of a book. To read a book does not involve any act infringing copyright; it is only the photocopying of a book that raises copyright issues. Therefore a book is not 'licensed' to readers as such.[12]

The presence of no licence at all is interpreted in English law as an 'implied licence'. Since 1 January 1998 what is and is not allowed in this situation has been much more precisely defined by the new Statutory Instrument. There is still a large grey area of which both users and publishers should be aware.

Scenario 5

As an example, suppose that a UK-based organization puts up a large database on the Web. There is no licence agreement and no copyright statement indicated on the front pages of the website. A Web surfer happens upon the site and knows that her company will benefit from the information contained in the database. She starts searching the database and downloading the documents she finds. After she has found all the documents her company is likely to be interested in, about 200 altogether, she republishes them on her company's intranet, acknowledging the original site from which they were extracted.

She has now violated both the database maker's copyright and database rights and her company is liable for her actions. Her use of and extractions from the database are most definitely for commercial reasons. The publisher has certain rights regardless of the presence of a copyright statement or written licence agreement. The question is what did the original publisher intend?

The publisher could have made the issue absolutely clear by including a licence agreement on the website giving users whatever permissions the publisher chooses to grant and stating any limitations of permission and/or liability.

When the surfer copied the documents onto her company's intranet, she became a publisher. She should have been aware at least to a basic level of the existence of copyright issues. At the very least the directors of her company should have ensured that she or her supervisor was educated in these matters. If she had been, she would have contacted the original publishers requesting permission for her reuse of the data.

Apart from the very limited use permitted by the new definitions of 'fair dealing' with regard to databases, almost any use of an electronic database requires a licence. End users can either contact each data owner every time they want to do something with their data, and publishers can deal with many different end users on an *ad hoc* basis *or* publishers can save everyone trouble by making an appropriate licence agreement available with the database.

For an example of this, look at the series of letters on the HMSO website.[13] HMSO has produced what amounts to licence agreements for various activities in the form of letters or notices. These letters were sent out by them to known interested parties and also published on the Web. The letters are addressed 'Dear Publisher', 'Dear Librarian', etc., and cover just about every possible way in which Crown copyright or parliamentary copyright material might be used.

Here is an extract from the 'Dear Publisher' letter:

REPRODUCTION OF STATUTORY PUBLICATIONS AND PRESS RELEASES

4.1 For the following specified types of Crown copyright material, reproduction in any media, other than the uses described at paras 9 and 11.3, is permitted worldwide in all languages without prior permission and free of charge: Acts of Parliament, Statutory Instruments and Statutory Rules and Orders; Press Releases from departments, agencies or other Crown bodies. Whilst these are obviously for unrestricted use at time of issue, they may also be freely reproduced thereafter, singly or in compilation, but not for the sole purpose of providing a commercial press release service.

4.2 Such reproduction is subject to the following conditions being complied with:

(i) the material is reproduced in a value-added context, i.e. where the official text has had value added to it by compilation with other related text, analysis, commentary, annotation, indexing or cross-referencing (this may be taken as covering both commercially published and in-house databases);

(ii) that an acknowledgement of Crown copyright is featured as well as a statement of the source. The copyright acknowledgement will generally be in the following form: Reproduced with the permission of the Controller of Her Majesty's Stationery Office;

(iii) the material is reproduced accurately and in a form and context which is in no way misleading as to the intended meaning of the material.

A written licence agreement to access a database gives advantages to both end-users and publishers. Issues of liability and permitted use can be clearly stated. Obviously the licence cannot override those permissions and limitations of liability which are granted in law. A good user licence should clarify the issues. Unfortunately, licences are an area where legalese runs rampant.

If you do not consult a lawyer on any other aspect of your publishing business, you should seriously consider it when it comes to drafting a licence.

The Electronic Information Publishers Action Group (formerly, CD-ROM SPAG) commissioned a study in May 1995 into the issues of CD-ROM licensing. The result was a 73-page document that outlined the then current practices of CD-ROM publishers, but more importantly gave a thorough set of guidelines for drafting a good licence. Although the study dealt with CD-ROMs, the issues raised apply equally to online and Web publishers.[14]

Piracy

Piracy affects both software on its own and electronic publications, along with music, videos, etc. The website of the [US] Software Publishers Association (SPA) contains an excellent definition of piracy.[15] Of course the SPA's focus is on software, but their definitions apply equally well to electronic information:

What is Software Piracy?

Software piracy is the unauthorized use of software. Piracy includes:

1. purchasing a single user license and loading it onto multiple computers or a server ('softloading');

2. making, distributing and/or selling copies that appear to be from an authorized source ('counterfeiting');

3. renting software without permission from the copyright holder;

4. distributing and/or selling software that has been 'unbundled', or separated from, from the products with which it was intended to be 'bundled'; and

5. downloading copyrighted software from the Internet or bulletin boards without permission from the copyright holders.

SPA's anti-piracy efforts include organizing the Copyright Protection Campaign (CPC): 'CPC has developed comprehensive education and enforcement programs to help promote and protect copyright . . . A variety of information pertaining to legal software use is available online. In addition, SPA has developed the Internet Anti-Piracy Campaign (IAPC).'

The amount of commercial damage caused by piracy, both small and on a commercial scale, is substantial. Numerous surveys have been conducted in the past few years attempting to quantify the total damage. Generally these surveys concentrate on software or video or music CDs. Lost revenue in Western Europe for software alone is usually reported in hundreds of millions if not billions of pounds (a 1995 survey conducted by International Planning and Research estimated software piracy losses in Western Europe as exceeding US$ 3.5 billion). If one gives any credence to these figures at all, electronic publishers should assume that some level of piracy is occurring with their products.

Other groups involved in anti-piracy activities are the Business Software Alliance (BSA) and the Federation Against Software Theft (FAST).

From their website, BSA says the following:

BSA wants software piracy to end. Our presence can be found across the globe with enforcement programs in 65 countries and anti-piracy hotlines operating in nearly all nations. Litigation, raids, and audits are all means BSA employs against 'Warez' websites, corporate end users, hardware dealers, bulletin board operators, and other persons or entities suspected of violating copyright laws protecting computer software. Settlements from the BSA's enforcement activities fund future policy, anti-piracy and education programs.[16]

FAST's website has this to say:

Founded in 1984, FAST is a not-for-profit organization supported by the software industry. The aim of FAST is to promote the legal use of software. This is achieved through education and promotion of the legalization message and enforcement of the copyright laws thorough criminal prosecutions. Its members in the software industry come from a wide range of companies led by the major software publishers. Its corporate membership scheme is now supported by over 900 private and public sector companies in the UK.

FAST also lobbies for improvements to the current legislation covering copyright and works with similar bodies internationally. In addition FAST works on behalf of the vendors of datasets through the Datafed group, promoting the better use of data and defending the copyright of members within the publishing industry.[17]

FAST has spun off a number of related organizations, including the FAST Legal Advisory Group (FLAG) and Datafed. FLAG is a forum for legal practitioners, both those in private practice and in-house lawyers, to discuss and keep abreast of legal developments related to software protection. Datafed is an interest group within FAST specifically dealing with dataset licensing issues. Its work is explained on the FAST website as follows:

Its work in educating users and advising data providers about dataset usage helps to ensure better use of datasets and [fewer] situations in which users may be abusing the terms of their dataset licence. As a significant interest group of FAST, Datafed capitalizes on the substantial body of knowledge which FAST has in the area of copyright law and offers the same digital enforcement resource [that] FAST's software industry members enjoy . . .

As with software many organizations are managing the important resource poorly such that datasets may be copied without regard to the copyright protection they enjoy, exposing the company to possible prosecution.

Permitted acts; prohibited acts

Copyright and Rights in Databases Regulations 1997 section 9 says: .

Acts permitted in relation to databases.
50D. – (1) It is not an infringement of copyright in a database for a person who has a right to use the database or any part of the database (whether under a licence to do any of the acts restricted by the copyright in the database or otherwise) to do, in the exercise of that right, anything which is necessary for the purposes of access to and use of the contents of the database or of that part of the database.

Public domain

This is a term applied to material where any copyright protection has expired or the author has given global permission to reproduce or republish the material. Neither publishers nor end users should assume that any material is public domain. For example one could assume that text as old as the *Bible* would be public domain, but modern translations or interpretations may constitute new works and therefore be subject to copyright.

Trade marks

The Trade Marks Act 1994 implemented an EU directive, No. 89/104/EEC, harmonizing trade mark legislation within member states. In Section 1(1), it defines a trade-mark as being:

> any sign capable of being represented graphically which is capable of distinguishing goods or services of one undertaking from those of other undertakings.
>
> A trade mark may, in particular, consist of words (including personal names), designs, letters, numerals or the shape of goods or their packaging.

Publishers should ensure that in the naming of their products, and in the choice of domain name if publishing on the Web, that they are not violating the trade marks of others. They should also seriously consider registering their own trade marks. UK and EU trade-mark registration can be done without professional assistance. Forms (and copious instructions) are available from the UK Patent Office.[18] Alternatively a reputable trade-mark agency can be employed to complete the process. Depending on whether the decision is made to register in just the UK or throughout the EU, and assuming that there are no previous registrations or any objections to the proposed trade mark, the cost of registering a trade mark can range from about £250 to over £3000.

Summary

- *Educate yourself.* Make yourself aware of your own rights and responsibilities as a publisher as well as those of authors, end users, software suppliers, data owners, etc. that are involved in your publication activities.
- *Seek specialist advice* where necessary. Many of the areas you will be entering into are very new. You need good quality advice from lawyers or other professionals who have proven expertise in the particular areas that affect your publishing activities.

- *Write agreements carefully.* End-user licence agreements, distribution agreements, assignments of copyright, contracts with joint venture partners – all of these should be drafted very carefully. Once written they should be reviewed regularly. Changes in legislation and technology frequently make perfectly good clauses out of date or even unlawful.
- *Keep an eye on developments.* The law and technology are changing very quickly. You should keep yourself aware of how possible future developments might effect you as a publisher. Your reaction times are going to have to be very fast, especially if you hope to remain a commercially successful electronic publisher.
- *Don't be paranoid* but don't be naive either. Make yourself aware of the changing attitudes of your markets.

References

1   Worldwide Piracy Initiative [homepage], http://www.piracy.com/ [visited 11/02/1999].
2   Office for Official Publications of the European Communities, COM (97) 628 final, ISSN 0254-1475, ISBN 92-78-29745, 9.
3   Bullock, P., 'The millennium time bomb: legal issues for suppliers and users', *Computers and law,* 7 (4), (Oct/Nov 1996), 5–6.
4   'Northern Light caught in copyright wrangle', *Information world review,* 134 (March 1998), 1.
5   Office for Official Publications of the European Communities, op. cit.
6   Council Directive 91/250/EEC on the legal protection of computer programs, OJ L 122, 17.5.1991.
7   Council Directive 96/9/EC on the legal protection of databases, OJ L 77, 27.3.1996.
8   Office for Official Publications of the European Communities, op. cit., Section B (14), 16.
9   Ibid., 19.
10 Ibid., 51.
11 Business Software Alliance, news release, 26 February 1998, http://www.bsa.org/pressbox/index.html [visited on 17/07/98].
12 Electronic Information Publishers Action Group, *CD-ROM licencing issues for publishers, a report prepared for the CD-ROM Standards and Practices Action Group by Electronic Publishing Services Limited and Bird & Bird,* London, Bird & Bird.
13 HMSO Copyright Unit, 'Letters', http://www.hmso.gov.uk/copy.htm [visited on 17/07/98].
14 Electronic Information Publishers Action Group, op. cit.
15 Software Publishers Association: http://www.spa.org/piracy/ [visited on 17/07/98].

16 Business Software Alliance:
    http://www.bsa.org [visited on 17/07/98].
17 Federation Against Software Theft:
    http://www.fast.org.uk [visited on 17/07/98].
18 UK Patent Office, 'Trade marks',
    http://www.patent.gov.uk/dtrademk/index.html [visited on 17/07/98].

Recommended reading

Bowes, R. and others, 'New copyright law fails to reflect copyright permissions of
    importance to user community', *Managing information*, 5 (2), 1998, 13–15 [an
    exchange of letters on the new Statutory Instrument].
The Copyright and Rights in Databases Regulations 1997, SI No. 3032. ISBN 0 11 065110 3,
    http://194.128.65.3/si/si1997/06511001.htm [read the explanatory note at the end
    if nothing else].
Smedinghoff, T. J. (ed.), *Online law: the SPA's legal guide to doing business on the
    Internet*, New York, Addison-Wesley, 1996, ISBN 0-201-48980-5 [US oriented].
Vinje, T. C., 'Who owns the information', *Supplement to information technology and
    public policy*, 13 (3), 1995 ISSN 0266 85 13, 30–8 [a very interesting fictional case
    study touching on many intellectual property issues while focusing on multimedia
    and US law].
Wall, R. A., 'Copyright forum', *Managing information*, 3 (3), 1996, 25–32 [covers some
    of the current EU proposals and programmes that may impact on electronic pub-
    lishers].

Useful websites

Business Software Alliance:
    http://www.bsa.org/piracy/piracy.html
Federation Against Software Theft:
    http://www.fast.org.uk
HMSO Copyright Unit:
    http://www.hmso.gov.uk/copy.htm
Software Publishers Association:
    http://www.spa.org/piracy/

Index